"A Totally Alien Life-Form"

Other Books by Sydney Lewis

*Hospital: An Oral History of
Cook County Hospital*

"A Totally Alien Life-Form"

TEENAGERS

Sydney Lewis

The New Press | New York

Library of Congress
Cataloging-in-Publication Data
Lewis, Sydney.
"A Totally Alien Life-Form": Teenagers / Sydney Lewis.
p.   cm.
ISBN 1-56584-282-0 (hardcover)
1. Teenagers—United States--Interviews.
2. Teenagers—United States--Social Conditions.
I. Title.
HQ796.S3995   1996
305.23'5'0973—dc20   96-5574
CIP

Published in
the United States by
The New Press, New York
Distributed by
W. W. Norton & Company, Inc.,
New York

Established in 1990 as a major
alternative to the large, commercial
publishing houses, The New Press is
a full-scale nonprofit American book
publisher outside of the university presses.
The Press is operated editorially
in the public interest, rather than
for private gain; it is committed to
publishing in innovative ways
works of educational, cultural,
and community value that,
despite their intellectual merits,
might not normally be commercially viable.
The New Press's editorial offices
are located at the
City University of New York.

Book design by Paul Carlos
Production management
by Kim Waymer
Printed in
the United States of America

9 8 7 6 5 4 3 2 1

For Studs Terkel

"During adolescence,
Rousseau said, 'the blood
ferments and is agitated;
a superabundance of life seeks
to extend itself outward.'
During adolescence
imagination is boundless.
The urge toward self-
perfection is at its peak. And
with all their self-absorption
and personalized dreams
of glory, youth are in pursuit
of something larger than
personal passions, some values
or ideals to which they might
attach their imaginations.
Their energies are poised to
transform personal narcissistic
interests into a concern for
the common good."

Louise J. Kaplan
Adolescence:
The Farewell to Childhood

——————

"Youth culture reflects the
tension between what adults
prefer to believe about
themselves and how they
actually go about preparing
young people to take their
place in society. What we, as
adults, see in the youth
culture tells us things we
would prefer not to know
about ourselves."

Gary Schwartz
Beyond Conformity
or Rebellion:
Youth and Authority
in America

Contents

X. *Moms and Dads: Anything Can Happen*

XI. *The Need to Work*

XII. *Coming From, Going Toward*

Acknowledgments

A number of people helped in a multitude of ways, and I offer a tremendous thank you to the whole great lot of them: Carol Anshaw, Bill Ayers, Lois Barliant, Lois Baum, Jennifer Bogart, Lucy and Lenni Bukowski, Amelia Buescher, Jack Clark, Murphy Davis, George Drury, Mary Gaffney, Steve Grossman, Jean and Peter Guest, Deborah Handler, Susan Hinckle, Jane Jacobs, Sara Johnston, David Krupp, Alec Lee, Jack and Julie Marshall, Brian Murray, Jane Mushaback, Mary Nisbet, Marc Pokempner, The Redheds, Larry Rock, Janet Roderick, Ben Sandmel, Michael Scott, Tim Sheils, Lizabeth Sipes, Alex Skene, Nick Smith, Penny Spokes, Bill Stamets, Dale Tippin, Mary Beth Valentine, Michelle Weaver, and Dave and Laura Winkleblack.

My gratitude, also, to an assortment of people and organizations who dedicate themselves to working with young people: David Jones of Anchor Graphics, Leah Mayer of the Anixter Center Factory Branch School, Cori Anderson of the Gateway Foundation, Andy Humm of the Hetrick-Martin Institute, Elvis Gomez and Ruth Hernandez of Hudson Guild, Duffie Adelson of the Merit Music Program, Garfield Phillpotts and Dennis Sykes of New Expression, and Pearl Wolf of the Looking Glass/New Roads Program.

At The New Press, all thanks to my editor and publisher, André Schiffrin, whose interest in what the young have to say prompted my own. Thanks also to Ellen Reeves and Jessica Blatt for their wise suggestions; to Ted Byfield for copy editing with great skill; to Grace Farrell for shepherding the manuscript with attention and patience;

and to Lisa Bernstein, Allegra D'Adamo, Jodie Patterson, and Matt Weiland, for their comments and kinship.

I owe an immense debt to Elissa Guest, with whom I've discussed books and writing since our grade school days. Her early and astute reading of the manuscript, insightful comments, and thoughtful suggestions were invaluable. As for my patron saints Denise DeClue and Tim Kazurinsky, there is no way I can ever repay their generosity, enthusiasm and friendship. I also thank my parents, whose pride in me is equaled by mine in them.

Finally, my thanks to the young storytellers who agreed to talk about their lives. I was so happily engaged in their worlds that I forged on, even when I knew I had more than enough material for a book. As a result, a number of interviews do not appear in these pages. The choices were difficult to make, and I offer my apologies to those absent—their stories are no less engaging than these.

A NOTE ABOUT NAMES AND LOCATIONS: Those under the age of eighteen have been given new names. Those eighteen and older were given a choice—most chose to use their real names. In all cases, the first names of family members, and the names of all friends and others mentioned, have been changed. On occasion, I've changed a parent's profession, and in a very few instances I've moved storytellers to different locations than those in which they actually reside.

Introduction

Over the course of a year and some months, I interviewed close to sixty young people for this oral history. Their stories settled inside me, thoroughly engaging my thoughts and emotions: they had me in their grip. So much so that recently I dreamt I was in a crowd of adults, and when someone asked how old I was, I said, "Eighteen." When awake I found myself saying "like" and "you know" way too often for someone over thirty. OK, way over thirty. But mostly I had a blast. I enjoyed spending time with young people; they can be really good company. Of course, being with them brought back many memories of my own adolescence: both of the thrills of discovery, and the pain of being alternately unable or unwilling to communicate with my parents. It made me glad I was young when I was young. There's so much more to worry about now.

The young people in this book are of many different backgrounds. What is common across class, race, and age lines is a quizzical and sometimes prickly wonder at the giant magnifying glass of the adult eye. An eighteen-year-old sums it up: "People look at teenagers like we're a totally alien life form." I noticed, again and again, adults staking claim on adolescence because they once belonged there even as they yet look at current teenagers with utter confusion, if not outright terror—as though visited by ghosts they somehow know but cannot recognize. I heard certain adults say with a touch of impatience, "I know all about being a teenager." But what I wanted was what no one else could know: the weight and texture of these lives, their experiences of being young in this country now, as we near the end of the millennium.

A long-standing cliché is that the young don't recognize their own mortality. But for decades they have recognized the possibility of a larger mortality—that of the species. Unlike our parents, my generation was born under the sign of the mushroom cloud; we knew about the Bomb in the way that we knew about the planets—as part of our world. And today's teenagers are ever-more concerned for the planet itself, in terms of what might happen to it in war and in peace. They do not take its survival for granted.

They're concerned about violating the planet and about being violated by others. Almost every young urban person interviewed knew how to get his or her hands on a gun, and for those outside of cities there is no escape from at least an awareness of violence. But nothing is more widespread than the availability of drugs. Everyone everywhere knew how to go about getting their hands on something illegal. The war on drugs seems about as successful a strategy as was our campaign against the North Vietnamese. Also widespread are concerns about the quality of education: from coast to coast, they know how essential it is to their success in what remains of the labor market.

When I was young we worried about unwanted pregnancies and sexually transmitted diseases—but the pill was available and the diseases easily treatable. During the time I worked on this book, politicians spoke harshly about the number of teen pregnancies, until reports surfaced noting that a significant number of the fathers were well out of their teens. And I was shocked to find that despite the horrifying emergence of AIDS, many parents still avoid talking about sex with their children. The one thing that hasn't changed is the adolescent need to bond—like small herd animals, most young people prefer to travel in packs.

The second half of the sixties was my time of adolescence. Back then, the streets of New York City were ours to run. At eleven we were wandering the parks; in later years, we simply wandered—everywhere. We eluded our share of rough kids, subway flashers, and street creeps, but as a rule we didn't fear for our lives. Manhattan was our home town, our village, and meandering its streets was what we did for fun. The haunting faces of missing children did not yet grace our milk cartons. We walked, talked, looked, went to movies, piled into coffee and donut shops, and spent as much time as possible out of our parents' sight lines. When trapped indoors we listened to music, loud—Bob Dylan, Jimi Hendrix, Al Green, Doc Watson, Joni Mitchell, Billie Holiday, Aretha, the Rolling Stones. We had big ears, we loved it all—as long as there were words.

Back then we didn't have malls, we weren't yet the "youth market," and accumulating material possessions wasn't big on our agenda. We went to thrift and army-navy stores for aged, treasured items. It didn't cost a fortune to buy a pair of sneakers or a pair of blue jeans, and those who were dressing up were dressing wild. Mostly, we were busy protesting the war, or prowling the perimeters of a Central Park Be-In, or trekking through the weekend circus that was Greenwich Village. Whatever we did, there was a sense of community, of people acting in concert.

When we met young folks from different neighborhoods, the suburbs, other states, other ways of life, we could always find a common ground. We might have radically different backgrounds, but we were in that seemingly isolated, misunderstood stage of life, and could find collective comfort assembling at the gates of a universal high school for a rage-fest or massing to mutter about the numerous idiocies of authorities-at-large, parents included. The future looked pretty good, vital at least: higher education at reputable universities was affordable for many, and community and city colleges were a decent fallback. There were exciting careers awaiting us at best; perhaps boring, but nevertheless paying jobs at worst. We would do as well as, if not better than, our parents—or so we thought. There were reasons to be upset, but to be despairing, not really. It is different now.

Before embarking on the interviewing work for this book, I talked with educators, parents, psychologists, and others who work with or have contact with young people. I sought their advice, and through many of them found people to interview. The rest came by word of mouth, and chance. This is not a scientifically exact study; rather, my intent was to gather as evocative a group as possible, differing widely in age, as well as in geographic, racial, and social backgrounds.

Setting out, I knew little about current teenagers, and most of it was by proxy. I have no children, and my friends' children are for the most part younger. Through work on my first oral history, *Hospital: An Oral History of Cook County Hospital*, I'd become aware of the tragic number of young victims of violent assault, sexual and other. Relying on the media would have led me to believe that, at worst, most teenagers are reducible to being either victims or perpetrators of evil—and that, at best, they are generally empty vessels without insight into their own lives or into ours. I wasn't at all certain I could get teenagers to really talk to me. However, my many years of observing Studs Terkel, both as transcriber and as assistant on his daily radio program, held me in good stead. I adopted his approach to conversation—I had only four or five basic questions. The point was to let the conversation follow each storyteller's lead, cleaving to what seemed to matter the most to them.

Many people have asked me what most surprised or shocked me about today's adolescents. It's hard for me to say—maybe because, in many ways, during my own youth I was something of an anomaly. In a time when interracial marriages were even more uncommon and unwelcome than they are now, my Jamaican mother was an upset to my father's white Anglo-Saxon Protestant family. People were always finding new and creative ways to ask me exactly what I was. In a time when divorce was a stigma, my parents were apart, and had been since I was six. I was a latchkey kid: my mother worked as a nurse, and when I was old enough to be left alone, she often worked nights. In a time when domestic violence was truly taken for granted, my stepfather was my mother's persistent batterer. Though long absent by the time of my adolescence, he haunted my dreams well into my twenties, and in them he was always going to kill me. And in a time when the horizons of substance abuse were expanding wildly, yet discussions of alcoholism were confined to Alcoholic's Anonymous meetings, my parents were both serious drinkers.

But ours is a remarkably resilient species, and the youngest of us no less so. It is amazing how capable children are of seeking out what they need, of weaving nets of support from the thinnest of materials. My parents loved me, but their own problems interfered with the act of parenting. So I found second homes through my friends and their families; in a sense, I created my own child-raising village. And I read voraciously—I never went anywhere without a book. The worlds I experienced through literature fed my imagination, and on a deep level literally sustained and nurtured me. In these ways, I survived.

Yet, what I experienced kept me from feeling especially shocked or judgmental about what I heard from my young acquaintances.

Neither shocking nor surprising is the fact that this generation's pulse runs fast. There's a sense of hurry, of things running out—educational opportunities, jobs, space, peace, oxygen. They're anxious. Information floods their systems: with radios, multi-channeled TVs, videos, movies, computers, videogames, they're the most plugged-in generation ever. Geographical distance notwithstanding, in many ways they all breathe the same UV-ray-infested air. MTV brings gangsta rap to rural America—there are now "farm gangs" in Wisconsin—and thanks to adult appropriation of youth culture, everybody knows everything about them, almost before they know it about themselves.

Reactions to the notion of an oral history of teenagers ranged from, "Fantastic!" to a skeptical, "You're interviewing teenagers? What's *that* like?" How much could a teenager have to say? Plenty, it turns out. They know about and have experienced a lot, and they are much more sophisticated overall than were my peers at that stage of life.

In our culture, adolescence is a period during which a young person undergoes physical, emotional, intellectual, social, and spiritual growth. While who they are reveals itself slowly, and often in deep, intangible ways, they are actively, moment by moment, establishing who they are not by testing the tethers which bind them to parents, teachers, and peers. It requires great energy to undertake the passage from family to worldly life; and great understanding, attention, and concern on the part of parents who must come to know their children anew.

I did not meet all of these teenagers' parents, but my dealings with those I did meet were noteworthy for the immense trust they placed in their children and in me. Friends led me to some of the young people in this book, and occasionally I'd linger for a social visit with a parent. Over tea, one young man's mother asked how it went, "Fine, great," I said. We spoke on other matters, but I could sense some interior struggle on her part. Finally, she lunged across the table: "Just tell me one thing. Did he mention *anything* about a girlfriend? Just as quickly she burst out laughing, embarrassed by her lack of self-control. To another mother, I made mention of the kind nature of her child's words about a sibling. "Oh, I'd like to see *that* reflected in reality," she scoffed. There's no question that I was sometimes getting a slightly colorized version of day-to-day events—but, I thought, wouldn't that be the case with adults too?

What their parents have to say about them is fraught with the tension involved in letting go and holding back, all in one motion. What the culture has to say about them is fraught with commerce's agenda. They are both a market to be courted and a vehicle for selling; their usefulness to the advertising world is inestimable. From the selling to of clothes, music, and technology's entertainment toys, to the co-opting of their every creative expression, they're worth way more than their sometimes anorectic weight in gold. When adult culture isn't frantically tending the seeds of young people's consumerism and dangling before their eyes the tantalizing and glamorized adult world of sex, cigarettes, and booze, it's busily portraying them as willing sex objects, rebels without a cause, or violent, amoral criminals. Their use as villains goes unquestioned: the president refers to the "scourge of juvenile violence," while the Congress contemplates eradicating as many after-school, substance abuse prevention, and job-training programs as it possibly can. Meanwhile, the fact that guns and assault weapons are fewer than six degrees of separation from adolescent hands is considered unremarkable.

The phrase "family values" has been trotted out to denounce and defend all sorts of public policy agendas. It sounds positively surreal when falling from the lips of those who would eviscerate the long-standing social safety nets that many children rely on. These very nets have made a world of difference to some of the young people in this book. An unprecedented battle rages, allegedly over disposing of the deficit, but really over what kind of a nation we will be in the next century. We can argue over what defines family, and family values, but there is no arguing about the fragile nature of family in modern society, and about the difficulties increasing numbers of people face in caring for their own. Though the current battle is waged in the name of protecting the future for our children, feeding, housing, and educating them now seems strangely uninteresting to these budget warriors—as does any firm commitment to safe-guarding their environment and ours.

A final note. Obviously, who I am and who my contacts were had an effect on whom I found; someone else might have ended up with an entirely different book. A universal truth, though, is that these and all young people carry our past into our future. And what moved me most about those I spoke with was their savvy assessment of the complicated and stressful world they find themselves in, and their strength and courage in the face of it. In many cases, they want to make a difference, to do something good for the world. In all cases, their heartbeats reverberate, as do any adult's, with the need to be loved, and to have meaning of some kind, somehow, somewhere. What is different is that just like pinballs reacting to the flick of a lever, flashing off the ball posts, they are in constant motion, both literal and figurative. These, then, are oral portraits, snapshots of a quicksilver moment in time: the speakers' thoughts, beliefs, and feelings evolving even as the tape recorder clicks off.

Three at Thirteen

Annie Garcias

Manhattan, New York

W*e meet at Hudson Guild, an activity center for young peo-ple, in the Fulton Projects. Our interview begins late because there is a group meeting of girls. One of the girls, Nicki, has said she was raped. A Hudson Guild worker wants to talk things over with the other girls. Annie is tiny, four feet nine or so, and very pretty in a fresh, open, country-girl way.*

If I had to flee what would I take? The most important thing is my green card. 'Cause I wasn't born here, I have to travel with that every-where I go. But if I could take something else? I'm embarrassed to say. [laughs] The doll that my father gave me. That's my most impor-tant thing. 'Cause my father—I remember he gave me that with a lot of love. I'll never forget that.

I'm from the Dominican Republic. I never wanted to leave my country. I've been here five years. I live at Fulton—it's a project. First we used to live over on Avenue D, in a two-room thing. We had a cur-tain in our bedroom: the boys used to sleep on one side, the girls on the other. It was like five beds in one bedroom—I got used to it. Sometimes it's hard because when you fight with your sisters, you just want them to get away from you, you don't even want to see them. But when you're thinking about the family, you be like, "That's all right, I'll get used to it." Because we're a family, so we're supposed to share.

My bigger sister is twenty-four, my brother is twenty-two, my other brother's twenty, my little sister is twelve. I had a twin brother—he died at birth. I wish he could be alive. Sometimes it's fun, but sometimes having brothers is a pain in the ass. [laughs] They bother me, they're always picking on me: "Annie this, Annie that." They embarrass me in front of people.

My bigger brother, he's the smartest one in the house. I'm smart, but he studies hard. He goes to school, and works; he lives at home. I'm proud that those are my brothers. We fight a lot, but I really love them. My brothers used to be guys from the streets all the time, but my bigger brother, now he's Christian—he's Charismatic. I don't know what happened, but God touched his heart. My other brother's still on the street. [affectionately] I'm *always* beating him up. I learn how to fight with him. He used to deal drugs. I didn't know nothing about the drugs. But once I saw him take a lot of money home and I was like, "This is strange." And then he brung a gun to my house, and I was like, "This is *real* strange." I took the gun—it was a BB gun, really small. I saw where he put the money at, and I told my father about it. My father went like a detective after my brother—he followed him.

I asked my brother why was he doing that, and he told me because he needed money. I'm like, "But you could get money by working." He said that he didn't have enough money. I was like, "But let me tell you, Alonzo, I would look up to you. If I look up to you, you're supposed to try to be doing the correct things, not the bad things." He really thought about it, and I think that is the thing that made him change. My brother, now he doesn't sell drugs, he went back to school, and he's working. But he's still on the streets, he's always on the streets, playing around.

My father used to be a chef. [sadly] Then he started getting cancer. He had two operations in his stomach and one in the back. I was ten when he got sick. The day they told me he had to be operated on, I was crying my heart out, 'cause I didn't want him to die. I couldn't go visit him in the hospital, so I stood without seeing him a month. I used to pray to God to come save him. You could think that I'm one of these girls from the streets, but I believe in God. I got two attitudes: when I'm in the street I'm a bad girl, but when I'm home I go to church every Sunday, I'm a very Christian girl.

Now we get welfare, and a check for my father, 'cause he can't work. That money is not enough, because we have five kids in the house. I want a job to get money to buy clothes for my own self. I'm always asking my mother, "Let me get a dollar, let me get this for my lunch, money for this." I feel like she's not a bank to be asking everyday. My mother thinks I changed a lot since living in this neighborhood. I got skinnier. Before I got skinny I used to take karate, but then I left my karate lessons and my video classes. My mother was like, "She's leaving everything." But I'm not bad, bad, like some of these girls. In my house, I'm an angel, I don't do nothing. I can't throw paper in my house because my mother would slap my hand, so in the street I'm throwing things on the ground, I don't care. I think that's a bad habit that I got, hanging around with the girls. I didn't used to be like that.

My parents are real strict. If I do something wrong, it's a punishment. It's not like I do something wrong and *next* time they'll punish me. That's the way that my mother and my father grew up, and that's the way they're teaching us how to grow up. Sometimes my mother is like, "Do this." And if she says it more than three times and I don't— you know how Dominican people are . . . More than three times, it's with the belt. In the Dominican Republic, in school, if you don't do your homework you get hit with the belt. That's how they are.

My father don't hit me for just anything, but if I do something real real wrong he *does*. When he hits me, I'm like, "Damn, I hate him! He's too strict with me." And in my house, you can't curse. In the streets I'm used to cursing and stuff. But in my house, I'm like, "*Oh!*" [She claps her hand over her mouth] When I'm lying to my father, he just have to look at my eyes, and he's like, "You're lying to me." I'm like, "*OK, OK*, I was *lying.*" He knows—because I get nervous, and I, like, turn pale. If I get out of school at two thirty, and I get home at four o'clock, I'm like, "I was in detention." He'll be like, [serious, inquisitive look]—I'm like, "*OK, OK*, I was on Fourteenth Street buying something." [laughs] I don't hardly lie to my father. He's the boss of the family.

Once I came to my house smelling like cigarettes, but I was not smoking. My father goes, "Are you smoking?" I went [exhaling with gusto] "I'm not smoking." When I'm not lying I look him straight in the eye, but when I'm lying I'm like, [shifts eyes] "Um, um"—I'm always changing the conversation. He's like, "You're lying to me." I'm like, "*No, I'm not! For real, for real!* I was down with the guys and they was smoking outside, on the corner." He doesn't want me hanging around out there, 'cause a lot of trouble be going on.

My friend Dalida ran away from home. One night she slept over my house. She was like, "Come on, let's cut school," so we cut, and spent the whole day in a park. I was working at Hudson Guild at the time, taking care of the little kids, helping them with their homework. I go to my job, my big sister comes to pick me up with my little sister, and I found that strange. My little sister always comes to pick me up, but not my bigger sister. I was like, "Something's going on in my house." I was nervous, I was pale, I felt like throwing up, I felt like running. I don't know what I felt like doing, but I just went home.

My father asked me, "Where were you?" I was like, "At school." And he goes, "Where you left Dalida?" I was like, "I left her in front of school." "*You sure?*" So I was like, "*OK, OK!* I was in the Twenty-eighth Street Park." I told him I left her at my sister's school: she said she was going to make a phone call, and she never came back. The police was looking for her, and they came to the apartment and grabbed me by my shirt and said, "*Where the F--- were you?*" I was like, "Oh my God—" I turned pale, and I don't know what happened because I kind of fainted. They found her in another friend's house. Dalida told her mother and the cops that she was getting harassment by her stepfather—that's why she ran away. Her stepfather got arrested.

I didn't get in really trouble at home. My father said it was good by one way that I cut school with her, but it was bad by the other 'cause "You know what you're gonna get." I was like, [pleading] "*Please, poppy, don't give me that.*" He let that go, he let that pass. The day we cut school was my father's birthday, and I was sorry. He was *down* on his birthday, he had so much pain; his birthday was the worst day of his life. But it touched my heart, what I heard from her, that her stepfather was harassing her. I felt sorry for her, so that's why I cut school.

My junior high is a really good, friendly school. You can't see nobody without hugging them or kissing them. I love that school. There are all kind of kids, but there's more Chinese kids than anything. The Chinese are together, and all the black, Spanish, and like that, we are together; and all the white people are together like that. It's because they know their own languages. But everybody gets along —we're all friends. Racism is the fault of the parents. If there's a black man right there and a white woman and a kid, and the black man is getting next to the little kid, the mother will push the baby, and go, [whispers] "Don't get next to him." And the baby thinks, "Oh, he's bad, so I can't get next to black people." That's how the kids grow up, and so when they're older they hate black people—for no good reason.

In school the boys are the worst ones—they just *talk*. They don't do no homework, no nothing. Some of the guys in my class got a crush on me. I don't really pay attention to the boys, I just like them them as my friend. I don't know what they find in me because I'm kinda crazy in class—I talk too much. My teacher, she'll be like, "*The parrot is talking.*" [laughs] She's like, "Annie, please, sit down and *shut up.*" I just like to talk!

The Chinese girls, they're real smart, but they never answer the questions. In my science class I'm the smartest one. Every question that my teacher asks, I'm like [waves hand wildly, squealing for attention]. With the homework, they'll be like, "Lend me your homework, lend me your homework." I lend it to them, 'cause they might get in trouble—they get detention if they don't do homework. It's not every day they don't do it. I don't lend it to the guys, 'cause they *never* do their homework. The girls in my class are really smart, but the only thing, they're too shy to wave their hands—they think they're gonna get it wrong.

When I'm with my little sister, I still feel like a child. She likes to play with dolls, she likes to play house—I play with her. Being a teenager is hard, especially when you're twelve to fourteen. In your house everybody's telling you you're too small for *this*, you're still little, but you're too big for *that*. You're big enough to wash the dishes, but you're too small to wear makeup—so I get confused. Before, my mother would never let me wear lipstick, and now she'll be, "Oh, I don't care, let her wear her little makeup." [laughs] Now I could go out by myself some places that before I couldn't. That's how I feel a little bit older.

On Saturday I was in a store, and this guy was rapping up, he was talking to me. [amused] He goes, "Hey cutie, can I have your number?" I go, "Too bad, I'm with my mother!" He goes, "*You're with your mother?!* Bye, see you." [laughs] They're afraid of the mothers. I don't know why, but that always works. It's not that I'm a lesbian or something, that I don't like guys, but I'm not ready for that—I'm too young. Especially to have sex real young, I don't think that's right. Girls in the street will be like, "Oh, you a virgin?" I'm like, "Yeah, I'm a virgin." They'll be like, "Oh, you're stupid. Why you don't lose your virginity?" I'm like, "I'm not stupid, I'm smart—because I haven't lose my virginity and that's *good* to have, to keep yourself a virgin until you get married." That's my only answer to them.

But most of the girls don't see it the same way. Some of them, they don't listen to their parents, they go out any time that they want. I have my curfew: I have to be home before nine o'clock. I hang out with my friends, but with my father's permission. Like my friend Nicki, she never listens to her mother, she always used to walk out. [sadly] I felt sorry for her. My brother told me like two o'clock in the morning he used to come home and see her in the streets. She needs strict parents —she doesn't listen to her mother. She's mad at me or something, I don't know why. I told her, "Where were you? Where you been the whole day." She comes up to me, she's like, "Why you tell the cops on me, where I was, where I slept?" I was like, "Nicki, I never said that." She goes, "I'm gonna slap you." And I was like, [emotionally] *"Slap me! Come on! Here—here's my face. Slap me!* I'm still you're friend. Whatever you do to me, I'm *still* your friend—I'm not gonna leave you because somebody told you I said something I never said."

The next day she said, "I'm sorry. The person that told me that said she was only kidding, to see the way that I was gonna act—if I was gonna fight." The problem is that I don't fight. This is how I am: if you're gonna fight me, I will fight you; but starting trouble with another person, I don't like that. The anger comes from your heart. When you have anger, your blood goes to your head. The only way they resolve the problem around here is punching, hitting, killing, and stuff like that. I'm not like those kind of girls. The way you solve a problem is talking, talking to each other.

When a person is gonna start trouble with me, I just walk away. Especially if it's a friend of mine, I can't fight. My tears comes out. They could punch me, they could slap me, but I can't fight them. My friend gets mad at me and I start laughing. That's how I am. I don't know, but my heart is like a real friendly heart.

I want to get married when I'm older—after twenty. I want to go to college, cause I want to be a doctor. After my grandfather died, I got that in my mind. He died two years ago. I'll never forget that day. He was throwing up blood, so we took him to the doctor, and I was crying. I was like, *"No, no, he can't die, he can't die!"* My father told me that God was gonna get him, that he was gonna go to a new place.

After that I just wanted to be a doctor, 'cause I want to help people. I want to help people that can't afford it. I want to be a doctor in the Dominican Republic, 'cause over there it's real poor. Every time my mother and me used to go and eat in the restaurant, there was little kids looking at me, and I'm like, "Mom, I'm not hungry." I'd tell the waiter to wrap it up and give it to them. My mother used to send another plate to give to them. Over there, they're real greedy— they prefer to throw out the food than give it to poor people! I don't know how people can be that way, that's real wrong. And here, I don't know how people can live in the street when it's cold outside. I saw someone sleeping on the sidewalk, right there. It's real sad. I don't know, but these people got a bad heart. Not me, I can't be like that. I'm different, I'm real different.

Melissa Tates

Manhattan, New York

*A*t Hudson Guild. Melissa is a friend of Annie's who was with Nicki the night she was allegedly raped. As I interviewed Annie, Melissa kept popping her multibraided head in the door, looking to see if we were done—she badly wanted to be interviewed too. She's black, direct in manner; her expression jack-in-the-box alert. She is thirteen.

I'm in seventh grade. I want to go to a Catholic high school, and I want to go to a university. I want to get an education. I want to get a scholarship for art, reading, and math—those are my best subjects. I just want to keep studying.

I live here in Fulton Housing Project. I have two brothers, one sister—I'm the youngest—and my father and my mother. We all live in an apartment, and we live very happily. My father's ex-wife had two kids, but one died; the other one, Michael, lives with us—he's the oldest. Then Charisse, Frankie, and me. My parents aren't married, they just live together. My mother works in Housing [NYC Housing Authority]; my father used to work in Housing, too, but he retired. When my mom's not there we all take care of ourself.

My brother, Frankie, he's fourteen, a year older than me. My mother was just telling me yesterday that when I was born, he didn't want me in his crib: he would kick me out, and try to put my head through the bars. We're always fighting. It starts with him saying my underarms stink or something, and then I start hitting him. My sister—

she's like the best one of the family. She's sixteen, and goes to an all-girls Catholic high school. My grandmother's real sick, and she has no one to stay with her and whatnot, so now my sister moved in with her, and my aunts moved in too. My grandma, we don't really sit down and talk—only on the holidays. When they start drinking they talk too much.

They call me Mel, in my house. My father, when he drinks he talks in his sleep. [amused] The other night he was like, "Mel, you better not go outside. *I'm gonna kick your butt.*" I was like, "Dad, wake up, wake up!" Me and my brothers were just sitting there watching him. He was like, "*Heh heh*"—laughing in his sleep! It doesn't bother me when they drink—only when they bother me. [tolerantly] Like when my mother's drunk, she calls me every other minute to do something for her. Even when I'm sleeping she wakes me up. Even when I'm sick. Like yesterday I was real sick, she was calling me, "Mel, come take off my shoes." Last night, my mother took me out to a bar. She was cooking for a party there, but they let her stay because she knew them. If this room was real hot right now you'd see my eyes getting red, and I would start sweating because of my fever and the bronchitis I have. That place was real hot, so my eyes was getting red. It was like one thirty when we left. I was having fun playing the jukebox—all the music they had. I liked it.

I like hip hop, reggae, and slow jams, house music. And I like two songs from the blues. My father, he listens to music, but the music he be listening to makes me fall asleep. He's got tons of books about the blues. I read them, they're interesting—but the music's not, it's slow. I have to have something with a beat; if it don't got no beat, I'm asleep.

My father was Muslim when he was younger, but you're not supposed to go to clubs and stuff like that, and my father, he just kept on doing that, so he had to put his religion aside. He's Catholic now. My brother has this friend who's Muslim, and he teaches me a lot about it. They pray, and when they close their eyes, they say they see God coming down and blessing them. I try to do it, but it never works. Me, I love religion, I go to church. To be in a Catholic community, it brings me closer to my family and whatnot.

I just came from confession the other day. When I go to confession I tell them everything that I've done in the past. They say that it's supposed to take everything off your mind and you won't think about it no more, but as soon as I finish I'm thinking about it, I'm right back on it. If I confess that I didn't do my homework, I'm still thinking about why I didn't do it. I still feel I'm a sinner.

I don't like fighting unless somebody starts with me. But I get a very bad temper when somebody says something wrong to me. If somebody bugs me, I get real mad and red, and go in the room by myself or I start screaming at them. Like one day the boys in the pool room here were saying some stuff about me, and I didn't like it. I went in another room, closed the door, turned off the light and was listening to music. All the boys came in, and I was like, *"Get out!"* I screamed, and I got in trouble—but, you know, they was all bothering me. They were saying some stupid stuff, like that I got a nice butt, and don't have no chest, stuff like that. They're from around the neighborhood.

There's no girls around here to really hang out with that you could trust as your friend—they all got big mouths. If you do something, they go rat on you. A real friend wouldn't rat on you or nothing. One of my best friends was Nicki, and Annie. Annie, sometimes me and her start arguing, but the next minute we're talking. The only boy in here I like is Louis. He doesn't spread rumors—he talks, but not about people. And he doesn't hang out with the wrong crowd that smokes and drinks and stuff. When he comes in here he's wild, because he's offa the streets and he feels better, safer. I do too.

What happened with me and Nicki? We was on the street, it was nine-thirty at night. This guy asked us if we wanted to go for a ride. I've seen him around—he's a drug dealer. He's like nineteen, twenty. He asked us, and I said, *"No,"* Nicki said, *"No."* We were walking on Eighth Avenue, and he was walking behind us. When we got to the corner he pushed Nicki into this car, and I was in front of her, and I got pushed in the car too. I thought she knew what was going on, and we were going for a joyride or something.

When we got on the West Side Highway I was scared. I didn't know where we was going, what we was doing. He could have killed us— we're lucky we're still alive. I thought about jumping outta the car, but in the highway you'd get hit by a car—and they had the doors locked. The guy driving the car let us out at some lady's house. The other guy took us in the living room, and then he called Nicki in the room . . . Well, he didn't call her—he *told* her to come in the room. She was like, "For what? I'm not coming in the room." Then he said, "Please." She was like, "*No.*" But then she went in the room, and they was talking. He told me to stay out there with this lady. She was playing cards and asked me if I wanted to play; so we was playing pittypat, and watching TV. My mother called the cops, saying that I was missing; and Nicki's parents did too.

Him and Nicki was in the room for over three hours. It was like one o'clock, and I kept on saying, "I have to leave, I have to be home at ten." Nicki, she came out like if she had cried—her eyes was real red. She has allergies, and so I thought she might have had her allergies and whatnot. When we got downstairs he went to go call for the car, and she started crying. She told me what happened, and I didn't believe her. I was looking at her real strange—and then she was like, "I have to tell somebody." The car came, and they took us back.

I had a feeling nothing happened to her because why would he take us back home? Sometimes she makes things up—it's something called "cry wolf." Her father thinks she wanted an excuse for why she came home late. Nicki's parents and my mom, they're real close, and they're always talking, hanging out, drinking. My mother was talking to her uncle, and he doesn't believe it, 'cause she lies so much. And Nicki keeps on telling a different story, and every time you say anything she starts crying.

We have to go to court tomorrow. I'm nervous—you know, I don't know if it's true, I wasn't in the room. I didn't think they was gonna take it to court; I didn't think they was gonna find him. If he did it, he wouldn't be stupid enough to come back around here. He was around here when they caught him—so to me, I think he didn't do it. Nicki probably just wanted an excuse. All I know is that she was in the room for a while, and that's it.

My mother, she talked to me about sex when I was like eight. She told me about what age to have sex at, and for the boy to use a condom —make sure he doesn't have a disease. And don't let nobody force you to do anything you don't want to do. She wants me to understand how to live my life and whatnot. People out on the street these days are doing drugs and stuff, and she doesn't want me to do that. [outraged] They have little kids selling drugs over here! *Little kids,* like ten and eleven years old, that I've seen myself sell drugs. If somebody asks them if they want to sell drugs, and they say yeah, it's *their* problem —it's really their fault. If somebody forces them that's different. And why would they force a little kid to sell drugs?! That's sick.

I still think I'm a kid because I'm not in high school. I don't wear makeup, I don't wear big earrings—only, like, if my mom's not home. I wear lipstick on special occasions. I'm getting older, and taller, but I'm not going to places on my own, like to clubs and discos and parties and stuff like that. I'm not sixteen—I can't drink, can't smoke, nothing like that. That's why I think I'm still a kid.

My sister gives me advice about being a teenager. She always tells me how to dress. In the summertime wear shorts not that short. And when I go to church and stuff don't dress like who hit it and ran. She said, "Don't wear miniskirts, wear dresses with creases in it. Don't go around looking like a hooker." If you wear a lot of makeup and tight clothes—like all the girls who come around here with tight clothes on, the boys are always looking at them. The boys talk like, "Hey baby, you got a nice butt." [feigning a sneer] "That girl think she all bad. This ain't her project. Let her get out of these projects."

If we bring somebody around here, people say, "Introduce"—they want to know who you bring around, they don't want no trouble to start. When trouble starts around here, the first thing they do is pull out knives or something—a gun, a blade, whatever—and start cutting, fighting. A few months ago, there was a fight between the Dominicans and the blacks. They were shooting and everything. They tell us when it's gonna happen; they tell us to go upstairs.

One day we was all out on a Friday—it was like one o'clock in the morning. We was with our parents and whatnot—it was the summer. They told us to go upstairs because there was gonna be a shootout. As soon as we heard shooting everybody ran upstairs. I know everybody was looking out their windows, 'cause I was. I seen this lady walking with her baby carriage, and the bullet went right by her head! I was, *"Oh my God"*—I was ready to cry. When I hear shooting when I'm asleep I'm scared, I be under my pillow and stuff. One time it was like three o'clock in the morning, they were shooting. It was like a forty-five millimeter, and I just keep on hearing bullets and bullets. Since then there hasn't been no shooting around here; everybody calmed

34

down. Everybody is in jail, but they *calmed down*. That's the way it is around here, that's the way it is mostly in a lot of places.

Annie is all Dominican, and I'm all black, and we have no problems against each other. My mother said, when I was little I didn't like no little white kids, I didn't like Puerto Rican kids. But I grew up, and I didn't want to just play with my race people. It doesn't matter what color you are, where you come from, just as long as you have a friend that you can really count on. Everybody's a different color, a different race, but in another way everybody's the same. I don't know how to say it, but your face . . . you can't really see your face. [touching her cheek] This is just an image in the mirror. Your face, who you are—is inside.

Louise Martin

Manhattan, New York

Louise has a calm, good-natured demeanor. In looks she is a prototypical Alice in Wonderland. She spent her childhood in a Chicago suburb, and moved to the New York City area when she was eleven. She is thirteen.

I live with my mother and my sister—she's eleven. My parents separated when we moved to New York. They get along well, though— it's like they're friends now, which is better than them always fighting. It may be a better situation for everybody.

I was born before my parents were married, so I took my mother's last name. After they were married my sister was born— she has a hyphenated last name. I think it's too long, so I'll keep what I'm used to. When I say my parents weren't married when I was born some people say, [raising eyebrows] "Oh, *really?*" But mostly people are used to it now—it's more common.

I was never that upset about moving, 'cause it's an exciting thing, moving to New York. My sister took it a lot worse. She'd be sitting in the apartment, she'd say, "I miss my friends"—and it was sad. Lately we've been kind of nostalgic, my mom and I. Cause where we lived was a very unique place. I'd walk down the streets and just know people. And there were always the greatest restaurants there, and different wood shops and bookstores. And I loved going into Chicago and looking at all the antique stores. I guess it was the way I was raised.

Up until I moved, I wasn't even in tune with the kind of music that kids were listening to. I was always hanging out with my parents. They're thirty-four, they're young; I have a lot of similar interests— like music and movies. They even like my friends. Everything we always seem to agree on. Well, other than the usual things, like how late I can stay out, and if I can sleep over at a friend's house on week- days and stuff. Those little things.

My sister? [sighs] Oh, my sister and I, our relationship has changed a lot. When she was like three to six, she did anything I asked her to, and it was great. A couple of months ago we were hav- ing this really hard time: it began where I was starting a lot of fights with her. And then she was like anything I said, I was saying it because I hated her. And it wasn't true—it was just her opinion of the situation. We'd be watching TV and I'd say, "Could we change the channel?" And she'd go, [irate] *"Don't tell me what to do, Louise!"* And I'd be, "I'm not *trying* to tell you what to do!" She'd bring up an old argument and say, "I hate it when you do that!" And we'd both start yelling at each other. "Remember when you did that?!" [laughs] Dwelling on past arguments.

I don't know what was going on. Maybe I was upset about the transi- tion from her idolizing me to being my enemy. [laughs] She's a little more emotional—she's also younger—so the littlest thing can send her into tears, and into her room. If she gets in an argument with my mother or father, then she's crying in her room, yelling, "Well, you love her best." I do a little bit of that also—but it doesn't send me into tears or anything. But I think we've mellowed out the past few months.

Since I've been getting older, my mom, she's much more patient with me, maybe 'cause we're closer. But sometimes I get aggravated, and I start yelling. My mom will go, [gently] "Oh, come on Louise." She won't really get that mad—which is better for me. Maybe it's because I'm becoming an adolescent. I don't feel like an adolescent yet. [laughs] I'm still the same person—in fact, I think I've always been the same height, and I've never grown, and I look the same. According to me, *nothing* has ever changed. It's like, I can't believe I was ever that short! No, I couldn't have been. No—I've *always* been this height, I've always been seeing things from the same perspective. In my thoughts, when I was in kindergarten, I thought I knew it all— and now I *still* think I know it all. [laughs]

My father directs a photography gallery in Manhattan, and my mother is vice president of something in a bank. We moved to New York because my mom got a higher job offer. The move hit my father hard—he's struggling with this gallery. My parents, they always loved each other, and they still do, but they're both very stubborn at times, and very opinionated. Their opinions were their opinions, and they'd get in fights over little, stupid things. My mom smoked cigarettes, and my dad drank, so, they'd fight about that. Sometimes it bothered me that he drank, because he's not a nice drunk. He wouldn't beat her or anything like that—it's just that when he's drunk and you get into a conversation with him, he gets to be even *more* stubborn, so a stupid conversation would just turn into an argument. I may have always known that them separating was going to happen.

To tell you the truth, I don't know what's happening with their relationship now. Sometimes my mom will peek in my room at night and go, "I'm going to go play pool with your father, OK? I'll be back later." I told my mom, "Who separates in their marriage just to date?"

I think I can basically cope with the situation pretty well. I don't get thrown totally off guard if something changes drastically in my life. Maybe it's because my parents have a good relationship, and I have a good relationship with them. Maybe if they were always trying to get back at each other through me it would be different. That would be very terrible, because I wouldn't want to have to choose. My sister and I, we don't have to be torn, because we can love them both and the other one accepts it. Not even just accepts it but *expects* it. They'll still stand up for each other. If I get in a fight with my mom, my dad will take her side—"Don't talk to your mother like that." They're still "the parents."

The first day of school after we moved was hard because I walked in late. The teacher goes, "*Well, find a place to sit.*" So I sit in the back of the room alone. And the kids go, "No, don't sit there. Mr. Clark says you can't sit in the back." I walked around and found a seat between two girls who looked like they'd be nice—and ended up making friends with them. I was very shy. At this point in my life, I'm not shy, but then I was just like, "Oh my gosh, I don't want to be here." Now I don't care—if they don't like me, then they don't like me. I don't have to be worried about that because I'm me—that's who I am.

It was very different when I first came in. [laughs] I was wearing sneakers and jeans, and I had them rolled up. I was wearing this silk scarf—which, you know, your mother wears a silk scarf—and no one else was. And I had two watches on, which was a cool style where I was before, one after the other—I walked in and people were just staring, looking at me like I was crazy. Did I wear two watches the next day? No. *Never* again. And I never wore a scarf again either. I don't like constantly getting made fun of. It's a real hurt to the pride; it damages your self-esteem.

I was in sixth grade, and I was flat-chested, so I was called "checkerboard," or "monopoly board," or any game board that they could find —that was me. It was horrible. I mean, I was in sixth grade, it's not *my* fault. [emotionally, a flush creeping up to her cheeks] I was humiliated half the time. I'd be walking with friends, and there'd be all these strangers around—and some boy would go, "Checkerboard!" It was *upsetting.* I would cringe, and turn around, and yell something like, "Shut up stupid" or "You're just a jerk," and I'd run to the bus with my friends. I never dreaded going to school, but I dreaded seeing the people. Like, it was a good day if they were absent. My friends would be, "Oh, don't worry about it." But you get that knot in your throat.

The school's a big mixture. They've got Asian kids, Russian, black, Hispanic, white—a little bit of everything. Most people get along pretty well. There's the real hip hop crowd, everyone's in that—white, Hispanic, black. And there's the grunge crowd. And the nerds— they're not really, they've just been labeled that because they're immigrants. A lot of Asian kids are in that, and Russian kids, 'cause they've just come here—and their parents don't have the money to buy designer jeans, and that's that.

Sleepaway camp, I really wanted to go to, because my friends went, but it was so expensive. It was like, "OK, Louise, if you save up five hundred dollars, you can go." It's very pricey, and not something that my parents can afford right now. One girl, she's at a five-thousand-dollar camp—her camp reunion was in Boca Raton. [laughs] Let me fly out to a camp reunion in Boca Raton. My friends will describe camp— they go paddle-boarding and rock climbing, and have the whole bunk thing—and I'll say, "Well, gee, I'd love to go to that." But it's not something that I'm gonna get to do unless I find five hundred dollars. [laughs]

Last summer I worked at Hudson Guild—it's a city camp for kids. Not all of them lived in the projects, although there were projects next door. A lot of the kids were deprived, but some weren't that bad off—by the way they dressed they seemed to be doing pretty good. Some of them weren't at the same level as maybe more upper-class kids would be. I got to experience their side of the story, and I got pretty attached to some of them. I also—this may sound, I don't know, cold—but I got something to put on a résumé.

Sometimes you'd bring in aspirin—you'd just be, "Oh, my goodness." These little kids, running around the stage screaming—it would get to you—and then you'd be screaming too. [muted yell] "OK everybody, line up." It was difficult, but there was a real sense of satisfaction, because after all this planning and hard work we had this great carnival. Everything worked out well: they wrote plays, and made up games. It was just like, "*Wow*, we did this!"

It was very independent for me, cause I was taking the train alone, and getting along on my own. I don't worry so much about stuff like what happened to that girl, Nicki. Well . . . it actually happened to me once. When I was six years old my parents' friend had a disorder in the head, and he took advantage of me—he lived with us at one point. I don't mind talking about it. He didn't ever penetrate or anything—but he, you know, touched me in places, and I was always uncomfortable around him. I blame him now, because I get uncomfortable around grown men, which I don't like—because I should feel free about liking and meeting people. And so I know what other people are going through when they go through something like this. But when you're younger you don't think about that; you don't think that something like that is gonna happen. You think, "Well, gee, maybe some riffraff might beat me up or chase me down the block," you know—but you never think about that until you get older. It's just some people are exposed to it younger.

What happened was, in first grade someone came to our school and talked about child abuse. I was like, "What?! He's abusing me? This is something that's not *supposed* to happen?" I went to my teacher and I was like, "This has happened to me—and this is something that's not normal? Other kids don't all go through this?" I thought, "This is just what happens—everyone, this happens to everyone." She said, "*Tell that woman.*" The woman and her partner were police officers, they took me to the station, and my parents came down.

It actually didn't traumatize me that much. I didn't like it at the time, you know, what he was doing. It wasn't something that I would actually cry about—I just didn't like being near this person. But afterward it was sort of exciting, going to the police station. It was all of a sudden getting me all this attention.

It's something that you shouldn't let ruin your life. Bad things that happen, they should be part of your life, but you should be able to overlook them in order to continue to function on a normal level. You should look past what happens to you, as something that happened that isn't going to destroy you . . . 'cause you have to continue with your life. If it's so terrible, you either continue with your life, or you end it. Either way, that's your own decision. But you can't let something that's someone else's awfulness or evilness, or even just disorder, rule your life—otherwise everyone else is gonna run your life, and everything is gonna be a task, it's gonna be a chore, you're never gonna have any fun.

I want to get married at an early age, like my parents. Not as early as my parents, 'cause I still want to explore the world a little bit. But I want to get married early enough so that I won't be like an old person to my kids. You see movies and TV shows where someone is always saying, "I can never meet the right person." I just feel like I'm gonna meet someone. In my mind it's always been, I'll be twenty and meet someone that I really, really like, and we'll get serious, and when I'm twenty-five we'll get married.

Work? Well, I've always wanted to be an actress, I've always wanted to be on the big screen. Lately though, I'm thinking, "What if I end up a starving artist, searching for a job?" So there are other things that I'd also like to do. I would like to learn how to speak another language, and sign language, 'cause I think you could do a lot of things with that. I'd like to be very computer literate. I plan to go to college.

My parents encourage what I like, but I've always been sort of worried that I won't make it for some reason. I think it is important to have what you want. I mean, to have to say to your kids, "No, you can't have this toy" . . . Well, that might sound like you're spoiling them—and I wouldn't want to spoil my kids—but I also wouldn't want to say, "No, *I* can't get this." I'd want to do well enough to live comfortably, to be able to send my kids to college [laughs] . . . summer camp.

I don't think people should have to be homeless, although sometimes it's their fault because they spend their money on drugs and lose their jobs. I look at the country and say, "Why is it so polluted? How come so many people can't find jobs? How come people aren't buying enough American products and the country is going farther into debt? How come it has to be this way? How come everyone can't just get a monthly check and everything can't be free? How come we don't live like in the stereotypical fifties when everyone was like upper- middle-class, like the Donna Reed family?" I look at crime, I look at the shelters and stuff, and a lot of the time it isn't their fault—sometimes there just isn't anything out there for your skills. And the Mayor's making all those budget cuts. I'm sure that there are things that you can cut that won't affect the less fortunate; I'm sure of that. How can every little bit of money in New York all be going to the schools and to the less fortunate? How come he can't cut something else?

We're middle-class. My father, his father died early on; he was very poor when he was growing up. We have a very close family. If you watch talk shows, you always see the families who hate each other and haven't seen each other in years—but my family, everyone knows and loves each other. Christmas we go and visit all our relatives. My grandparents live in a little town in the Midwest and they're old-fashioned: my grandmother bakes cookies, my grandfather works in his garden.

My grandmother is part of the reorganized Church of Latter Day Saints, or something like that—a reorganized Mormon. She goes to church every Sunday, and she's very kind. My grandfather, I don't think he's at all religious. My parents have always been atheist and raised me atheist, and for now that's what I am. I've thought about maybe becoming a Christian, but it's a really big commitment. If I get baptized, then I'm baptized for life. It's not a decision that I want to make right now. It's hard for me to grasp the idea of there being an entity up above my head. Having a creator—that's not very scientific in my mind.

I want to comfortably go in my sleep someday, when I'm about seventy. [laughs] I don't want to constantly be going to the hospital to save another organ, I'd rather just be taken off the respirator. If someone's still in good health, but they have an awful heart condition, and they can get a new heart, then that's a good thing—but if it's just to prolong an agonizing life . . . There was a case about a husband who helped his wife die. That was out of love: if she didn't want to be on this earth any longer, then why should she have to? And why do people think, "Oh, this person, they must have been crazy because they committed suicide"? If you don't want to be on this earth anymore, there should be a way to leave it. I think part of being alive is being able to enjoy it, and if you can't enjoy it anymore, then what's the point?

Pushing Limits

Rosie Piper

Baltimore, Maryland

W*e talk in the finished basement of the house where Rosie lives with her petite, gracious mother, Ella. Describing Rosie's behavior during puberty, Ella widens her eyes and says, "I did not know this child as mine." Rosie is African-American, large-boned, with a very pretty face beneath her backwards baseball cap. Her nails are long and perfectly painted. She is sixteen.*

Describe myself? Rosie Piper is a nice person. She's a stubborn person. Cares about people. Persistent—now she's coming to be more persistent, in high school. Eccentric, extremely creative, a neat freak—when it comes to certain things. Her room is different. [laughs] That's the creative side, really. But see, Ella, my mom, doesn't understand that, and so we fight about that a lot. I'm at a bit of a deficit because I have a friend living here. My room is not that big, and all this stuff is just double everything—there's not enough space for her clothes and mine. But my mom doesn't want to see that—she won't take that excuse.

Rosie doesn't like girls, cause girls don't get along. Men have that male bonding, they can agree on everything; and girls are just diverse, they don't get along with each other. I don't have all that many girl-friends. Let's see, I perceive people well, like the first time I meet 'em. I can have this attitude about you: I like you or I don't. And sometimes it's a bit of a downfall for me because I just won't open up to somebody, won't let them know who I am.

My school is the largest school on the East Coast, the largest building. I think inside too, the number of students—twenty-three hundred students there, and about half are girls. And they're all ghetto. I can't stand them. I hate how they talk, I hate how they dress, just how they *act.* If you go to my school you see girls dressed up to go on a date, to, like, an evening, black-tie affair. And I can't stand it. *What's the point of going to school dressing up like that?!* They do it for attention, to get boys—you know, so everybody can look at them and see the latest fashion. Some apply theirselves, some don't; some look good and are smart; some look good and are really dumb. I myself, I just dress comfortably every day. I mean, everyone wants to look nice. I have this attitude: I would like to have the latest fashion and the latest clothes. I don't have the money. I've just had to come to grips with not having. But some people didn't even go to school the first day because they didn't have the outfit they wanted. And that's really dumb.

I'm in the eleventh grade. But my ninth and tenth grade, I went to a school for the performing arts. I really liked that school at first. I was in theater production. No one cared about how you looked: it was just you and your talent. But last year I started to deteriorate, and so I left. Actually, I got dismissed because I did not do the work. My grades were plummeting. My mom, well, I bullshitted her all the time. Oh yeah . . . . [amused] I was like, "I'm doing well, I'm doin' *real* good." I bullshitted in middle school too. Back then I was going through that puberty thing, and so I just rebelled and didn't do any work. Middle school, boy—that was *rough.*

My mother told me about body stuff, she bought this book for me. I said, "What the hell are you buying this for me, man?" But it really helped me out. It's like a reference to everything about a girl, and what boys go through. We had a health class in middle school, which made me aware. I got my period when I was in sixth grade, and I didn't even think twice. I said, "Mom, I'm getting my period," and she was, "*Really?!*" That wasn't a big thing, but mentally and emotionally I didn't know what the hell was going on.

My father used to play professional football, and now he's an artist. He did that. [She points to a striking portrait of Frederick Douglass.] He's always been in the picture, but he and my mom were never married. I always thought that eventually they would, but when I was in the eighth grade I found out that he married this other lady, and I wasn't invited to the wedding. I didn't even know her. I was shocked. And so, I think, subconsciously I just held that anger in and took it out on everybody, and took it out on myself. At school I didn't do any work, I gave all my teachers a hard time—*all* of them. If a teacher approached the class the wrong way, to me, that was it. My mother was up at my old school all the time, up there trying to bail me out.

I have a half-brother and sister, my father's children from two other women. I was nine or ten when I found out. When he told me, I was like, "You're lying, I don't have no brothers and sisters." We're a year apart. When I met 'em, it was alright. Everybody was like, "How you doing?" It was interesting. I remember one time when he took us to Philadelphia for Christmas to meet my grandmother. It was weird because they'd never met me—they'd heard about me, had pictures of me—and I didn't know who these people were. My father, he left us there at the house and went somewhere, and I was the big sister. That was when I had to prove myself to them. We all slept in the same bed, and they were scared, cause it was a weird bed, a weird room; they heard little noises, and they were crying and stuff. I was just like, "It's going to be OK." Once I found out I was the oldest I was like, "*Yes!*" 'cause I always like being the leader.

It's hard being the leader at my new school because there's so many people there. The first day I was scared, I was *so* scared. I played it cool, though. My mom didn't know I was scared at first, but I admitted it to her: [timidly] "I'm afraid, I'm afraid." 'Cause I wasn't used to being in a big old ocean, you know, I was usually the big fish in a small pond. And now it's just so different.

I really regretted messing up. I felt so bad, like I was gonna have this big old stigma against me. I thought, "Man, I'm out of the arts school, I'm not gonna be a star"—you know what I'm saying? Then I thought, "A lot of famous people come from butt-ugly schools and never went to college, but they're big people now." So I turned that around. My mother felt like she'd failed, not keeping me in line. After a while she realized it wasn't her fault, it was my fault. She said she was just gonna deal with me being dismissed and getting me into a new school. Now it's cool because I'm really doing well. I'm on the honor roll.

My mom's a professional photographer and a professor. She knows a lot—she's really smart. I really love my mom, I think she's a really good mother: she taught me how to be a good person, and gave me everything I need to know about life pretty much. And she's beautiful too. But we used to fight and stuff—about anything. I remember one time we had this fight because she didn't tell me the food was ready. I was down here, and she was cooking upstairs. I was hungry, I just assumed she knew I was hungry. I ran upstairs and she was sitting in the kitchen, and, man, I called her a *bitch*. And she took these tennis shoes and whipped me, hit my butt. Oh, God, that stuff *stung*. Oh my *God*, it *hurt*. I didn't know she was going to retaliate like that. She was right to do it, though.

We was fighting all the time. She'd put her hands on me. I'd say, "Why you trying to hit me and stuff?" We was just fighting. Physical. That was like when we were the same size, but she won't do that no more, 'cause I'm bigger. [laughs] One time she said, "I'm gonna call the police on you." I just thought she was bluffing. Next thing you know, *ring-ring*. She was down here washing clothes, and I heard the doorbell. I looked out the window and there were these policemen, a woman and a man. Oh my God. I came down here, "*You called the police on me!*" She said, "They're here that quick?" She went upstairs and opened the door. I stayed down here in the basement, locked in the cedar closet. I covered myself with all these clothes and stuff, and I stayed in there for four hours. I heard 'em talking, and I heard the door close. She finally went to work, and I got up and I left.

Another time she called the cops on me and this big fat white man came to the door. You know when you get that knot in your throat? Boy. He was talking to me, I couldn't say *nuthin*. I was crying, I was so scared. He was like, "You hear me talking to you?" [in a strangled voice] "*Yeah.*" I couldn't get it out. He said, "You was hitting your mother." I said, "Yeah, she's mean." That was the last time the cops came in my house. Things have been calm for a while. I was always a hard head, I always learn things the hard way. I just know I'm too old for that stuff now. But I know that when I start driving things are gonna get rough, 'cause I'm gonna really want the car, and she's gonna say no. [laughs]

I remember talking about boys with my mom—not talking about "how to," but how boys *are*—like how boys hit you because they like you. "Boys act dumb, Rosie, and they really don't know what they want." I really never knew the value of giving up your virginity. I remember when she found out I wasn't a virgin. I was thirteen. This is the story. I had a best friend and she moved away, and we would write each other. I wrote her a letter telling her I lost my virginity. Ella found the note and read it. This was on a Sunday, we just came home from church—I thought everything was hunky dory. Oh my gosh, then it came out: *"I read your letter."* [cringing, squirming, groaning] Oh my God. [face flushed] That was so rough. I was speechless. She was like, "Now I told you, if there's something you don't want me to see . . . ." She was like, "Who is this boy?" and "When did this happen?" "How many times?" "Did he penetrate?" I remember that question. Oh boy. She jacked me up, she jacked me up big time. She pulled me up, she choked me. [tugs at shirt dramatically] Oh, she was *mad!* We kept on that whole day, that whole week so to speak.

I came home from school one day, always fix myself a snack, I hear the doorbell. I looked out the window and it was my father. I was like, "Oh my God, this is not over." I said, "Hi, Daddy." My mother came home and we were sitting in the living room talking. I told them he was [small voice] seventeen—four years older than me. Like a dummy I wrote down every time he came over. My mother found the calendar, and it was on the nights that she worked late, so she, that just, *oh* . . . They thought that he took advantage of me, but I don't think he did, 'cause we would talk, you know—he was nice.

But he was a bad boy, he was a drug dealer. I didn't tell them—they found out though. It was like February, and he had been shot, but he had a vest on. I was scared. I wrote down: "George got shot." She read that, she was like, *"What?!"* That was just the hardest thing. My father was like, "Is he a drug dealer?" You know, I couldn't say anything, because I was just so totally in the wrong. I was so humble then. And I was so afraid that he was gonna hit me or something, bein' he's so big. My mother, she jacked me up right then and there. She beat the mess out of me. My father had to pull her off me.

Nowadays I use condoms. I wish my mother would buy me condoms, because they're expensive. I ask the boy to provide them, and I don't engage in sex that much either. Unless it's really intense and passionate, you know. It's not often like it was when my last boyfriend was here and we were together. He's moved on, he's in college now.

Everybody I know who's having sex uses condoms, they're responsible. I know people who have AIDS and stuff. I worry all the time. I was thinking about what if I had it, what would I *do?* Crap like that. It scares me, man. I'm scared all the time. We talk about it, me and the girls. We're like, "What would you do if you had AIDS?" "Yo, I'd give it to everybody." 'Cause that's like your first instinct, 'cause you know you're gonna die. Why should *you* die when everybody else is alive? That was like the first thing . . . And then I thought if I had it, I'd probably be a teenage advocate, go around to schools and stuff. That's what I'd like to do, turn it around and make it a positive thing.

[sadly] But my worst thing is that I die before my mother. I've even wondered about, what would it be like at my funeral? I always see my mother crying, alone —'cause she's not married. Her father died over a year ago, and that was real rough . . . [Her eyes fill with tears.] She was strong, she was *real* strong. I remember when I found out he died. There was all these cars on the street, and I thought, "Oh, it's a family meeting." I went into the house and I seen all these people from this church—'cause he was a minister. I'm like, "What are all these people doing here?" And then I see my uncle sitting there with my grandmother—she'd been crying. Then I seen my mother—she's crying. I looked at her, she said, "Grandaddy died," and *pshew* . . . [choking up, voice thick] That was it for me, boy. I was outta there. I *wailed.* I was crying, for a long, long time. I couldn't take it . . . [She cries again.]

My grandmother was like, "You want to go see him?" I was like, "No, I don't wanna go see him. *No, no, no!* I want to remember him *alive!"* But then the coroner came, and I knew, after he went in there, the next time I was gonna see him in a coffin. I went upstairs, I saw him: he was sitting in a chair, looked real peaceful. His hands were white. He was cold. He was dead. My grandmother said he died like this: [clasps hands across chest] like he was holding his heart. He died of a heart attack. And so they laid him down. I kissed him, I held his hand . . . [sighs] That was it. They took him away.

Family's really important. They should always be there for you, to back you up. The nagging is supposed to be there, and support, and a shoulder to cry on. I value that. Some people just don't have it, and I feel sorry, 'cause they don't know what they're missing. I've come to see that, 'cause a lot of people I know, they don't have good families.

When I graduate from high school I'm going to go to college. I have a lot of interest in photography, theater production. But artists don't make money—and production is money, but it's not enough. I really want to make a lot of money: you can't survive without money. I want to live as well as my mom. Being a single parent, my mother did real well—I give her a lot of credit.

I have a strong, strong, strong feeling for chemistry, so I think I want to be a chemist. The world is so competitive, kids really have to be a bit ahead of theirselves to know what they want. It worries me. Years ago, when you graduated from college you usually went to where people were looking for graduates in your field to work for them. And it's not like that anymore—you really have to have an idea, you have to be special. And so I want to be a special person—I just want to know it now, what I want to do. There's a lot of people out there, and it's not that easy for African-Americans anyway.

I was thinking about interracial relationships, and I really don't have a problem with them. As long as two people like each other and understand their heritage, you know, how that came about—and understand their culture and can accept it—then I don't see nothing wrong with it.

It's like the big issue—people talk *white*. Well, there ain't nothing wrong with people talking white: it's just using proper English and articulating. But you can't say that to anybody because they're like, "You like the white man, and you want to be like him," and all that mess. It's just the real ghetto girls, or the real ghetto niggers, the ones who are strictly from the streets, who've grown up in the poverty and stricken environment. They talk dirty, they just don't know how to talk. That's how that is. They don't give a lick about school, don't really want to learn how to speak the proper English, or they never had the opportunity. It's unfortunate—I think that's sad. Some people don't know how to get dressed and how to act in an interview. When you're applying for a job, you're supposed to be courteous and polite to the store manager. And some people just don't know.

When I started going to the new school, a lot of these teachers, they thought that I was just like everybody else. I went, "Come on now, I don't know you, you don't know me, so this attitude is not called for, 'cause I'm not like everybody else." [angry] They'd always be smart with me and talk to me like I was a little girl. I was like, "Nuh-uh, that's not right." At first I thought I was gonna get in trouble with the teachers maybe, with some lip—but that wouldnt've been well thought out. It's not worth it. I'm trying to graduate—I'm just trying to focus now, 'cause I really want to go to college. I don't have the time to get in trouble—that can be eliminated. Yeah, I'm making priorities for myself. Got to. I have to. I just want to be treated with respect.

Carl Randall

Eugene, Oregon

H*is family has just moved from outside a very small, increasingly conservative town in Oregon, to a newly renovated house in the hills about ten miles outside of the more metropolitan and liberal city of Eugene. Their view of the grand and graceful Three Sisters Mountain range is breathtaking. More important to Carl is the fact that his dad has finally put a basketball hoop in the driveway. He is gangly, and dark-complected. He seems to puzzle out his thoughts and examine them carefully before setting them forth. He notes that he will be fifteen in a matter of days, but at the time of the interview he is fourteen.*

I have a little brother named Sam—he's eleven. My mom and my dad both live with me. They're potters—they make pottery and ceramics—and they work at home in that barn studio out there. It's nice because I can always call home and I know they'll be there, but . . . um, I sometimes wish they'd go away. [laughs] They go to arts and crafts shows, about ten a year, but mostly they're in Oregon. Sometimes Sam and I stay with family friends, but mostly we go. For our next show I'll probably help drive, because I'll be getting my permit. I *hope* to help drive. I don't know if they'll let me drive the van full of pottery. [grins]

The car trips get pretty long, but I enjoy them mostly. I can't explain why, really—just that I like to be traveling, just with family. Yeah, I know the stereotypes about teenagers not wanting to have anything to do with their parents. Sometimes that's true, but most of the time I can stand them. [smiles]

We eat dinner together every night whenever we're here. It's not like "family time," it's just a routine. Living out here, it's hard to like, "OK, I'm gonna go out right now." Even if I wanted to ride my bike all the way to town or something, it's a long way, and unless it's something really important, it's not worth it to go. I think it's all a big scheme, a plan to keep me at home.

I wanna live in town when I grow up—some town. I've always lived in the country. Where we used to live, everybody was Christian, everybody was right-wing and *really* conservative. There's not a lot of diversity in that town . . . [laughs] And because there's such little diversity, they run away from it. My mom's background is Jewish and my dad's is German, Christian. I couldn't really relate to most of the people there, 'cause my family's liberal, and I've been raised to be more left-wing.

There was a measure on the ballot in Oregon, against gay rights— like that you could fire somebody on account of their being gay. During that time—seventh grade, or maybe eighth—we had a school thing where a teacher read off the different measures, and we voted, and I voted "no" on Measure 9, which was the gay rights measure. It was really weird, people were like totally fighting about it. He read off of the actual voter's pamphlet, and we raised our hands. Everybody was voting yes on it, and I was like, "*What?!*" He asked if anybody wanted to go up and speak, and I went up and said why I voted no.

I can't really remember what I said, but it just kind of escalated into an argument—it was "special rights," *they* said—and people were yelling, "*Fag.*" They just totally couldn't even see where I was coming from. I wasn't the only one who voted no. There was one other girl—whose parents just happened to be good friends with my parents. [laughs] Did that change the way people treated me? Just for like a week or something. It wasn't the first time I realized that they didn't share my beliefs, 'cause I knew it was mostly a Christian town. It was just—it brought it all to *me*, personally . . . [small laugh] After that I decided not to voice my political opinions very much. It wasn't like I was scared to, but I didn't really feel like arguing. It just got me so frustrated when I would, because I would try to show people my side, and they couldn't see it. It was really weird.

People knew that racism was bad; there wasn't a lot of open racism, like there was antigay things. There was like one black family there, and the kids went to school. You could tell that people were uncomfortable when a black kid would sit in a classroom. I could see they were uncomfortable, because I was . . . because I wasn't used to it—I wasn't used to any kind of diversity. I didn't feel scared, I just knew that that was different, and I noticed it, you know, more than somebody who grew up in a big city would. I knew that I shouldn't feel uncomfortable, and by the time I moved up here I didn't, but it was different. The difference between me and some others is that I didn't think different was bad.

I think everybody in this family probably could go back to where we used to live, except for me. When we moved I was really relieved, I was glad to get out of there. I have nightmares about having to go back. It's so much more comfortable here. I don't have to pretend to be what those people need me to be just to be friends with them. I didn't know what that was like until I moved. Here I can be myself without being an outcast.

I'm a freshman in high school. There's like six hundred kids in the class. At my old middle school there were two hundred fifty in the whole school. I bet it'd be scary if there were five hundred kids crowded around me at the same time. But you don't see a lot of kids except when they're in the halls, and you ignore all the people and just try to get to your locker, and to your class. It was different because, in my old school, I'd walk down the hall and I'd know every single face.

I just prescheduled my classes for next year, my sophomore year. It was weird because there are classes that I *have* to take to get into college. It kind of freaked me out because it was too much. That was probably when I first realized, you know, how far along I'm getting—college isn't even that far away. I feel nostalgic about my childhood. I think about when I was a kid and all the things I could do, and I try to do as many things as I can now. Like not sit and wish I had those years back, but *do* things.

My best friend's Mexican, and mostly my friends are Mexican. But on my basketball team, there's two white kids, two Native Americans, two Mexicans, and a black kid. It's not like I wouldn't be friends with a white guy if he came up to me, but it's just—[shrugs] I don't know why I hang out more with the Mexican kids. Maybe it's because I look kind of Mexican, because I'm dark.

My first math teacher this year, we had a lot of run-ins. He was like a Nazi, I swear. The first day of school there was a Hispanic girl, and he couldn't say her name right. Everybody could say it right, you know, but just because it wasn't Smith or Williams or something, he couldn't pronounce it. I got mad at him right then, I said, "I don't like this guy"—because he wasn't even trying. He said I was his biggest problem, and I kind of wanted to live up to the challenge. I didn't want to be, like, *bad* in his class, but if he was gonna point me out for every little thing that went wrong . . . A lot of the time I was frustrated because it felt like he just wanted to pick fights with me; it felt like he was so much more immature than I was. And that frustrates me, when people in authority are less mature than you.

My parents aren't that strict. They'll give me a chance to go over to a friend's house after school, and go wherever I want, if I can make it out there. I feel they trust me, and it's all about earning their trust. If I blow it, I have to earn it back—and they *will* do that. That's just another reason not to break their trust! [laughs] They might be a little more strict if we actually lived in town. They wait for me to call and tell them whose house I'm at; they don't, like, call around—"Is Carl there?" See, their strategy is, they'll give me freedom, and if I blow it, I don't get it. If I get grounded I can't do much of anything—no hanging out after school, any of that. I gradually have to work for my freedom back. I think it's a pretty fair way.

Once I got suspended from school for three days, and that was the biggest thing that's happened to me since we moved here. I don't really like to talk about it because it was something I totally regret doing, and it was one of the more stupid things I've ever done. Um, I stole a jacket is what I did. It was left in a classroom, and I picked it up—it was that simple. I got caught and got suspended. In my other school they knew you—the principal would be like, "Now, I know you're not the type of kid that would do this, so I'm gonna let you off this time." But here there are so many kids, and it's like, "You did this? You're gone. See ya."

I got suspended Thursday, and that weekend I had to stay with a friend of the family while my parents went to a show. They almost didn't go; they felt really uncomfortable leaving me. I realized how when something like that happens, it totally breaks their trust . . . [swallows hard] That was kind of a reality check—the turning point where I stopped trying to push the limits of stuff. Now, whenever I think of doing something, I remember that—and I don't.

Like just recently I had a substitute teacher that was almost as bad as my math teacher. Our regular teacher is laid back, and this teacher comes in, and she's *totally* strict. Three people got kicked out in the first two minutes of class. We were talking, and she says something like, "This is what's wrong with society today." And she meant us *kids* —and we were just doing our regular thing. One girl stood up and said, "I think *you're* what's wrong with society—you overbearing teachers." And the teacher was like, "*Get out!*" There's one. Her friend stands up, he says, "I think people should be able to voice their opinion in this class." There's two. I wanted to get up, but I [sing-song] remembered what happened, and I didn't want to get in trouble—I didn't want to see the principal again—and I made it through the period.

We watched an informational movie, and took a quiz on it afterwards, and I aced the quiz. She was surprised, 'cause of the way I dressed or something. I dress like everybody else—baggy clothes. I didn't dress like . . . [sighs] what she would think was acceptable, with a tie, or something. She saw my paper, and she looked up at me, [quizzically] and I was like, [nodding] "Yeah, it's me." She goes, "*Oh,* good job."

I think teenagers get stereotyped. The people that run those TV shows aren't teenagers, but they can vaguely remember being a teenager, and maybe they went to their parents and asked what they were like, and their parents said, "Oh, you were like this and this." But society changes, and I think teenagers are a lot more grown-up now—I think there's more stress to deal with now. I have two parents living at home who've been married since I was born, since before I was born. And there's not a lot of that now. There's kids who grow up without a mother, without a father, and they have to take care of their younger brother or sister, and they have to grow up faster—there's more responsibility. And that's just one example I can think of. Then there's teenagers in gangs and that.

There's violence here. It's a small town, but it's a big little town.

Just this weekend, this girl I know, her friend got stabbed and died. She said it was stupid, that it was over fifty dollars that a guy owed him. He didn't have the money, and they got into a scuffle about it, and the guy's dead. And she had to deal with that, and she's fourteen. It's not any different than in a big city, it's just less people.

There's a measure that is just taking effect right now—I think it's Measure 5. It says if you're over fifteen you can be charged as an adult in, like, worse than third-degree charges of anything. You can be tried as an adult and be sent to prison. The other day I was reading about this guy who killed his son and got six years. In our high school newspaper, it had all these different instances: so-and-so killed his grandmother, charged as an adult, got fifteen years. And there was this kid who broke a guy's jaw, and he can get, say, five years in prison. But the guy that kills his kid goes to jail for six. Now that's where I think the system falls off. If they're gonna escalate it that much they should do it throughout, for everybody.

My parents have had a sex and drugs and rock 'n' roll type talk with me. I smoked pot, for the first time over Christmas break, and I got caught. That was about the same time I got suspended. [shamefaced] I was with my cousin, we came home, and my mom pretended to be giving me a hug, and she was like—[inhales deeply] I went and sat down, I was like . . . [slumps, tries to look very small] I was just . . . [sighs] 'Cause I knew. I looked over at my cousin, [eyes darting guiltily] and went like [mouthing it] *"We're caught."* And she was like, "No, we're not—we're fine." And then my mom comes in and goes, [somber] "C'm here."

I didn't get in trouble, really, 'cause they knew it was my first time *and* my last time. My mom talked to me and forgave me right then. My dad didn't talk to me for three days. He *wouldn't* talk to me. I guess he felt that if he did, he'd blow up, 'cause he was still so mad. It got to where I was like begging him to give me a talk. [laughs] *Yell! Do something!* I think that it was good that I got caught my first time. Maybe if I hadn't, I might still be doing it, but I remember how it hurt my parents, and that gives me incentive not to. It's behind us, I think. I hope it is. It is for me.

I don't know what made me do it. Um—everybody has done it, my age. My mom said, "You're too young to be doing this"—and I know that's true. But I told her later, she should be having this talk with Sam, because I know that kids are doing it right now, in seventh grade, sixth grade. I know people who hate their siblings with a *passion*, and they really don't care what they do; but I feel like I kinda have to look out for him, because my parents don't really know what he has to deal with in school. Twenty kids in the sixth grade got busted for alcohol because some guy brought it and gave it to them. And I know that that happens, and I gotta kind of watch for that. Sometimes I ask Sam what's going on, 'cause he'll tell me the real story—not just tell me about classes, but, like, what went on *between* classes.

I can do some stuff with him, but he's just, like, going through the phase of being totally moody. Sometimes, just because I'm his brother, he won't want to do anything, he'll totally disagree with everything I say. Or maybe he just can't stand me. Sometimes he can—you gotta catch him on a good day. It's kind of frustrating, but then, he's my little brother. [He sighs. Different parts of his face register big brother expressions of love, annoyance, resentment, and resignation.]

Do I torture him? He'll say I do, but no, I don't think I do. There are certain times he just *really* gets on my nerves. [laughs] Most of the time I don't interact with him very much, because when I go into his room, he freaks. I hope this is just a stage, I hope he's not like this for the rest of his life. [laughs] Don't get me wrong, most of the time he's all right. It's just . . . like today—he came back from his friend's house, and he tried to act like everything was his, and he owned it— and unless I was his best friend . . . You know? But I'm his—I'm his *brother.* [perplexed] I guess he doesn't want me to take the place of his best friend or something. I don't know.

Yeah, I think people expect teenagers to be difficult. Maybe that's why a lot of parents complain about their teenagers, because they're supposed to. 'cause the word teenager is synonymous with, like, headaches. I've made the transition, I've gotten in my trouble, and now I'm just, you know, going with it. Just going with the flow. I know everybody tells people this, but, really—you have to be your own person, not try to live up to anybody else's standards, and not try to live down to anybody else's standards. And people like you for it—[brief pause] I *think* . . .

Outcasts

Phoebe Lens

Bolinas, California

A tiny town north of San Francisco, on the other side of Mount Tamalpaid, referred to by locals as "Mount Tam" or "the hill." There are few paved roads, and it seems to have the largest number of Volkswagon buses anywhere outside of Albuquerque, New Mexico. Phoebe is quite tall, with long blond hair, a wide, open face, and very pale skin. Her voice is almost creaky, like an elderly woman's. She is fourteen.

I want to be an actress and horseback rider. That's my dream. Riding, I could teach, be a trainer, or a breeder—something to do with horses. And then acting—I want to play Hamlet. Sarah Bernhardt played Hamlet, way back. I like the play, it's full of everything I love—revenge, romance. In the olden days the males played the women, so why can't the women play the males? Most of Shakespeare's main characters aren't women, and even if the women are main characters, they don't have as many lines as the male characters. So why not be a woman who plays Hamlet? I don't think I have a big feminist attitude. It's just, you know, I think women should have the exact same rights as men.

I'm an only child. If I had a sibling, I've always wished it to be an older brother—a younger kid you end up having to take care of, and I don't want that responsibility. [laughs] And then an older brother, they could help you out with math problems or whatever. I go to my dad, "Can you help me with this?" He goes on this long explanation like he knows what he's doing, and I'm like, "Dad, that's not it. Don't even try that, that's even further from the answer!" [laughs]

I've lived here since I was born. It's space, and I really like space—I love the ocean. I get claustrophobic in cities. I go into San Francisco for an acting class, and if I haven't been doing it for a while, I just stare at the buildings and I'm like shaking. [laughs] I don't actually shake, but I feel tight, and when I step in that elevator to go up just eight floors, it's like, *"Oh my God."* Cities are *so* busy and *so* fast. Everything out here is so slow. You have time, and it's so beautiful and spacious—it has the ocean and it has hills. When I ride my horse up onto the mountain I look down over Stinson Beach and the lagoon and the beaches, and it's just like, "Wow!" I don't take it for granted. I don't know what I'd be doing if I were in a city. I'd probably be a couch potato, you know, and just sit around and watch TV.

I'm doing independent study this year, so I have a teacher that I meet with once a week, who gives me work. Doing independent study gives you even more time, because you can get a week's worth of normal schoolwork done in, three or four four-hour days. Basically, I wake up whenever I wake up, and I work. I'm learning—you get work done faster by yourself, no interruptions. I was really sick of the lectures five times a day: "If you don't behave we're gonna take your study hall away. These are privileges we have given you," and then, "Sit outside, you're disrupting the class"—and it just goes on and on and on. I'm like, "Give me a break! I'm not doing *anything.* I know this is for the other kids, but I don't wanna hear it." You waste so much time. What's nice about this is you can fluctuate your schedule. You can say, "Today I'm gonna read a book," and you can start your work the next day. And the teacher will give you credit for reading that whole day, and that whole book. As long as you get your work done, it doesn't matter.

I go to the barn around three, and I ride two horses every afternoon. I have a job to pay for my horse—I ride another horse. I have to keep track of horse stuff, but I don't pay much attention to economics. When I'm grown up and old enough to deal with it, I'm gonna *have* to deal with it, so I figure don't worry about it until I have to: don't put more stress on yourself than you already have. My mom's always kind of secured me, and so getting a job and helping support my habit makes me more independent. Like, "You guys have done it for me, but now I can do it too." It gives me self-confidence. I usually don't come home till like six thirty, and the nights just seem to fly by. We probably won't eat till eight, and then I'll talk to my parents about something, and maybe read some, and go to bed.

I watch TV about two, three hours a week. My mother kind of throws a fit when I turn on the television and she's in the house. It's a waste of time. When I'm really exhausted and I don't have the brain-power to think about reading, I get sucked into television. We only get five channels out here. [laughs] I channel surf between those five and find whatever sitcom is on—and I *love* watching sports.

My mother is really old-fashioned. We went down to L.A. to visit some relatives, and I heard my cousin say, "Does your daughter do drugs?" And my parents were like, [quizzical] "My daughter do drugs?" It's, like, not a concept to them. My mother looks at me some-times and goes, "You're so different." And I go, "Mom, I'm more nor-mal than a lot of kids—I'm more old-fashioned." I try and explain to her that I'm not way out there, I don't do what a lot of kids do today. I don't even know what they do today. [laughs]

Every night I'll just, like, get into a conversation with my parents, and one thing'll lead to the next. Most kids, they don't have that free-dom. Maybe it's not freedom, but they don't interact with their par-ents that way, have conversations every night. We sit down to dinner, and then we just talk, and the night's gone. It's not like we plan to have a little family talk—it's just I ask questions. It could be anything from history questions to "What were you doing in the fifth grade? What did you used to do at my age?"

My parents are both in travel companies. My dad goes to Alaska, Oregon, and Idaho, and runs river trips there during the summer—I went on my first river trip when I was four months old. My mom runs art trips around the world, like to Bali, and right now she's doing France. We have an office at the house, and they go out there every morning, and there they are. I like that because to get up, drive in—at least an hour—why do that? After a long day of commuting they come home and they'll just be all stressed out. So it's not as stressful on them, which makes it not as stressful on me.

I've traveled to Japan, and France, and Tahiti, and [laughs, glancing at a large wall map of the world] so many places—and I was so young, it's hard to remember. It's neat to go other places and discover other cultures. Lots of people don't know that so many different cultures exist. And being in third-world countries, and then Japan, and Singapore. And then there's Bali, and everything's so peaceful: people aren't murdered, people aren't killed, there aren't mass bombings or whatever. It's just a nice culture. And you get to busy Japan, but then you walk up into the mountains and it's, *wow,* how beautiful it is.

It's nice to know, in my mind, that there are places where violence is not happening. It gives some hope to our country, to other countries. When you watch TV, they have these news breaks: So-and-so was just shot in Sacramento—and that's so close to here. It's scary. It could happen to anybody. I have a friend, her dad went out to get the mail, and in a drive-by shooting he was killed. He didn't do anything to those people. Why did they take their anger out on him?

I see the newspapers sometimes, but it's like, I don't even want to know about it. I try to hide. [suddenly serious] It's something I don't like, but I try to hide from the truth, because it's so awful, disgusting, you know. I can't handle real situations, things that actually happen. I have to go to these fantasy worlds, like Alexander Dumas and *The Three Musketeers.* They go through all these adventures and stuff, and everything ends up right in the end.

I don't like the truth. We're living in such a corrupted state, country, world, that it's just, you know, let me live my life and leave me alone. Why get involved? I mean, everyone is involved somehow, but it's just so awful, so bad. I'm out here, and it's like, *can these things actually happen?* And they *do.* Murders and suicides, and everything . . . You look at such a beautiful place and think how could anything like that happen in this beautiful world? I want to think of it as a beautiful world. [unhappily] But you can't.

Like the Oklahoma bombing, that's so awful. [on the verge of tears] So many innocent people—all the children, all the babies. It's so sad . . . It's like there's no peace—war is going on all the time. I don't know how many people are shot per minute, or per second now, but it's just like, will it ever end? I can handle it if I have to, but I don't like to if I don't have to, and I don't have to cause of where I live.

I don't get out a lot. I might go over the hill once a month. This is just, like, where I live. I don't really know what other kids do. I spent a few days over at my friend's house, and basically they call up the other classmates, and talk all afternoon; then turn on the TV, and then talk all night. It's such a waste of time. And here they come the next morning, "Do you have your homework?" "Uh . . . no, I was too busy to do it." Give me a *break*.

In third grade I went to a private school. How long did I make it there? Half a year? The kids were so snobby and rude, and mean. Just playing rope, I'd say, "Can I join in?"—and they're all, "*No*, you're not part of *our group.*" The clique thing. And that clique thing really bugs me. It's these groups of kids who like each other, have something in common, and they just don't like you for some reason, and they won't, you know, [with a trace of pain] they *reject* you: "Sorry, we don't like you." But they don't even say sorry, they just go, "We don't like you. You're not gonna be our friend." And maybe there's one girl who's part of a clique but who accepts you as a friend—and that's what happened with me. But, you know, one friend in a school of I don't know how many, in a grade of a hundred or something . . . it's not enough.

We had to wear these sailor's dresses things. I can't really stand dresses. And we had to wear these [with loathing] *checkered white-and-red pinafores* . . . It was like kindergarten through third grade must wear these pinafores and fourth through eighth must wear something else—because we need to be able to tell you apart from the lower kids. [heatedly] It's your size, your personality. Can't you tell that? I can understand why they have you wear uniforms to prevent gangs from going, "Oh, you're wearing the color purple, and you're wearing your hat this way, so you're our enemy, I'm going to blow your head off"—but that's not a problem in that school. They could've at least had us wear something more comfortable. I like big flowing dresses, but I spend most of my day in sweat pants. I won't even put on jeans unless I'm going out to see someone, or I'm going to school where kids will go, "Ew, you're wearing sweatpants."

People, they've just teased me my whole life, and I have never figured out why. It's something I'm used to, that I've learned to ignore—to say, "Well, *you're* the insecure person." They tease me for riding horses, oh, a whole number of things. It's so long a list, I've kind of forgotten. I used to wear sweats to school in the fourth grade, and they'd tease me out of my mind for that. Or if my hair wasn't a certain way. Everyone wears their hair down, I always wear my hair in a pony tail. Wearing your hair down, it may look nice, but it gets in your way. And being around horses, your hands are full of mud, and [acting it out] you're going, "Oh, let's get this *strand* out my face." [laughs]

But being teased hurt for a long time. I bet it's left its toll. It's just something you have to learn to live with—there's no way to get rid of it. In the sixth grade, I went to a different private school, and they had all their cliques. But they had cliques within cliques, so it was even more complicated. My mom always used to say, "Sticks and stones may break your bones, but words may never hurt you." She'd tell me that all the time when I'd come home and the kids had been awful to me. And so it stuck in my mind. I mean, some words do hurt, but some you just gotta learn to ignore, let pass right by you. Just turn away.

My parents really wanted me to stay in that school, because it's a good education, and the local school is not the greatest education, let me tell you that. [laughs] But I'd come home and I'd cry every single night. I hated that place so much. I was in pain, and so they set me up with this person to talk to. I think I was in such a dilemma—and I couldn't stand it anymore—that I'd give almost anything a try. By seeing this person I could say, "You know Mom, I'm sorry, this is not helping the situation at school. It's helping me, but it's not gonna change anything." It was kind of a way to say, "Mom, I'm sorry, I'm not going to this school anymore."

It helped me get this attitude that I have now. We didn't just work on that, we worked a little on my claustrophobia and stuff. Sometimes I feel like I'm gonna hyperventilate. I don't, not so other people can notice: I can put on a total calm when I feel like I'm about to explode. I may look really pale or something . . . other than that you couldn't tell. But I'm totally tense, there's this big knot, and I just hold my breath. Claustrophobia, you're just wanting *space*, you know? Maybe it's cause I'm tall—I'm five nine—but I've always had it. And I've always been shy.

In class I participate, I do all my work and everything, but I don't raise my hand. If they call on me, I kind of stumble out and answer, and I blush and get all anxious. I don't know what it is. I can't control the blushing, it just happens. Even in front of my friends—boys or girls, it doesn't matter. [voice rising higher and higher] It's like, we'll just be talking, and we'll catch eyes, and I'll go completely red. It's so embarrassing. [laughs] I'll turn bright red and I'll feel the heat, and it's *really* embarrassing, because they look at you closer, and then you get even more embarrassed. I think I've always blushed, 'cause I've always been shy, but I'm not gonna let this happen my whole life. It's not something, you know, that I like. [laughs] But I don't know what I can do about it.

Because I've gone on my mother's trips, I'm really good at talking to adults, and all the adults say, "Oh, you're so mature." But I talk to the kids and they're all, "Oh, you're so immature." And it's like [gentle yell] *arrgh*. I don't know why they say that. I don't think I act that stupid around kids—no more goofy than my friends get.

My parents won't allow me to do independent study in high school. I'm gonna go over the hill to a private school. It'll probably be hard for me too, because I feel protected here, and secure. And so to go out, it's like, [anxious] "I *have to* go out?" It's kind of scary. [baby voice] "Well your mommy's not there to protect you, so what are you gonna do?" I guess you could say live one day at a time, you know; one hour at a time, one minute at a time. Just see what happens, and play it by ear. That's my attitude. And then, if people are mean to you, just ignore it, it's their problem and not yours—they're the ones who are insecure. Be who you are. People are more likely to like you as being yourself. If you're playing this kissy-up girl, or this hotshot or whatever, then you have to switch and change your other, good personality. If you have to make a new personality to be popular, to be somebody's type, I don't think you should make that sacrifice—it's not worth it. Your own personality is your best one.

If the girls are gonna be crappy, I'll just try making friends with the boys. [laughs] Boys aren't as cliquey as girls. I don't know why that is, I've wondered about that a lot. But I'm not gonna worry about social things anymore. If they don't like me, they don't like me. If they don't like me, I won't like them. I'm just gonna go through school, get my work done, and come home to my friends. And that's gonna be what I do. I've worried about it enough for one kid in one lifetime.

Eduardo Alcocer

Chicago, Illinois

I t is late afternoon of a Republican
sweep Election Day. We meet at
the offices of the Merit Music Program, where Eduardo studies as a
pianist. He is a tense young man, with a nervous tic–like laugh,
yet there is something centered about him, a certain maturity. He
is sixteen.

"I don't know why I'm nervous . . . It's two things. Despite the fact
that I'm proud of being an outcast, I'm secretly afraid of saying something that's like, "Oh my God, he's strange." It's like an internal self- con-
sciousness that I can't quite get rid of. And that's kind of one thing that
would make you nervous. And another thing is sounding stupid: I always
want to try to say something that's profound, and not just say something
for the sake of saying it. That's mainly my two nervous things."

I'm Puerto Rican. My parents grew up there. They met when they
were in grade school. My father drives around a forklift and that sort
of thing—I don't know for what company. My mom teaches in a public school, bilingual Spanish and English.

I was born here, raised here, but we visit Puerto Rico too. I'm not
into it there—my grandparents were farmers, and so we're in the
countryside. No technology. I'm more into my cubbyhole, my plea-
sures, you know, my TV. [laughs] I mean, they have TV, but it's in
Spanish, and I don't speak Spanish that well, so there's a language
barrier. I understand it, so if they, like, want to hide something from
me, Spanish wouldn't be a way. But in speaking it, there's like a little

mental block, I guess. My parents say it's because when I was a baby my babysitters were English, and I grew up with the English language first. My brothers and sisters speak not as good as my parents, but they're *way* better than me. [laughs]

I have two brothers and two sisters—I'm the baby. The closest one is five years. My brother and my sisters, everybody's in college, it's just the quality of colleges that are different. [laughs] My sisters are in . . . it's not quite junior college, but it's that level—they're like learning algebra. They're at home . . . they go to colleges around here —and my brother is at Ohio State. He was determined to be a football player, and he had an injury, so he couldn't play football; but he could play baseball, and that's what he's doing now—and hopefully he can do that professionally. My parents are telling him to always have another goal in mind, he might graduate with a degree in history. They want him to get a degree in education, so he can teach history, otherwise, without it, what is he going to do, really? I don't know about my sisters, I don't know what's their goal. I hear rumblings like, "I want to get married." [laughs] I don't know if that's a big goal. They work already, but it's not, "I want to do this, I want to be somebody." It's just, "I want to get married." I mean, it's something—but I think they could do better—if they really wanted to.

I'm a freak. I am the freak in the family. Yeah—and proud of it. I get mocked all the time. I help them with their homework, though, so it's all even. But we get along. As long as we have something, you know —just being a family. That's very important to all of us—as long as we still have that, we're OK.

We have dinner together—it's almost always Puerto Rican food. It's kind of hard to get 'em all together, but we try. We sit around the table, and discuss and argue—the usual "How was your day?" sort of thing. I'm usually the one that comes up with a comment: "Why are the Republicans taking over?" And my father says something like, "Because people are scared." We have that sort of discussion. I call my parents independent: they go for who is the best candidate for that situation. I'm the same, and I'm looking forward to when I can vote. It's important because it's a unique chance to actually decide who's running the government. And if you spoil that, your ideas might not be represented, and that's a shame.

My parents are middle-class. The neighborhood is on the West Side, right by Oak Park [a middle- to upper-middle class suburb]. We rent the upstairs of a house. It's a pretty good neighborhood, but it's getting bad. It's like they're spreading out—the gangs, drug dealers, all the bad things. Ten years from now they'll be in the suburbs.

I commute to a private school. I'm a junior; I transferred sophomore year. They gave me money. [laughs] Good reason to go. I went to a public magnet school before. In terms of education, it's better—it's better *a lot.* But the social atmosphere, it's so different. As a commuter I don't live near the school, and the majority of the people do. They make plans to do stuff in the after-school and I can't, 'cause I have a ride to get to. I'm more of an outsider there. And it's very small, the school is like two-fifty, three hundred. And, um, they're very cliquey.

It's sort of by common interests. I guess my group tends to be . . . we're all into computers. I wouldn't call it a clique—kind of like a clique of outcasts . . . [laughs] Something tells me that having popularity kind of blends in with stupidity. [laughs] That's not always true. I really don't judge stupid by grades, it's just I can tell—it's intuitive. I don't say, "Ah, this person doesn't know things," 'cause I'm bad in math and I don't think I'm stupid. It's just an attitude about what's important—priorities. Instead of concentrating on schoolwork, it's like, "I'm gonna call so-and-so." I guess smart people would, like, consider school and college. I'm not talking about a robot-like, [machine staccato] "I want to go to school." [laughs] I mean balance. But it has to be pretty high up there, the desire to learn. And if that's not up there, that's idiocy. Why are you in school? Is this just some big socializing activity?

I wouldn't say I'm an overachiever—just an achiever. I guess my parents had the plan when I was little, and I was kind of guided—and now I'm guiding myself. Part of it is becoming a teenager; the more you learn the more you want to learn. Learning for the sake of learning—which is hard to do, I guess, for most kids—as opposed to learning to get a job and make lots of money.

And now basically the split is my parents want me to get a high-paying job, and I want to be an English major. And my parents are, "No, you'll be a *bum.*" [laughs] And I'm telling them that money doesn't really matter, that it's something that I want to do. I guess it's hard for them to understand, because they always had it hard, and when you have it hard you want your kids to do better than you. They're always worried about that, and I'm more into the happiness thing—which doesn't mean money. [laughs] My parents say, "Be a lawyer." [laughs] Lawyer, doctor. Lawyers are creative—they do use a lot of the skills that English majors use—but it's not something that I want to do personally. But they never give up. It annoys me sometimes . . . But I understand their position. They don't think I do, but I do.

I'd like to do something that allows me to do not a lot of work but still make a lot of money—like something that fills a need. Maybe a very good script for a movie or something. I might compose a song, a pop song, just to amuse myself, and maybe it'll sell. [laughs] Something mundane, in the meantime, while I have the big plan in the background: to write books that challenge the mind, like maybe try to write a novel. I want to write more than a man does this, a man does this, and it's a nice plot, nice plot twists. I don't care about plot. It's more theme-based, and message-based. So that's one of my goals: to make money and do it as quickly as possible, so I can get into the other things of life.

I pretend to write. Well . . . I don't have confidence—I'm like, *"Don't look!"* I write short stories, poems, I'm trying to do a novel. But one of my problems is following through. I have this idea and I write a couple pages out, and then I stop—and then I don't know where to go from there, or I'm unsatisfied with what I've written and I have to do it all over again. I'm not used to saying, "No, this is wrong," or "I don't want to do this anymore." I want to start something and finish it—instantly! So it's either my self-esteem getting in the way or my lack of following through.

I'm always, like, having a script, and whenever things stray away from the script I kind of get angry, depressed, you know, that sort of thing. But it doesn't happen that often. I try to compensate for whenever that happens. My psyche is almost computeresque. I'm like, "Don't be depressed." Sometimes it works—most of the time, in fact—and I'm happy again, and I can go on. Mainly, again, because I have a sense of goals, I have a purpose. And maybe if I fail that purpose, then I'll be excessively depressed, but as long as I have something to work towards . . .

Recently there was a point in my life where I wasn't sure about piano. It was like conflicting interests. I mean, I really was into the English thing. I've been doing piano for all of my life, and after a certain point it doesn't make sense to quit; because, you know, you've invested so much, why quit now? It was not so much losing the love for music as gaining love of English, and being afraid to balance the two, because I would, like, get lost. What I told myself is that I should keep on doing what I'm doing, because I feel that eventually this might come in handy too—the piano—help me in the sense of discipline, you know: the lesson thing, the practice. And without that I do feel empty. So that was the resolution to that. But that was a very traumatic period—it was a week.

I don't think of piano as a career. It's very difficult. It's always so competitive, and I don't think I'm competitive enough to actually do something—except like maybe be a teacher or an accompanist, and I wouldn't be satisfied in doing that. I would want to be, you know, *concert pianist*. If you're going to do a dream, do a big dream. [laughs] Being an accompanist would be, you know, cog. And I want to be *a* cog. [laughs]

I have a Baldwin upright. I practice two hours a day, most of the time—sometimes it doesn't work cause of the homework thing. Ideally, I try to do two—I *want* to. I started playing when I was six. We had an old computer, and there was a program that turned the computer into a musical keyboard, and my father heard me tinkering with it: "Oh, he must be talented!" So he enrolled me in a free program.

I have a modem with my computer, and my parents are always yelling, "*Get off the phone line!*" And then I'm on the computer, period, a lot of the time, and they're, "*Get off the computer!*" And I don't understand that, really. It's not television; it's not like you just sit—it's interactive, you're actually *thinking*. And my parents don't seem to understand that. I think their reason is that I spend too much time on it, it's addictive—I'm using too much of my mental energy. But that's what I like. I don't like not thinking, I don't like just sitting there and vegetating in front of a TV—I'd rather *do* something. I guess it's just that my parents are from a different generation, and have kind of like the aversion to technology thing . . . And anyone using technology should be shot. [laughs]

I wanted to use my modem because I needed a game. Notice I said "needed." [laughs] And my parents said no—and I got it anyway. I got caught. It's kind of easy for me to get caught, because the computer is twenty-five feet away from the phone line—there's a cable running along the floor. All my parents have to do is look down, and I'm caught. They see the phone line: "Eduardo, ah-ah . . ." Then they ground me from the computer—I can't use it. [laughs] Do something bad, the computer goes—and then I'm trapped in the house, and I watch TV [laughs]. It's hard to discipline somebody like me. I don't misbehave that often, so it's kind of hard being creative about it— they have to do *something* that I won't like. But the computer—I mean, you actually do use the computer for a tool, and the computer is also a gateway to the outside world for me sometimes, most of the time. [laughs] I have my e-mail thing. I communicate with people around the country, around the world.

You know about the Internet? Some parts frighten me. It's just this huge information claw, and private companies are now trying to form their own Internet. And if you want to be totally paranoid, it's like eventually information will be the gold of the next millennium—and whoever controls information will have power. That sounds crazy, but it's being done now. There is, like, the Clipper chip. Let me explain: the Clipper chip was like an encryption standard for cellular phones, so you could digitize your voice over a phone line—no one could intercept it. And the government had a key to the Clipper chip, so if they wanted to get information—if they wanted to, like, bug some-one's line—they could do it. But the key was split up. The plan was the National Security Agency would have a key, and the local police would have a key, and if they really wanted to get somebody they would combine together. But the very existence of the key is frighten-ing, because Big Brother is watching. In the end they turned it down because lots of people from the Internet were flooding the White House with mail, like, "No, this is not a good idea." But even that they were thinking about it is scary.

Just the idea of the year two thousand itself scares me. I mean, you think about a new millennium, a new century, a new everything really. And what will happen? It's so unclear, the direction we're going. I mean, Republicans take over—all is lost. Why are the Republicans actually gaining control? And a good reason for me would be people are scared—and I guess when people are scared they go to something conservative. People are afraid, and that's sad. It's really sad, because I don't see conservatives actually saving the world. [laughs]

I think that something drastic needs to be done, almost radical. I tend to read science fiction a lot, 'cause I like that genre: it's really based on metaphor, if you think about it. It's like taking one aspect of something that exists in this culture, expanding it, and showing us a mirror of what might happen if we let this problem go on. I see society going in a downhill curve, and as society goes in a downhill curve, the people, they're clinging to something old, like something from way back when, something from the good old days. Society going downhill stems from pride and greed, the way I see it.

Like racism can be traced to pride, you know. Like maybe: I am white, I have pride in my race, therefore I am better than so-and-so race, and then I don't like that so-and-so race, so I'll burn them. And if the government won't let me burn them, then I'll separate myself from them. I consider racism an old value, something that we can't even perceive as being good, we can't see any benefits. That's the way we are now. We meaning kids, our generation, whatever. [laughs]

My friends are Asian, black—it's really mixed. I *see* racism, but it's never affected me directly. I've been lucky. I think if we learn about each other, then we develop respect for each other. Because if we don't know anything, then we just assume that we're the best and they're inferior.

I think the socioeconomic thing takes effect really early, and the more educated you are the less of a problem race is, because you have education. So because you're black or because you're Hispanic, that's not getting you down so much because you're smart, and you know what to do with yourself.

I don't think we can try to interfere with some other government, some other culture, without really understanding it. I guess that might be a reason why we have so much trouble with China, because they have their own set of values and their own set of beliefs, and we don't understand that because we're Western. And without really understanding who they are we can't really communicate well.

I see the nineties as a transition decade, as all the values that we had back then are slowly fading away, and we're trying to find new values to uphold, or maybe no values at all. [laughs] Trying to find an identity.

My family, they don't go to church, but I'd call them fundamentalist Christian. The Bible is the literal word of God. Not symbolic—literal. [laughs] They really stick to the letter. I studied a lot of religions as I grew up, and I kind of thought they were all the same, and the only difference was proper nouns—like, Allah, God, you know, same thing. And they all want you to do one thing, which is do good. And they all have different rules about what is good. And so what I thought was, just toss those aside and define good as doing something that you know as right, and evil as doing something that you know is wrong, and doing it *anyway*. And so, really, judging yourself by your own laws. Not a view supported by many, but . . . [laughs]

I believe that there is a force, something beyond which we can explain: call it God, call it chance, call it chaos theory, whatever. [laughs] And when we die? Let me see, we go somewhere, because I don't think the plan was to cease existence. We might exist in another form, but I can't even perceive lack of existence. But why bother thinking about death when you still want to be a lawyer? [laughs] No. My parents really leave me alone about religion, because they consider me a lost cause in that aspect. My other siblings are kind of on the same level as my parents, which means I'm in trouble . . . [laughs] I'm the outcast once again.

Drugs—never. Why? Because one, I was never offered any. [laughs] So that kind of gets in the way. And two, I don't see any benefits. And again, there's the plan. Nothing else matters. I want to get from point A to point B, and I don't want anything getting in my way. And drugs do that. I've seen people do drugs at school. I guess it's kind of like a depression thing, you know, searching for an escape. And I don't know what to tell them—I'm not qualified in that aspect, there's not much I can do. I should talk to them, but I kind of get the feeling that kids don't listen to kids; that they need someone older than them, someone that they actually respect, or awe, to tell them. I mean, there's peer pressure—that works—but it's kind of hard to do peer pressure with one person. Cause not many people care as much as I do, like, "Oh my God, how can this person do drugs?" [with real concern] I mean, that's frightening to me.

The general feeling I get from other kids is a lack of concern and thought about what's going on. It's like they think, "Why care what's going on around us when there's a new TV show?" [laughs] That's what I miss about being a kid—not caring. The ignorance of childhood, just living for the next chance to play with your toy, or the next episode of "Sesame Street." And as you get older you get more concerned about the world around you. That's kind of the thing I miss— being ignorant. And being able to get away with it.

But I need to do something for the world. I feel like I want to do something positive. It doesn't have to be big, but some positive contribution. And that's part of the plan too. [laughs]

The Way It Is

Joe Zefran

Chicago, Illinois

Joe is large-framed, with a scruffy beard. In 1994 he decided to run for alderman. He is eighteen. "I just don't like being how I am sometimes. I hate belonging to the same race, or the same gender, or the same sexual orientation, as the oppressors. There are days when I want to be a female, African-American, homosexual, Jewish person, just to not be the oppressor."

I ran for alderman 'cause I needed something to do. [laughs] But also, I wanted to let people know that there are eighteen-year-olds out there who are interested in politics. When I was going around to collect signatures for alderman, this woman opens the door, sees me and says, "Oh, no, go away—I read about you, you're too young." And part of me wanted to say, "I don't think you should be able to vote, 'cause you're too old, 'cause you're senile." I don't believe that, but the automatic assumption—"You're too old you're senile; you're too young, you're not experienced enough; you're black, you're dumb; you're a woman, you're a second-class citizen; you're a disabled, you can't do as much as we can . . ." People look at teenagers like we're a totally alien life-form.

I didn't get on the ballot because I didn't have enough valid petition signatures. The weird, funky law, is that in order to get signatures, you have to be a registered voter in the ward. And I don't know that many registered voters in the ward who would want to go out every night and collect signatures—with the exception of my parents. So that was a major problem. I was three short.

My parents were supportive, they were cool about it, but they're like that in a lot of things. I let them know I wasn't a virgin, and they were like, "Oh, OK." And it's not like they're not caring, it's just they're how I think a lot of parents should be: they look at me as a person, not as "my child." Of course, my mom wrote me in [as a candidate] because I was her child. [laughs]

Every reporter asked what my parents thought. That's what they're gonna ask, because that's how this society views teenagers: still living at home and kind of their parents' possession. This whole parental responsibility movement—if kids graffiti a wall they want the parents to be responsible and pay for the cleanup. *I don't think so.* There's only so much a parent can be responsible for. What they're doing while they're not at home, I don't think is the parents' responsibility —in fact, it's the teen's responsibility. If somebody graffitis a wall, I get pissed at them.

My ward is incredibly diverse, which is why I love it. Most wards have one, maybe two different nationalities, whereas this has Hispanic, Korean, Arabic, and white. It doesn't have a large black makeup. On my block alone there's all these different languages that are spoken— Rumanian, Filipino, Spanish, Gypsy, Korean, Yugoslavian, and Jewish Yugoslavian. Diversity is the lifeblood of this country. It *should* be. I think a lot of times people forget that.

I'm Slovenian and Irish. We'd probably be middle- or upper-middle-class, I guess. My parents are both trained as social workers, but then they decided to get pay jobs. My mom's an occupational therapist, and my dad is a social work manager. I have one sister, sixteen months younger. My mom, she got arrested in the sixties for protesting and all that stuff, and my dad was one percent of the people who voted for McGovern. They weren't hippies, they were more along the line of war protesters. War protesters, I think, were a little more responsible and less chemically oriented. [laughs] I attribute a lot of my political initiative to them.

I went to a small private grade school. My graduating class had nine kids in it, so there were certain social graces that I wasn't that good at. In seventh grade I went to a different school, for that one year. It was disastrous—I guess my hormones were like a year ahead of everybody else's, so I went through a bad experience when other people weren't.

Part of it was that I didn't have any allies in the school—I didn't know anybody for years and years and years, like a lot of the other kids did.

I was very much in my own world. I remember a lot of things vividly—obviously, it's not that long ago. But, it's bizarre. I was doing a lot of things, like staring at girls, and calling somebody up numerous times for a date, and she would repeatedly say no, and I wouldn't get the hint. Stuff like that. Yeah, I was a little child-stalker, you could say that, a little out of control. And I think it's because there wasn't anybody to say, "Hey, you're out of control." I was confused, I denied a lot. I said, "Well, she said no because she's busy, she didn't mean no." Now I'm just the opposite. Somebody'll move an eyebrow and I'll think they don't like me. [laughs]

In high school I went to public school—Lane Tech [a magnet school offering special instruction in technical skills]. It's selective to a certain extent, but it's not like you have to be supersmart to get in. But there was an obvious difference between the kind of kids that went there and the kind that went to regular high schools, just in terms of the potential intelligence—not necessarily intelligence but the *potential* to be smart. There are kids who, in the way they were raised, their grade-school education, weren't given exposure to different things. There are kids who in fourth grade haven't done an addition problem. As a result, once they get into high school, they're not gonna be that good at math—and they won't really have the potential to be that good at math.

There's a lot of growth that goes on in grade school, and once you reach high school that's really the expansion. And there's a difference between growth and expansion. Growth is like the tree gets a height, and expansion is the tree expands with its leaves, and its buds, and its flowers. So if you don't nourish a kid when they're young, it'll be a smaller tree.

I started my social career freshman year. My freshman year was very similar to people's seventh grade year in terms of the awkwardness, and the rejection, and the "Will I get to play in the truth or dare game, or won't I?" Like I asked nine people to homecoming, and I still went by myself. [laughs] I grew a lot in high school. My first girlfriend was sophomore year. Thank God for the drama program, [laughs] cause fifty percent of my girlfriends were through that.

I'll admit—and I hope that every other teenager will admit, because for the most part it's true—that the media has influenced some of the things that I do. It's these subtle messages inserted in certain areas—on billboards, on TV, on the radio, at concerts, and in music videos. They're drinking or they're smoking. I don't think there are a lot of kids out there saying, "Oh yeah, MTV affects my life," when in fact it does, as far as what bands are popular and what ones aren't, how kids dress, how kids act. There's this turnaround of white culture, especially in the youth, of becoming kind of everything but white. It's the bullshit on MTV—I blame MTV for a whole bunch of stuff. One of the best quotes I heard was from Kurt Cobain—and other alternative rockers have said this: when they play their concerts they look out in the audience and see the same people that would beat them up in high school. And I think that's directly attributed to MTV. It reaches Nebraska and the suburbs—normally places those bands wouldn't reach.

In a music video, or at a concert up on stage, musicians'll drink or smoke, and as a result kids will think, "Oh, if my hero's doing it, it's OK." But the main reason that kids drink and do drugs and smoke and have sex is because it's fun. A lot of people out there who are trying to get kids off drugs forget that. They release these stupid PSAs [public service announcements] and these stupid brochures about peer pressure and about the dangers of drugs, and they don't work. It's other people telling teenagers what to do; it's authority figures who they don't want to hear from.

In my junior year there were people from some organization handing out booklets, and I think condoms as well. The booklets were full of real blunt facts about teen sex, getting protection and stuff, and those worked. They were more peer-based, and a lot of the people handing them out were in their early twenties, and they were a lot more realistic. "Yeah, we know you're having sex, but at least do this and this and this. Use protection, and watch your back."

Teenagers are independent-minded. They hit age fourteen, and they're making their own decisions, with the exception of things that they can't make their own decisions on because of the law restricting them, like curfew. Curfew is one of those laws based on adults being able to control kids, that's the prime thing. And yes it helps against the gangs—but *Jesus*, I mean, it hurts so many other kids. It's society telling them, "We don't trust you after a certain hour." The majority of teenagers just want to hang out. Whether we hang out at ten or at two, we're gonna do the same thing. We're gonna go to a coffee shop and talk, or go to a play, or whatever. And yeah, there's that ten percent of teenagers who'll go and wreck things, or get drunk on alcohol, or whatever. But there's ten percent of every group that'll do that, because there's ten percent of society that'll do that. It's kind of like the class thing—where two people cheat in a class, so the whole class gets an F on the test.

But it's like this whole problem I have with building more prisons, as opposed to doing more prevention. We need more prevention programs. There's a *lot* more kids doing pot than doing cocaine, and not just because of the cost. There are kids out there who realize that crack and heroin and cocaine and hard drugs are stupid. I don't think pot's all that bad. I've never done it, but I think it's less lethal than alcohol.

Part of what might help is to go to the reason why kids do this: not only is it fun, but they literally want to escape reality. It's fucking boring! It's *fucking boring* in Nebraska and in the suburbs—I mean, there's *nothing* to do. Give them something to do—and don't give them these dumb *recreation centers!* Give them a reality that they'll like. I enjoy my reality, and that's why I don't need to do drugs—but I've had to search it out myself, and I've had to bust my butt to do it. And my reality is getting worse and worse as my bank account shrinks. [laughs]

I talk to a lot of teenagers from the suburbs and the only place they go when they come to the city is downtown, and to Belmont and Clark [an area with teenage-friendly shops and a favorite hangout—the parking lot of a Dunkin Donuts]. They may not only be afraid to go anywhere else themselves, but it could be that their parents don't let them. A few years ago I didn't know that many people in the suburbs, but I've met a lot more people, and I've asked them, "What is it like? What do you do?" "Oh, I go to the mall, smoke pot, and have sex . . . see a movie once in a while." So I say it's boring out in the suburbs because that's what I hear.

I've met them through America On-Line, and through the youth group that I'm in—it's part of the Unity Church. I think that really helped in terms of how I grew socially in high school. I started when I was in seventh grade. My parents were Catholics and they wanted to look around for another church, and they found the Unity Church. I started going to the youth group and I liked it—there were cute girls there. [laughs] And it's a very loving environment, very accepting.

My whole thing is there's the spiritual plane, and then there's the physical plane, and sometimes they can intermix, and sometimes they can't. This is the problem you get into with the whole prolife issue, and these born-again Christians, who are on the spiritual plane in their beliefs, and believe that God is the top power. And sometimes they bring it over into the physical, and say that God is bigger than the president. But the president is the leader of the country in the physical world—not God.

I like Clinton idealistically, but he can't do what he wants to do— he has to compromise too much. As a result he's passed some shit amendments. Even the crime bill was a load of crap in my mind, because it was too weak on gun control—too much prison, not enough prevention. I'd like us to be like England. There's not a single reason that people should have guns: we don't need to hunt anymore, 'cause we have grocery stores—and the British are pretty much a non-threat! The reason the Second Amendment was created was for hunting and to protect us from the British. I don't see why people can't admit that there are outdated amendments in the Constitution.

Here's where I'll go into my spiel about teenagers. Back in the teens, women fought for the right to vote—they got it. Back in the sixties, blacks fought for equal rights—they got it. In the eighties and now, homosexuals are fighting for equal rights and acceptance. There's nobody out there defending teenagers. There's nobody in Congress or the state legislature or the city council; there's no organizations like the gays and lesbians have, there's no NAACP or Rainbow Coalition, there's no NOW. The Children's Defense Fund is for children. Part of me wants to start up this organization, an NAACP for teenagers, a NAAT, or something.

There's a zero tolerance law that Illinois just passed saying any alcohol on somebody under twenty-one's breath, they lose their license. Why not have that for everybody? I don't think that teenagers are any less responsible than a lot of people in their forties who drink.

The perception of teenagers is a lot of them aren't as mature as you, but you can look at some people your age and say they aren't as mature as you. It's the same thing. And even if teenagers have less sense of mortality, drunk is drunk. I think teenagers are gonna put themselves more at personal risk jumping off bridges or doing cocaine or something.

In the media, with the exception of the bullshit extra effort award and stuff like that, the only teenager story that you'll see is the victims of Jeffrey Dahmer, or the kids who shoot and kill, or are doing weird stuff, or are pregnant. I stood around in my workplace, where there are people from the age of twenty-five to forty—and these are very liberal, open-minded people—but, literally, this conversation went on: "I went into a Taco Bell the other day and there were a bunch of teenagers in there." "Oh, I hate that, they're so rowdy, and they're so loud, and I get so scared they're gonna take my money." I'm thinking the exact same conversation went on all over the country about blacks twenty-five years ago. And it's wrong when it's about blacks, but everybody was chiming in and saying, "Oh yes, I agree," about teenagers. What I want is a greater awareness, a perception change. People say, "All these teenagers, they don't respect us." Well, gee, I wonder why? We're the Rodney Dangerfields of the human race.

My mom gave me a book about sex—she didn't really talk about it. I think it's *Our Bodies, Ourselves.* That was real informative for somebody who's twelve and thirteen, and just wondering. It cleared up a lot of questions for me. [laughs] Actually, later on I wowed a lot of girls, because sometimes I knew more than they did. Like I rattled off the female's most fertile time, and girls were [feigns dumbfoundedness] "How the hell did you know that?"

A lot of times sex gets thrown in with drugs, cigarettes, and alcohol, and it's totally separate in the teen world. Yeah, I know the argument that sex is more than physical, it's emotional. And what? Kids don't have emotions? That's what I say to that. A lot of people will argue, "They should wait until they're ready." People aren't ready until they're fifteen? I waited until I was ready, and whether that was fifteen or eighteen, that was my own thing. I know people who are ready when they're fourteen. I know people who practice safer sex at the age of thirteen and fourteen, than at the age of twenty-two.

And peer pressure—I think it's boyfriend pressure, personally. There's a lot of male pressure: guys who pressure females into sex, or certain sexual activities, like oral sex or something. I ask my friends, "Why did you do it?" "Well, he wanted me to, and I wanted to please him." I'm like, "But did you want to?" "No, not really, I don't like it." It doesn't make sense—that's just *weird.*

The danger comes when you have to conceal things, when you have to hide things. Get to a point where your kids don't have to hide anything from you, and they'll be safer. That's number one. Number two, I fully endorse condom distribution in schools. There's different arguments about this, like it's gonna encourage teens to have sex. The argument to that is: teens are having sex already. Then it is: kids won't necessarily use these condoms, they'll have unsafe sex with or without the condom—they won't want to break the mood. And the argument for that is, well, at least they have the option. At least they have the option. If it saves one kid from getting AIDS, it's worth it. It's not hard for me now, but two years ago it was hard as hell for me to buy condoms in a drugstore. I didn't need to buy them back then, and I was just timid. Especially if there's a female checkout person or an older person—like if you go to the corner drugstore and it's a pharmacist that you've been getting acne medication from your whole life. [laughs]

I wish I had my own place, but financially it wasn't possible. I'm sure my parents, in part of their mind, wish I was already gone—and so do I. The letting-go. Like when I bought a six-pack of Guinness and stowed it in my room: my mom had to let go of the fact that I'm not a little boy, and that I'm probably going to have an occasional beer. She knows that I'm responsible, and that I'm not gonna get drunk, or drink and drive or anything. Which I'm not. So I think her trust is well warranted, and I try and live up to that.

I've worked in a flower shop, I've done the grease job at a fast-food restaurant. I worked at an ice cream shop—I stopped working there 'cause it was held up. I was working the cash register. The goofiest thing is it was *three days before Christmas*—the guy had to be stupid as all hell to hold up an ice cream shop! And then I've done a lot of production, radio and video, and been a mobile DJ for a number of years. So my resume looks interesting.

I've been working to get money to go to college. I want to major in film, but I'm going to do a lot of TV production, journalism, radio, poli-sci. I'm hoping I can go next year, but there's a good chance I won't, just 'cause of financial bullshit. I sure as hell can't get as many scholarships as a lot of people can, because, let's see, I'm white, male, heterosexual. The Irish have no money, and there are no Slovenian scholarships. [laughs]

I believe in affirmative action, 'cause there are still people saying blacks are stupid, and unfortunately, they're probably the people who're hiring. I'd like to eventually see it change. I'd like affirmative action's prime purpose to be awareness, as opposed to getting more jobs for more minorities. I'd like to see it happen naturally and not by force.

I want to get married and have a family, but not till I'm thirty. My life will be a little easier then, I think. If I'm going to be a disc jockey or a journalist, I'm gonna have to go to a bunch of different markets, and that'll be tough for a family—you don't want to drag somebody around the country and say, "You have to get this job here, because *I* have to live in this city." I think by the time I'm thirty I'll probably be in L.A., so I'll be a little more settled. Plus I want to have just like a lot of casual sex when I'm in my twenties! [laughs]

Remo Imparato

Towson, Maryland

A t his parents' home in a suburb of Baltimore. He's about
six feet tall, really skinny, with jet-black hair, a goatee, and wire-rims. He looks as though he stepped right out of a thirties photo of a group of anarchists. He lives in another part of town, having moved out four months earlier. He is eighteen.

Imparato—it's Italian. My father was Italian. Well, is—he *is* Italian, he lives in Italy. I'm with my real mother and my stepfather. He used to have all these little food shops, but he's a stockbroker now. My mom's a writer—she's writing a novel—and she edits, and also designs peoples' gardens. I have a half-brother, who's nine. My full-blood sister is twenty-one—she moved to San Francisco. Then I have a stepbrother, from my stepdad's previous marriage, who's twenty-two and lives in Utah.

I guess I was three when my parents got divorced. We moved to Illinois to live with my grandparents, and we moved here when I was seven. I was still young, so my memories of my real father are scat- tered—you know, bits. After they got divorced I saw him a couple times, and then he moved to Italy. He called every once in awhile though, wrote letters. He came from Italy to Maryland maybe five years ago. I knew him because I've talked to him on the phone, but it's more like a pen pal than a father—an uncle, more like an uncle. I haven't heard much of him since.

My mom remarried when I was six. I didn't have a problem with the change—it was just change, and usually I take change kind of matter-of-factly—I'm flexible. I think of him as my dad, I call him dad. He's more of a father than my other father was. He's pretty cool. I really can't say what my sister felt. We were always getting into fights, just the sibling type of thing. I like her now. Once she moved out she started being cool—we were out of each other's hair.

Baltimore's on the south side of the Mason-Dixon Line, but I really can't say I feel like a Southerner at all. Towson's a nice place, not much crime. Well—when I was growing up there wasn't much crime. It's changed, there's more now. I guess Baltimore would be on the top ten list of most random violence in the country. Like in Illinois there's parts of town that you know if you go there, you'll probably get mugged or beat up. Where here you can get beat up on the East Side, the West Side, North, South, in the middle. This neighborhood is upper-middle-class, I'd say. It's mostly a white neighborhood— around here it's really segregated. Where I live now, whenever a black family's looking for a place to live, they'll advise against one area and say, "This one's probably better for you."

I went to public school. [resignedly] I guess you want to hear about that. It had maybe a couple thousand people. There were black students, Asian students; but it was mainly white. No one was really racist at my school. If you had a black student that was into football, and he was a jock, he'd be with the jocks. I mean, I noticed some racism, but just from a scattered few. I think my generation's a lot more open-minded.

I remember in the beginning, in my freshman year, there were cliques: you had to be this way or no way at all. The art students dressed in black and were morbid and whatnot; the actors were more aloof and empty-headed; the jocks were big and empty-headed. I was friends with just about anybody, so I wasn't in any clique—unless there's a clique for not being in a clique. By the time I was a senior most of the cliques had dissolved.

Cheating? There's plenty of cheating at Towson High. It wasn't a big deal. If I saw somebody doing it I wouldn't say anything about it —it's their business. Maybe they did it because if they didn't they would've maybe failed the test; and if they failed the test, they would've gotten a lower grade; and if they got lower grades, maybe their parents would ground them. There's too much stress on grades.

The grading system doesn't mean anything until, like, your senior year—for college. All I did my freshman and sophomore year was what I had to do. If they made your grades have a direct result on what you took the next year, and you had more options about what classes too take, I think students would do better. Freshman and sophomore year I was getting Cs and Ds. Junior and senior year I was getting As and Bs because I did my homework. I knew I had to get good grades to go to college and move out.

I needed to move out to grow. You only grow to the size of your environment, and I'd grown to the size of this environment. I'm not saying that I don't like it around here—like I'm meeting a friend tonight that I've been friends with for years—but when I was here it was like I was stuck doing the same thing every day, every night. I'd come home from school or from work, call up my friend: "What are you doing?" "Nuthin—why don't you come over?" "Alright, I'll come over." Get to his house, say, "What are we doing tonight?" "I don't know. Nuthin—we'll just sit around here all night." We'd have laughs and whatnot, but it's just the same old thing. But then again, what am I saying? I'm going to my friend's house, and I'll be sitting around. Arrgh. [laughs]

Normally I was hardly ever home—I'd come in, eat, call, leave, come back at nine or ten, go to bed, wake up, go to school. I kinda regret it now, just because of my music situation. [laughs] I don't have any. It's just one of those small things, but I think about it. I'm like, maybe I should've spent more time at home, I would've saved more money, and I'd have better music to listen to now.

I guess if there was a marker to not feeling like a teenager, moving out would be it. Yeah, when the bills arrive. Ooooh boy! When it's time to *pay.* I don't think I was fully prepared to move out. I *wasn't* prepared—nobody prepared me. I knew I'd need to pay rent, and I'd have responsibilities and whatnot. It was just that all the small things weren't taken into account. Like, the music situation . . . cooking, eating, groceries. Just, I don't know, um, [small voice] furniture. I moved out with my clothes, two desks, a stereo, a computer, a bed. But there's things . . . [wistfully] I could use a TV and VCR.

When I was living here and everything I needed was paid for, if somebody had said, "Maybe you want to save some money to buy this or that when you move out, because you're not taking my stuff," then I would've probably saved money. I just didn't think of it. I knew I had to buy groceries, but it's another thing to have to plan it. Would I have listened if my mom had sat me down? [smiling] Well, I wouldn't have listened at the time, but I wouldn't have ignored what she said. I would've gotten a little more prepared. She'd say it, I'd blow it off, but I'd be driving down the road and it would pop into my head: "Maybe I should save some money to blah-blah blah-blah blah." [laughs]

I come here for lunch. [grins] My mom will direct me to what to eat. What's about to be thrown away is what I have to eat. [laughs] I'm sure my mom was figuring I was gonna live in a dorm, but I was like, "An apartment is cheaper for twelve months than it is for a dorm for nine months," and, "Would you help me pay for it?" I'd rather do this than live in a dorm. To avoid my generation is why. There's a definite mind-set of people my age—they all seem ditzy, a lot of people are just airheads. Dorm life would be living next-door to all the people that I didn't like in high school. I'm ready to take on responsibility. [swaggeringly] People don't need to watch over me anymore, I know what I'm doing well enough. When you're living with your parents, they're constantly teaching you, "Don't do it that way." I have my own ways of doing things. I don't have a problem with advice—"What do you think I should do?" I'll accept the advice. It's just, I don't need it offered all the time.

Religion? The way I see religion is, a prophet—like Jesus, or Zoroaster, or Krishna or Baha u Llah—comes to guide the human race. They give it advice based on the current problems. Christians say, "Christ is the Lord, Christ is the one," but all his teachings are two thousand years old—and yeah, they're good teachings if you're two thousand years old. A lot of them are just out of date. My mom's devoted to the Baha'i faith, which is what? a hundred and fifty years old. Baha u Llah says by the year two thousand there will be a lesser world peace where all the governments will get along, but before that there's gonna be a problem. Some people say it was World War I and World War II; others say it's still coming. He's into a peace, equality-type thing, where there's equality between races, between sexes, between whatnot. The man had good ideas, and I'd have to agree with him. But all the religions have restrictions on what you can and cannot do—you must be pious and all that stuff.

Did I get the sex and drugs talk? Well, my dad tried a couple times, when I was twelve, thirteen, but I already knew it all. He was like, "Do you have any questions about anything?" I was like, "No, I don't. You're too late—I learned this when I was four." It's not like kids are ignorant—there's the wonderful invention of TV. Parents should talk to their kids when they're young—seven or eight. When they're twelve or thirteen they already know it all, and maybe they know some wrong stuff. Talk to them before they get the firsthand advice from Joey across the street. I'm assuming my little brother knows. If he does, I don't think he'll tell me or my mom, just because he'll be like, "I don't know—maybe I'll get in trouble if I tell." [laughs]

There's always that thing between the parents and child: "Maybe they'll punish me." Most parents do too much punishment, too much grounding, go to your room type thing. You should punish maybe after you've taught them. If it's the first time, and they didn't know—because kids just don't know—then you shouldn't punish them. You should teach them, be like, "That's not right," and talk to them in a calm voice. Raised voices will upset a kid, they'll get frightened. If a mother sees their kid running in the street, they'll start yelling and screaming and going all over the place, [feigns hysteria] "*I don't want you to get hurt,*" and blah blah blah. But they're yelling, and the kid'll be frightened. So just *back off.*

I didn't get grounded much compared to my friends. My mother was good about it. I didn't start getting grounded till I was a freshman in high school, and my grounding was not very strict. "You're grounded for a week," and raa-raa-raa-raa—the rest of the lecture. But I did get in trouble—for *everything.* Sneaking out at night and getting picked up by the cops. [smiling] Being brought home at three in the morning, when I was supposed to be too sick for school, that type of thing. I wasn't a good kid, but it was just little stuff.

For senior year I did a Career and Development Program. You take a half day of school, and the other half you go on a job which you think you might wanna do. It's for students going to college. The job that I got was at a civil engineering firm. I'm still working with them now, but I don't want to be a civil engineer. Senior year I said I'd do mechanical engineering, but I really didn't know what it was. I thought it was gonna be studying the mechanics of all these levers, engines, machinery, that type of thing—and instead it's heating and air-conditioning ducts, and sprinkler systems for fires. [laughs] I said, "That doesn't sound like fun at all." One of the main reasons for the program is so you see the job that you think you wanna do, decide if you like it before college—before you spend four years of your life or more, and ten thousand dollars, to find out that you don't like what you're doing. I would like to do aerospace engineering, but NASA's going down the tubes. But there's a lot to learn in space. I think there is intelligent life out there, just due to the size of the universe.

I used to worry about the environment, but I can't say I do anymore. I believe in recycling—it's just, I don't know, all the big corporations seem to be against environmental safety. I don't want to see the world go into like in the sci-fi movies where everything's a desert. What kills the ozone layer is the fluorocarbon. Theoretically, one particle of it could destroy the whole ozone layer, because it doesn't die: it mixes with the O_3, which is the ozone, and then they do their thing, and the final product is a dead ozone and a new fluorocarbon.

The hole now is back from '78, and that doesn't even touch what we just put out last year. I'm starting to think it's almost too late to do anything about it. It's discouraging. Maybe that's also why I want to do chemistry: there's the chance that I'd figure something out to stop the problem, fix the problem, help the problem. If I had the opportunity to get a car that didn't run on gasoline—a hydroengine, one that runs on water—I'd do it. But if they come out with that car, it's gonna cost a hundred thousand dollars or some nonsense like that. The oil company won't let it happen anyway: they'll just buy the patent and throw it away.

I'm suspicious of large corporations. They run the government, they run the U.S. today. The elite run the economic system for the country, and the elite is the heads of corporations. The government is afraid of change—they're afraid that there is actual proof of extraterrestrial life. I think it's all about money, personally. If we found out, they'd lose money, because they're gonna lose their position, because the balance of power will change. Like if there is extraterrestrial life, maybe people won't really listen to the government any more, like, they're just nothing—there's so much more out there. If we're just this little [with thumb and index finger a smidgen apart] in space, then what's this little boundary between the U.S. and Canada got to do with anything—people would just go back and forth. It's not just the U.S. government—I don't trust most governments, because it's all based on money. I don't have a political stand. I wouldn't mind just knowing the truth, but everybody's hiding something—they're definitely hiding a lot.

Another thing I don't like about my generation is they seem oblivious. We're dumb: everybody's too feeble, because everything's handed to us. The United States was formed on the Bill of Rights, freedom of speech, everybody has these rights. It took work to get it. We're living in a system that's already been made, and we don't do anything, we don't have any great achievements. No one's thinking for themselves. And no one has any sense of honor anymore. If my grandfather's boss said, "Here, I'll give you advance pay, but will you do this thing?" he would have definitely done it. Definitely: he gave his word, he would have done it. Now it's like, "Well, he gave me the money, I'm skipping town." That might be why there's that cheating thing—nobody has a sense of honor. If there was more honor, I think there'd be a lot less violence, and a lot more achievements. People would be proud of what they did, would *try* to do things.

It's like the Dodo bird: it lived on Australia for a long time, and it had no natural enemies on the island. And then people came, and their pet dogs killed all of them—because they had evolved into fat lazy birds that sat on the ground all day and couldn't fly. Challenge is good—challenge leads to change, and change is usually good. If there's struggle then something good will come out of it. But we're not struggling—we're just coasting.

Gretchen Dee
Chicago, Illinois

*S*he is big boned, with long, tousled blond hair, and a strong, attractive face. Her energy is almost overwhelming: words gallop like horses shot loose from a starting gate. She is a sophomore in college; visiting her home in Schaumburg, Illinois, for Christmas break. She is nineteen.

People call Schaumburg the big-hair capitol of the world. It *is* the stereotypical suburb: it's people with their lawns, it's people with their baby strollers, it's low culture, new money—mostly upper-middle-class. It's people who are involved in their church groups, and women in their sweatsuits who go walking in the morning and power shopping at the mall. My parents were hippies, and they're city people in heart and soul—they're Democrats in a Republican area. They ended up in Schaumburg for safety. I don't want my kids to grow up in the suburbs, I want my kids to grow up in the city. Of course, in an urban environment it's drugs and gangs,and I would not even pretend to have any experience with that—I lived a very sheltered life. But in the suburbs you feel it too, it's heading that way.

I got involved with peer jury when I was in eighth grade. The police department had this pilot program where if you get caught shoplifting or something—it's a misdemeanor kind of a crime, and you're a teenager—you can appear before the peer jury. And they ask the questions, they act as lawyers and judges. Guilt is assumed; the questions that we ask are intended to establish motivation. We take into account how much peer pressure was a factor, and then we decide the sentence—it's always community service hours. And we assign research papers on different issues. Like, if you were caught in possession of marijuana, you might do a paper on the side effects of marijuana. The whole experience of being there is very scary: you have to stand at the microphone in a courtroom; your parents are there; the police officer's there; and the adults who oversee the program are there. But the teenagers kind of run it. I guess that had an impact, the fact that someone your own age was saying, "This is stupid. You don't have to do this."

We saw kids from the lower-income subsidized apartment housing and from brand-new, beautiful, three-hundred-thousand-dollar homes. It was a really eye-opening experience: it gave me an idea of what kids are going through, of how important peer pressure is. I could not *believe* the affects of peer pressure: "I did it because he said he wouldn't be my friend if I didn't." And they meant it. I always thought peer pressure was something glamorized by the media, and it isn't, it really is there. I hate to push family values, 'cause I think that single parents are fine, and that working mothers are a reality. But the collapse of families is a big issue; and also how affected kids are by not having parents home, how not in-touch kids are with their parents; how the kids didn't think about things before they acted. It was a good look into how teenagers react and work.

Alcohol is a very big issue for teenagers. Drinking is a huge part of college, the drug culture is huge too: a lot of shrooming, a lot of acid. Pot is *everywhere*, from the football players, to the musicians, to the highly intellectual people—nerds, geeks, freaks, everyone. Pot was everywhere in high school, but it was still very easy to stay away from it. The kind of friends I had, we really weren't into stealing, or doing drugs or drinking. My social group was very tame: we went to plays, we went bowling, we went to movies. We were good kids, the girl-next-door kind of people.

I was very successful in my high school. I was always very—not a kissass—but I was interested in my teachers and I cared about the school. I love being protected, but I think there is a natural instinct to move on. That's a really huge part of all these problems that teenagers have with their parents. Like my brother, who's seventeen. My mom says, and I agree, that if we were cavemen he would have his own cave now. My sister just suffers from being the youngest. She's the big rebel, she's the black lipstick and Doc Martens—the punk of the family. She wants to cut and dye her hair. My mom says, "Don't you want long, pretty, curly hair?" [feigns anger] "*I don't want to look like Gretchen, and I don't want a flowered room like Gretchen.*" [laughs] So, independence!

But for me, going to college—I didn't want to go. I thought my life was good. I thought, "I have this great trusting relationship with my parents, they're very loose—I have no curfew." I was satisfied with my social life. I was feeling maybe I needed a new start, to get away from all the stereotypes in high school, but it wasn't enough of an urge to overpower the comfortableness with my family and my home.

In high school I was plagued by not having a boyfriend—I really didn't have any serious boyfriends until I got to college. I always had trouble in relationships because I was so outspoken. I had a prom my senior year, and I could've gotten a date, but I was too proud to go with someone that I didn't want to go with. And that will stay with me the rest of my life. I had enough attention, it's that no one ever seemed to want to date me seriously. I felt and still feel every day like I'm not good enough. When I meet a guy I'll be like, "Oh, he'll never like me 'cause I'm not pretty enough or I'm not smart enough." I'm not worthy. I can say to myself, "Look at your grades, look at where you've come in your life," but it doesn't matter—it's still that rejection.

All my friends had boyfriends, always. I don't look at other girls who don't have boyfriends and say, "There's something wrong with that person." But I always felt people looked at me that way. Not just boys, but everyone. "Gretchen has no boyfriend, it must be because there's something wrong with her." I don't know where it comes from, but I have to believe it's partly the fact that you turn on TV or open a magazine and every girl has a boyfriend, every girl is a hundred and twenty pounds, and beautiful. You should be thin, you should have a boyfriend, and you should be smart too. The culture tells you also, not too smart, not too self-empowered, not too independent. And you shouldn't be too good either, because that's not fun.

I've always been at the top of my class academically and involved in volunteer activities. I was Miss Involved, the perfect college candidate.

But at the same time, I was so hugely affected by wanting to fit in. I didn't realize how low my self-esteem was, my self-image. I still have body-image problems, I have eating disorders. I'm a self-empowered woman and a feminist, and I believe I can do all these things, and I see how successful I've been in my life—but at the same time I am so affected by not feeling pretty enough, not feeling thin enough.

I've definitely changed a lot going to college. I go to a small college in Minnesota, it's known for being highly liberal and highly intense. As a general rule they get students that were social outcasts in high school—the majority of them are out to be different, weird. It puts me in the absolute norm, and all of a sudden I come off as being really good-looking. What I realized in college was how damaged I was, like emotionally, by the silliest things . . . Like the fact that I didn't make cheerleading when I was younger, or the fact that I always felt fat, and how that had a huge, huge, huge, huge impact on my life. I don't think there's ever been a time, in the last eight years, when I haven't been on a diet. My perspective is: I am heavier than everybody else. [sighs] I'm not anorexic or bulimic, but I definitely have a bad relationship with food.

I never enjoy food, there's always the guilt. Guilt, guilt, guilt. If I eat too much today, then I won't eat tomorrow at all. I weigh myself every single day without fail, and if I gain a pound it affects my mood the whole day. I tie food to emotions. When I'm upset I have two reactions: binge or starve—eat celery and water for a week, or eat a whole pizza. I just can't seem to ever eat normally. When I'm in public—when I go out for dinner, when I am at the college cafeteria—I eat nothing.

My roommates were the ones that said, "Gretchen, something's wrong—you're totally binging." They made me get help, they begged me for months. They were like, "We're calling your parents if you don't." Finally my roommate made the appointment. I said, "Fine, I'll go once"—and I went three times. But oh my God, to this day I'm still denying the fact that I have an eating disorder. Or I see it as, "Lots of people have eating disorders, mine isn't serious—there are people with much worse problems." So when I talk about this it's not me speaking, it's not my true feeling. It's what I've come to accept, and I'm trying to talk myself into it.

How am I gonna stop the "I'm not worthy" stuff? [sighs] You know what is really pathetic? When my therapist asked me that, I answered, "Lose fifteen pounds." [laughs] And part of me believes that if I just lose the weight I'll be OK. Isn't that awful? And I know that's wrong— I know life's not easier for beautiful people. But you get cut a break here and there when you're beautiful: you get more attention, you get taken more seriously. It's no joke that as an overweight person it's harder for you, and that success is sometimes tied to physical appearance.

The media says everyone should be thin and pretty, and I think that's a *huge* influence on all teenagers. There's such a high expectation to be something they can't be. I think they're uncomfortable, they feel kind of dumped on, like the expectations of them are too much. It's the loss of innocence. We have teenagers growing up with adult issues, and they're without all the emotional resources to deal with that. You're still a child in so many ways: you don't have the stability, the self-confidence yet, but you're *forced* to deal with things. There's nothing sacred about being a teenager anymore—you grow up *so* fast.

Teenagers years ago didn't have as much pressure because they weren't as exposed to things. There was no *Seventeen* magazine and *Mademoiselle,* and *90210* and *Melrose Place.* They weren't being marketed to as heavily. I think that without knowing it teenagers feel degraded, and that's detrimental, it really is—it reinforces a stereotype. Adults can say, "They're just lazy, and they don't want to do anything. And selfish"—because that's what the media says. And that's what books say, and TV, and movies.

In this book *Revolution X* it says, "Are you sick of being labeled and packaged?" And that's what I've always felt: I'm sick of being a teen spirit and bubblegum, and not being taken seriously. It's OK to recognize teenagers as generationally separate: you're not twenty, you're not ten—they're growing years, those are interesting years. And I don't even mind being targeted, being looked at as being a *teenager.* But I hate people doing it in a way that is degrading, and I don't think you have to be intelligent or ambitious or hardworking or an overachiever to feel it's degrading.

Teenagers have a sense that something is wrong, and that culture is going down. The media says, "Look at the gangs, look at the urban violence, look at drugs." The news is the scariest thing on TV! I think teenagers are very concerned about the fall of the infrastructure and the rise of crime, and the change in what it means to be a teenager in this country—especially in the city. I don't think they realize how the government's screwing them over, and killing their future. They don't realize the economic side, how serious that is.

In high school I was always, [rolling eyes] economics, GNP, GDP, you know, supply and demand—God, I don't want to think about that. But the last couple of years I've become a political science major and been forced to do reading and research. Basically, the deficit is so bad, and people my age, they have not a clue. We're a consumption society, and when you consume more than you invest, that's when economic societies fall. And that's what we're doing.

Spending is killing us, the deficit, and then everyone wants their perk. And it's this whole, "Well it's them." It's gonna be so easy if we just get "those" people out of Congress, if we get "those" interest groups out, that bad congressman. Everyone thinks it's them, but who is the them? The them is us. I was thinking, "Well, I'm not affected by interest group politics," but my father works for a company that gets tax breaks or subsidies from the government, which affects my father —which affects my income, which affects my college education. So don't take my dad's company's tax break away, because it affects me. Everyone's affected, everyone has to sacrifice.

We're facing generational war. My mom jokes about this, "Oh, you're going to be fighting against me—there's going to be a war." But there is! *Right now.* And it's scary for me to think about. I love my parents, we're very close. And they've both worked hard, they're not rich, they're middle-class people. [sighs] Gosh, this is such a big source of guilt with me. [distressed] How am I gonna tell my parents, who paid for my college education and worked hard, that they gotta sacrifice for me? I work every summer, I work over Christmas break, I do everything I can to help pay for my college education. And I hope somehow I'll be economically stable enough to help them out when they're older. That's the way it should work—like it used to in the olden days when kids took care of their parents.

But it's gonna be "Do I wanna give my kids basic health care, or do I wanna support the medicaid system which provides my parents with health care?" [sounding frightened] Is it one or the other? What are you gonna do? I value my parents' life and their work, and I think they should have comfort in their old age, but I don't think it should be unlimited, untaxed comfort. But I can't see any way of saying that without making it seem like I think they don't deserve it. It's like me saying, "How can my parents not value my future?" You know, they don't mean for it to be that way, but that's the way it's looking. Their comfort and their having what they wanted in their day led to the future, my future, which is just screwed.

I used to say I wanted to be a senator when I grew up. I *used* to say that. [laughs] I always joked, "Oh, I'm going to change the world"; but the truth was that wasn't where my interest in politics stemmed from. My interest in politics stemmed from just loving the bullshit—I watch C-Span all day. I am so fascinated by the system and how it works and the problems: the pork-barreling, the special interest groups. How everything works together—not just the government— the whole society coming together to make policy and to run this country. And that's what I loved.

But I'm kind of disenchanted. I think people go into politics because they want to do some good, and they're trying, but they're just so entrenched by all these huge interest groups and the demands of the voters. I don't know what the answer is, and that scares me too. But I don't think that actually being a politician is where to go, I don't think things get done at that level. I think it's in being in an interest group or being a staffer—you could get to do policy creation and research and activism.

I want to make a lot of money, I want a beautiful house, and children, and a castle, and I want to be able to travel and see the world and be able to send my children to excellent schools. I want that, and I think part of me actually believes I'm gonna have that, but reality-speaking-wise, I know too much. I'll probably have to live in debt, and just make ends meet—especially if I want to work in the political field. I'm gonna drive a secondhand car and live in a small apartment, and probably not go out to dinner, and coupon-clip for the rest of my life. A couple years ago I thought, "I can't settle for that." Now I'm kind of like, "There's nothing wrong with that." I've come to realize that having a job you like is probably the most important thing.

I'm going to Washington, D.C., next term, through a program at school. I'm going to be working on the national deficit with an interest group that's Generation X, twenty-something politics. We're doing Social Security, reform, the environment, infrastructure, education. I was thinking about what I could do when I come back—like maybe talk to high school classes. Going back and just explaining in simple terms, the debt, the deficit, what it means, how it affects you. I know I was scared off by economic terms in high school, but it's not that hard to understand. I want people to know, that is my whole goal. Because they don't really know. And who's to blame? You don't see it on the news, you don't see it in the kids' papers or magazines. What about *Seventeen* magazine? For all their hair and looks and makeup and fashion, what about something on the deficit? The right things are not in the media. There's such an audience: they watch so much TV, they read so many magazines; it'd be so easy to reach them, yet no one's doing it. That's kind of where my focus is going to be.

I'm thinking if I were to have a claim to fame, that's where I'd like to make my name: to start an organization or to spread education—*do something.* Use the power of one human being in a thousand to take the energy and money and time. It amazes me, the power of human beings, one in a thousand, to really do something, to be unselfish. And that's why we're going to be OK—probably.

Noah Barnes

Chicago, Illinois

I*met Noah at the Chicago open-ing of* Hoop Dreams, *which ben-efited, in part,* New Expression, *the teen newspaper on which he works. He leaned toward me with a paper and said, "Here, please read this—I have two stories in here." He is African-American, with the broad shoulders of a football player and a confident manner. He is sixteen.*

I'm an only child. My father's a sales-something at Amtrak, and my mother is a teacher. We're between middle and lower-class. My neighborhood is predominantly white, and I hate to say that predominantly white neighborhoods are better than predominantly black neighborhoods, but, in fact, they are. I live in Beverly [a far South Side neighborhood], and it's just top-notch. It's really ethnically diverse now, but when I first moved there I was two or three, and it was all white. *All* white. So I kind of grew up alone. I think that's why I'm like this now. I'm social, but you can put me in a room by myself and I'd be perfectly fine. When I was a kid, I never just played with my toys, I made stories up—every little guy went through an adventure. Like how girls play house, I played stories. I was always by myself.

The people next door were *so* prejudiced. On their side was a metal gate, with a hole. Me and the boy next door, we'd sit right there, and talk to each other, play ball over the fence, stuff like that—'cause his grandmother wouldn't let us talk to each other. Kids can't see prejudice, it's just what they grow into, what they adapt to. If you grow up into an environment like, "Man, he's a nigger, and we don't like him," and "That white guy, he's a honkey, and you don't mess with him," then of course you're gonna grow up with that hatred of other people. The Bible says, "Train up a child in the way he should go, and when he is old he will not depart from it." Everybody is a version of their mother and father, and what your parents' values are, basically, your values are.

My immediate family, we're close—my parents and my mother's parents, and her sister. My father, on the other hand, grew up on the West Side of Chicago, and there was fifteen kids. One of my father's brothers was a leader of a street gang. That was his thing—he was in jail, stealing cars—that's what he did. My father kind of took the role of, "Man, we ain't got nothing, so I'm gonna get a job." My father could really play ball, but he had to stop cause he *had* to get a job.

I see my parents every night, but we don't do the family-type thing at dinner. I'll go in my room and watch TV. My grandparents, on the other hand, they have dinner: they make a plate, and you sit down and eat together. My grandmother's religious; my grandfather believes in God, but he's like the typical male that doesn't go to church, watches the game on Sunday—but he believes, my father, too; my mother and her sister, they're like that. I have a lot of doubts about religion, about all religion—I have my doubts. I believe in God, but I don't necessarily believe in the Bible. But I grew up in a religious background, and I go to church with my mother—she goes every week. My great-grandmother was one of the founders of the church, and it'd break my grandmother's heart if I said I was going to a different church, so I wouldn't do that. Our church is the old Mississippi-type kind of church.

I used to really try to be around my grandparents' house. [On the near South Side.] I didn't want to grow up to be a so-called sissy. 'Cause growing up with the black people that was by me, they were kind of bourgeois—kind of, "I'm better than all the other black people 'cause I live in Beverly." My father didn't want me to grow up to be kind of falsified in that sense, so I would always be over my grandmother's house. It's in kind of a ghetto area, and it toughened me up. Even though I did have a little something in life, I wasn't blind to everything else—reality—and I appreciate more what I got.

I'm not as tough as I would have been growing up in another neighborhood. Most of my friends that live in Beverly are going to college this year, most of them are going to school. They have two parents in the household that work and can afford things; they had a good background, a good foundation. On the other hand, the people that I grew up with over at my grandparents' house, one just went to jail two weeks ago for shooting somebody in the head—for twenty dollars. He's about fourteen, fifteen. Most of them I know over there are selling drugs. Another guy that got shot around there, he was my friend. He was sitting on his porch one day and somebody from the opposite gang came up and shot him in the head. They dragged him across the street to his girlfriend's porch and laid him there so she could walk out the house and find him. That was terrible. But most of the people that I grew up with in Beverly, they're trying to make something of their life. But that still doesn't put them aside the fact that anything can happen. *Anything* can happen to *anybody*. You could be the worst person in the world and still live through anything, or you could be a good person and still die. You're not immune to anything.

Now, this is the worst experience of my life: it was the day before Mother's Day last year, and my father decided to take my mother out to dinner that night, and so I decided to spend the night over at my grandmother's house. If I was home I would have went out with the guy nextdoor—I call him my brother—and his best friend, Curtis. But I said, "I ain't going out, I gotta go over my grandmother's house." They go to someone's house, and when they get there some guy's over there, and they get to arguing, and they're like, "Let's just go." Then they come back later, and all the lights was out in the house. My brother said a car drove up behind them. My brother's in the passenger seat, and Curtis is in the driver's seat. My brother's kind of stocky, big, and he'll fight: he don't back down for *nobody*. Usually he'd get out the car: "What you gonna do?" But, it's really ironic— this time he said, "Curtis, just drive off and forget it." [He starts to rush the words.] So Curtis puts the car in drive—next thing you know somebody got out and sprayed the back. The car smashed into a pole, and he reached over and pushed Curtis. His head hit the glass and blood started coming out the back of his head. He looked over, and got out the car and ran all the way to the police station.

The next morning, I'm over my grandmother's house, and he called me and he's like, "Man, Curtis *dead!*" He hung up the phone and I'm sitting there like, "Curtis dead? What's going on?" My mother picked me up and I was crying. This was Mother's Day and she's all happy. I said, "Curtis just got shot." She was mad, on one hand, and on the other hand, she was so happy that I wasn't *with* them—because when we go out in the van, it's always Curtis in the driver's seat, my brother in the front seat, and me sitting right behind the driver. Right behind *Curtis.* And he got shot in the back of his head. If my parents didn't go out, I'd have been, "Yeah, I'll go." I would have been the one that got shot.

The guy that shot him was in a gang. He said that he was just trying to scare him, but I don't buy that. Boy, that was the *saddest,* man. I'm not sad for him anymore—it's his mother: he was the only child, and his parents were divorced. Him and his mother was getting in a lot of arguments, so he left and was living with his father on the North Side. She said, "Well, you're gonna spend Mother's Day with me." He came back from the North Side to see his mother—so you *know* how guilty she's feeling. And it really isn't no reason for her to feel guilty, 'cause she just wanted to spend Mother's Day with her only child. She said, "I will never see true happiness again."

My freshman year, I went to a different public school, but it got *bad* there—it was a lot of gangbanging, just a whole bunch of mess. One of my friends there—he wasn't necessarily a gang member, he just knew a lot of people—but I kind of wanted to separate myself from him. The gang there had it in for him, and he never ran away like a chump—he always stood up to them. They kept wanting to come after him, and the opposite gang of that gang was like, "*Man,* he's standing up to them—yeah, I *like* him." He would get into fights and the opposite gang would help him. So then everybody thought he must be in a gang.

I was at the bus stop one day and some guys, they ran up to the bus stop, "*Aren't you blah-blah-blah's brother?*" [Tension seeps into his voice.] I was like, "No. Who are you?" They tried to put me in a circle, you know, three-sixty, and one of them hit me. I took my book bag and hit him back, and I ran to the police station. I didn't leave the school *exactly* after that, but I said maybe I should separate myself . . . For a while the police officer would walk me up to the bus stop every day—

and that didn't help: all the attention, and people like, "Man, Noah a *punk*, he got to walk with the police every day." I didn't care: it was saving me. I could care less about what people think.

I didn't like the school either. I had a lot of prejudiced teachers. Sometimes I'm kind of hard to get along with, a little bit. I'm very candid. There's supposed to be a line between respecting adults, and I rarely cross that, but I don't like to feel somebody is disrespecting me. If I'm being treated wrong, or if something is not right, then I'm gonna speak out about it, because *everybody* should be treated fairly; *everybody* should be treated right. I have a lot of teachers that was just plain silly, stuff that they did, the way they ran their class.

I go to a technical high school now. You have to take a test to get in, so it's children from all over the city, mostly African-American. I'm a good distance away from it, but it has a good program. Most of the kids from the neighborhood are thugs, but they don't really mess with people in school. There's a couple guys from around there that were smart enough to get in. Most of the kids there are smart, most of them have ambition and see further than what's out here on the street. The gang problem is a drug problem: drugs is the thing. The little kids are the ones that's out here beating up people and drive-by shooting. That's silly stuff. The ones that you see in all the fancy cars are the ones making big money. They're not really even for all that gangbanging stuff, they're just about making their money. If you stop the drugs, then you'll basically stop the gangs. Where gangs are really evident is in the projects, because you *have* to be in a certain gang because you *live* there. It's bad, but in a certain sense I think the media has escalated the problem. That's what they do with all African-American problems.

Like, I can put my two kids in a car and watch them drown, and they'll say, "Black man kills his two kids." But that lady, [Susan Smith] she can put two kids in her car, and the first words they say are, "Deranged lady drowns her kids"—a lady with something wrong with her. It's always an excuse why white people do something, but when *we* do it, then that's just us, that's just what we do. I don't think people mean to do it, it's just the way that you're brought up; and the way that society is, you're kind of reared into being prejudiced. It's just what you see.

The reason why white people get better educations is because in their neighborhood, at three, they know how to say their name, they know their telephone number, they know where they live. You know what I'm saying? They know their words, they know their colors, they know the alphabet. But at three years old at the Ida B. Wells projects, you don't know anything, you just know what you see around you: you see your father smoking drugs and selling drugs, you see your mother prostitute. That's what you're reared up into, that's what you see, and you think that there's no other hope. You live out your environment; by the time you're old enough to figure it out, you're either dead or in jail.

The environment has to change. You have to change the thinking of people, you have to change the *atmosphere* in order to change the thinking, and *then* people will change. It's a long road, and you have to start young. But all these free clinics, health clinics and the Head Start program, all that stuff that was helping people, especially single mothers—the governor's gonna cut all that. He doesn't care. His kids knew what their telephone number was and where they lived at when they were three—*they* had education. I think it's a lot of pocketing money that they're doing. My father's got an article clipped out, it said all the profits from the lottery will be for the schools. As much as I see people buying lottery tickets, these schools could be funded three times over.

I went to a Christian school since I was two. I entered the public school system when I was a freshman. They wanted to send me to a Catholic high school, but I didn't want to go because I was tired of wearing a uniform. I was *really* tired of that. And most of the Catholic schools, they was predominantly white, and I'd been accustomed to being around all black people. So, not that I'm prejudiced or nothing, I guess I just wanted to go to a public school. But sometimes I wish I'd gone to a Catholic school, because it's a better education. The experience that I've gotten from being around black people I wouldn't want to trade, but there's some things that you have to give up to get—to be better in life.

I think there should be more integrated schools, but it should be your choice whether you want to go. If you change the thinking of everybody, then it wouldn't matter what school you went to; you wouldn't be thinking black or white—that would be the *least* thing in your mind. But they should be more integrated, definitely—because if you don't have the money to afford to go to a small black college, then you're going to go to a college that definitely is more white—most colleges are eighty-five percent white. That's why I think you should get the experience, just to be around white people and see that it's no difference.

I was more sheltered till eighth grade. Then I started kind of doing a little bit more bad, or what I wasn't supposed to do. Nothing *real* bad. My grandmother said, "Anything that you can't do in Sunday school, you're not supposed to be doing." But doing a *little* bad, I didn't feel guilty. In an African-American's mind it's different: you turn on the radio and *every* song, everyone's smoking weed, and everybody's selling drugs; everybody's got big cars, and all the girls are sluts, shaking their booty, or they got babies, and everybody's thinking about sex . . . So that's what you grow up into.

My mother, she knows I go out with girls, but I don't think she wants to know about my sexual activity, 'cause I'm just her baby. My mother just always say, "Treat a girl like you would want somebody to treat me." But my father's like ghetto, West Side—he's open. He didn't really have a talk with me, he just kind of said, "Use a rubber," that male-type thing—but he made it clear to me. Once in a while he ask me—like the phone will ring a lot—"You messing around with them girls? You use a rubber." Or he'll see my face real clear and he'll say, "You ain't got no pimples or nuthin, you must be doing *something.*—you better be using a rubber." [laughs] In your mind you think sex is for pleasure, but if I was giving an honest opinion, I think God made sex for when a couple wants to reproduce, have a baby. But I think it's your decision, as long as you're safe about it. I'm realistic about it, but it's very confusing.

Drugs—I kinda got into that marijuana thing, just for a minute, just tried it out. But I know my limits, and I know I'll never try any other thing. One of my father's brothers, he's in recovery—crack, rock, whatever . . . He was telling me about when you first do crack: he's like, "It's the best, *best* feeling that you could *ever* have in your *life.*" And so it's, "*Man,* I want that feeling." And he said, "So you go do it again to get that feeling, and you *never, ever, ever, ever do.*" And then, from what I read and what I know, and what I seen, I don't want to have *no* part of that. And the health thing, too: in biology I was learning about the body, and learning about cells, and *every* cigarette you smoke takes seven minutes away from your life that you will not regain, *no way, no how.*

I'm looking for a job now. I stopped playing basketball 'cause I wanted a job. I have a car, and it seems I'm asking my mother for money more and more lately. From me playing ball, I know about a lot of these kids with all this talent, playing ball out here, and their grades are terrible. The guy that's the star of Chicago now, I think he's nineteen, and he's a junior. He's living the fantasy. And the boy, he can *jump out the gym*—he can *play.* I know that's what he's focusing on, and there's nobody telling him, "If you get hurt, you're going to have to do something else"—nobody's there to say, "Listen, you *need* to get your education, 'cause this basketball thing is one in a million. You could fall the wrong way playing ball; you could chase your little brother down the street and get hit by a car; fall down the stairs one day, and ruin your career. *And what do you have now?"* I don't wish no bad luck on him, 'cause he can *play*—I hope he gets all the money he can. All the ridiculous money he can. It *is* ridiculous— especially in college! And the way these kids have to live off their scholarship and they can't get money? I think Louisiana State University, the years that Shaquille O'Neal played, grossed like six, seven, eight million dollars, something like that. And your coach can't give you incentives?! Like, "Oh man, I need some extra money for my mother." They can't give you that! They make big bucks, *big* bucks. I just don't think it's fair.

The way boys are playing now, this high school thing is like college. A lot of them are making mega money. My school, from my basketball game, they'll make maybe ninety dollars from the people that go in there. A high school with a big player makes about two or three thousand dollars a night on every game! It's scouts that pay. Now, *who's* getting all that money? It's sure not the school system; and the player's not getting an education. So that's why I feel this recruiting thing is just taking it too far. But there's *so many* people making *so much* money—just like the gun thing and the cigarette thing—that *nobody's* gonna stop it.

With the gun thing, if you want to stop people from shooting people, stop making guns. What's the purpose? *What's the purpose?*

There's the National Rifle Association paying people off to keep passing these laws. If you want to stop people from smoking, make cigarettes illegal. But they don't want to stop it, because cigarette companies make so much money off these $2.59 packs of cigarettes. So they say, "Hey, Mr. Congressman, you take a little of this money here, and make sure it passes through Congress."

I hate to say it, but a lot of these legislators, they don't care about us, the inner-city people. I think it sad that we're gonna suffer 'cause so many people didn't vote. We need to reform a lot of things in today's society. Health care is a *big* problem, and I don't think the politicians really see the problems inner-city people have. I like the American way, that anybody can have a chance to be anything. Well, anybody *supposedly* can have a chance to be anything . . . If American views can mix with socialist views, you can say that everyone is required to have certain things.

When I'm older, I want to live in a house. I want my kids to have the same type of environment. I want to have more children—I wouldn't want my kid to be an only child. And I want my kids to be with my mother and father, 'cause I think that's important for a well-balanced child—the love generated from your grandparents: the grandfather sneaking money type thing, and the grandmother, the home-cooked meals, and the advice. But I don't want to have kids for a long time, because I'm young, and I want to stay young. A lot of people now are trying to leave *young* too quick.

I want to be a . . . [sighs] Sometimes I don't know. I want to be a journalist, sportswriter, writer. And I want to be a coach, because I love basketball, and it's important for older African-American guys to have relationships with younger kids, to be role models. Charles Barkley says, "I'm not a role model—your *parents* are role models." That's not true—when you get in front of the camera every night, when you play basketball, you immediately *are* a role model. I'm not saying that parents aren't supposed to be role models, but I think when you accepted that position, you accepted all them millions of dollars to play, you should be required to conduct yourself a certain way. Especially for the African-American kids that don't have all the role models that they should. I think that goes for anybody in entertainment or sports, in that limelight.

I want to write books. I want to be the poet laureate for Chicago or something like that. I'm writing a book now. It's about me and the guy I call my brother, and Curtis, and another friend. It's called *Maybe Manhood*. It's about us trying to grow up to be men. I talked to Curtis's mother two or three weeks ago, and she seemed to be getting better. I hate to even remind her about it, for her to think, "Mrs. Barnes, she has her Noah and he's going to be something, but my Curtis . . . " And that's something I'll make sure I tell my kids about —about Curtis.

A Foot in Two Worlds

Lily Wong

San Francisco, California

A conference room in a San Francisco Bay area private school. It's spring, and Lily is about to graduate. She is willowy, absolutely stunning, and nervous about the interview. I ask if she has any questions. She has only one: "Are there any wrong answers?" She is eighteen.

I'm Chinese—both my parents are from China. I'm first-generation, but my parents came over when they were in their early teens. They're still traditional, but they're kind of Americanized; they're strict, but not in the sense of traditional-Chinese-parents strict—they're more open. Before they were really strict about me dating, and they would be all, "Until you're eighteen, you go to college, you can't talk to guys on the phone." [laughs] And I'm all "*What?!* Oh my God!" But now they're strict in the sense of "You're a female, and you can't do anything your brother does"—and I feel that's a really big problem within our family, because there's a double standard.

It's like that in all families, I guess, 'cause the male has more freedom than the female, 'cause they're girls or whatever—'cause they're easily hurt. I don't know. My best friend, Sharon—her brother and her—she gets the same treatment I get, but she's black. But then also, traditional Chinese people believe that it's best to have a son, because they are everything: the male is better—he could support you, and live on in the last name, and nah-nah-nah-nah.

When I was little, I know that my big brother got so much more

119

attention—that's how I felt. My grandma, she stressed how important it was to have the son, and then I saw how she treated my aunt compared to my dad, and how she treated my mom. This is traditional Chinese belief: when you marry into a family, you have to do everything for the husband's family, especially for the mother-in-law. And whatever she does, whatever she says, you have to kowtow to. My grandma remarried three times; and one of my grandpa's sons from an earlier marriage, and his wife, the way they treated my grandma was in the traditional style . . . She'd give her massages and nah-nah-nah and make her food—but my mom was like, "I'm not gonna do that—I'm not gonna bow to anybody." She respected my grandmother, but her respecting and her giving her a backrub was completely different. She'd be all, "I'm my own independent person," and then my grandma would just give her so much, like, stuff, because of that. Can I swear? I'm all like, "Oh, I *can't* swear . . . " [laughs] She gave her shit.

I would feel the tension within our family. I remember when I was little my mom would come back crying, and my dad and her would always fight about that. My dad's a surgeon, and he has uniforms, and my brother's job was to wash the uniforms and fold them, and he'd get paid. But my grandma would be all, "Why is he doing that? Why can't Lily do it?" Because I'm a girl or something. And I would feel like, well she doesn't really respect me as a person. I, like, in a way, hated her because of the way she made me feel—that I wasn't important, because I was a female. When she died, I felt like, OK, it's *over* . . . I felt kind of guilty because of how I felt about her.

Over the summer me and my mom had this really big problem between us, and it couldn't be settled through talking, it couldn't be settled through anything. I was just going crazy, 'cause I couldn't deal with the whole way she viewed me, treated me, compared to my brother. And I'd be all, "Well, *he* can do this"—and she'd say, "Don't compare yourself with your brother, you're not the same." I just felt that there was some barrier in my life, and I couldn't deal with it because . . . [singsong] I don't know. I just saw it as my brother could get away with anything, and I couldn't—because I was Lily and he was Alex. And he could do anything because Alex was good, 'cause Alex got into a good college, and Alex is so smart, and he has Mary as his girlfriend, and she's just . . . oh, *everyone* in our family loves her—

and I love her too. But I felt like I couldn't live up to his standard of being, like I didn't have any standards of being Lily.

I don't know if my mom was following what my grandma was thinking, 'cause I don't know if she thinks my brother's better than I am. But I know there's that double standard within our family, and this summer I couldn't deal with it. So we had a lot of problems, and I guess I started hanging out with the wrong kind of people, just to be in your face—"I'm gonna do whatever I want to do." And I don't think that was good. My friends saw a change in me, and I think my parents thought I had some really bad problem, and they wanted [nervous laugh] to take me to some psychologist or something. I wasn't getting good grades, and they were, "Is this because you're hanging out with these kind of people?" and "Why don't you hang out with your old friends?" Whereas my old friends really were the people who were doing drugs and everything, but I didn't want to say anything. They kept on giving me lectures on marijuana use and all this—and I'm like, "I'm not *doing* drugs. *Leave me alone.*"

I started hanging out with more colored people, more racially diverse people. I have Latin, black, Asian friends . . . everything, I guess. I don't know why I changed, why I had this decline of grades. I don't know if it was just the high school experience, or I wasn't into school. This school is not really diverse, the way I see it—and my parents would be all, "Why don't you hang out with more Asian people?" and nah-nah-nah; and I'm all, "Well, there *aren't* any Asian people." And they're like, "Well, why don't you go to dances at other schools?" That's a big thing: they don't know my friends. They know Sharon. They say, "Black people—well, Sharon's a good kid." Well, that's the only black female they know, so Sharon's maybe like the spokesperson for the black race! [laughs]

Once I was gonna go out with this guy, and he was black, but my dad was like, "I don't want you to go out with him"—and we had this whole big uproar of, "*Why are you racist?* You don't want me to go out with this person because of his *skin color?*" And he just went off like, "No—it's because of the way people view you." And I was all, "Well, you didn't have a problem when I was going out with someone who was white. Why do you have a problem *now?*" They're like, "Go for Asian people, go for Asian people, 'cause it won't be that hard on you guys, the way people view you . . . " It makes me feel like, *open your eyes*—there are other people besides you around. You could learn from them and they could learn from you—and you don't have to be all, "Well, I know black people by their selling coke on the streets, or they're crack fiends, or they're nah-nah-nah." I don't like stereotypes.

I started hanging out with Asian people, and I guess that's when stuff turned bad . . . [laughs] It's just over the summer I got carried away: I was kind of like, "I am proud to be Asian—Asian pride. And Sharon and my other best friend Lydia—she's Latin, so it's like the Benetton, cross-color people [laughs]—they were just like, "Well, *something* has changed."

Some of my Asian friends would be all, "Don't you feel kind of funny when you hang out with all black people? Don't you feel uncomfortable?" And I'm all, [defensive] "I don't feel uncomfortable—they don't say, 'Who's the chink?'" But then, actually I *do* sometimes, because I think there's some connection between black and Latin people. That's what I think. [laughs] I just feel out of place sometimes, 'cause I'll be in a group and I'm the only Asian. But then I shouldn't feel that . . . why should I feel like we're separate? Everyone's the same. But also, I'd feel like everyone has friends outside of school, and my life was Sharon and Lydia—they go to school here. I felt like I didn't have my *own* people, people who I could relate to, on my own level —about me being a Chinese-American, me being a Chinese female, and just how that influences me.

And when I met my Asian friends, I felt like, "Wow, there's a whole new community out there." I was like, "What?! There's Asian dances and things for Asian teenagers!" I hadn't known that. I was just so caught up in it, because for once I felt like I was part of something. And I guess when I felt that, I kind of lost touch with my other friends. That's what happened over the whole summer: I started going to clubs more, and I started hanging out with the wrong kind of Asian people. I was like, "Oh, I love Chinatown." [laughs] I was like, "Chinatown gangs are my friends."

I feel like when I'm telling the story, in some way I'm kind of like, [cocky posture] "Ha, I know some gangs—I feel *cool.*" I felt like that before, and I don't know why, but . . . [laughs] I'm all, "Oh yeah, I started hanging out with Chinatown gang people this summer," and "Yeah, I went to their house, and I can't stand next to the window 'cause they'll shoot me or something." [giggles]

When I hung out with these people, I just felt like, "Wow, my mom doesn't know I'm doing this." [laughs] And my friends were like, "Why are you hanging out with them? We know you want to find your Asian self, but . . . " They were worried about me, I guess everyone was.

My old school was all Asian, and I was like, "When I go to high school, I want to be with all different kinds of people." I got here and first I was all, "Wow, white people"—and then I was, "Uh, where are all my friends?" I was like, "This is *too* different—I want my Asian people back." I felt completely lost.

This whole past year, I've just been like, "I want to go back to my roots." So last summer I went back to China on a cultural exchange thing. It was my first time in China, and I felt like an outsider at first. When I went back to visit my home village, I was just, "Oh, God, *this* is what it means to be Chinese!" I was all, "*Yes!*" I felt within, as one within the people of the village. I felt like now I know what it means to really be Chinese, 'cause I know where I came from, I know my roots, where my whole history began. It's hard to put into words—it's emotional. I was just taken in by everything.

Do I wish I felt more Chinese? Yeah, but what is that? I guess being a Chinese-American, I was kind of torn. I'm not really Chinese, 'cause when I went to China, obviously I'm not—I was an outsider. But then, here, I feel like an outsider in some ways too, cause I'm neither. I feel like I'm trapped between America and China—like there's some internal struggle within myself between these two worlds—and I don't know where I fit. And then I feel like if I hang out with more Chinese people, then I'm Chinese; but if I don't hang out with Chinese people, and I hang out with Sharon and black people, I'm blackwash you know. It's something my ex-boyfriend said—he's Chinese. He called me blackwash, as an insult. "Why do you talk black, why do you hang out with blacks? Why do you act that way?" After that, I guess subconsciously I felt the need to prove myself— like saying, "I'm Chinese." So maybe that's why I was hanging out with all these Chinese people.

So last summer, there was just a lot of conflict between me and my mother, mainly—not my dad so much. I feel like our whole story is like *The Joy Luck Club* or something. [laughs] I liked that movie. Sharon and Lydia—we're still best friends—are always saying, "You don't know what your worth is," 'cause I'll be all, "God, you know what my mom said to me? Nah-nah-nah-nah-nah." I'd just tell them about the fights we would have, and some of the things my dad would say. Like, "What do you want to do in life?" And I'm all, "Well, I kind of want to major in Asian studies." And my dad's all, "Well, what can you do with that? Maybe you should go into physical therapy—a lot of people are making a lot of money," and nah-nah-nah. And I'm all, "Why can't you accept that I want to do this?" And he's like, "Yeah, it's great to be into your culture, but what are you gonna do with it? You need something else."

I don't know if they're still set in this "Lily is our little girl, and she can't do anything, and we don't want her to grow up" or what. Sometimes I feel they don't listen to what I have to say. They're like, "Well, what do you want us to do?" And then I say . . . but they don't really listen to my answers. My mom speaks, and speaks, and speaks, and then she breaks. And when she breaks she thinks I'm supposed to say something. But I don't think she takes time to listen. And then my dad was saying, "I don't know how it's gonna be when you go to college. I don't know if we're still gonna fight. I just want to be able to talk to you." But they don't listen.

I can just picture our, like, lectures. I sit in the room, and they say, "What do you think?" And I say, "I don't know, I don't care." I always answer them with, [dispirited] "Whatever. I don't care. Yeah, uh huh, whatever." But then after I leave the room, I call my friend and I'm, [animated] "*You know what?* Nah-nah-nah-nah-nah." And I'm all, "Why can't I just say that to their faces?" But I can't, so, oh well . . . If they listen to my phone conversations, then I guess they would, like, know.

We've tried so many times to work out our problems. I don't know if this is how it's gonna be forever or . . . I don't know what it is between me and my parents, or why we act like this—if it's just a teenage thing. I guess it's just since I became an adolescent. At first I'm like, maybe it's some emotional roller coaster, like in those books —it's my hormones! [laughs] I feel like sometimes it's easier for me to

talk to Sharon's mom, 'cause she won't be biased, and she won't inter-
rupt me saying, "Well, nah-nah-nah-nah-nah; this is how I feel."
Maybe that's all I want, for someone just to listen to how I feel without
saying, "Why did you say that? That's wrong."

I end up just crying silently and saying, "Well, you don't understand me anyways, why should I even talk to you?" And then I go to
my room and lock the door. Then they knock on the door, or slam the
door . . . [laughs] Whatever. And then I'm all, "What? What do you
want?" And my mom's all, "What kind relationship we have? You
come home, you lock yourself up in your room. You come and eat dinner, and then you go back up to your room and we never talk. We
don't know how your life is." If I would tell them about my life—
which is I guess what they want—they would just be biased. Like if I
would say, "Well, I'm having this problem because one of my friends
smokes whatever," then she'd be all, "Well, you shouldn't be smoking." [exasperated]Aargh.

And they don't respect my privacy. It's not like they open my letters,
but I'm all, "Well, don't look at that"—and I purposefully place it in
some fashion on the table, so this lines up with that." [laughs] So I
know when it's out of order. I had gone to Boston, and I took pictures,
and I put them underneath my pillow. OK, like it's underneath my pillow, in my room, upstairs. Then I went on a trip to look at colleges
down in L.A., and I come back, the pictures are downstairs, in the
kitchen, near the phone. And I'm all, "What is *this* doing here? Why
are you looking at my pictures?" They're like, "We just wanted to see
how your trip was." Then in the corner of one of the pictures, there's
this big cardboard box, and it's all full of empty cigarette boxes. And
my mom and dad are, "We hate cigarette smokers, we want to kill all
cigarettes smokers!"—right? And after that they would just randomly,
every day, like, Xerox me copies of how teenage smokers have a higher
risk of sexual activity or something. And I wasn't smoking! Just
because my friends smoke does not mean that I'm going to. I bet they
think that I'm so weak of a person that I can't say no.

I feel that they expect little 'cause they're so used to me not doing
anything—and my brother, he's just like prize-champion-boy-son of
my dad and my mom. I feel like everything he does, it's like really positive. And I feel like I always fuck up in one way or another: my

grades, or the people who I hang out with, or what I do. I messed up with my grades. My lowest was a B minus or something, but I think I could do better, cause when I did try, I did good. [nearly inaudible] But I didn't get into the college I wanted. So I'm kind of like, OK. [pained laugh and shrug] And the ones I got into, I thought that they were just stupid-ass schools and that's why I got in.

What do I really want to do? I want to be an archaeologist, and I want to dig up tombs in China. [She lets out a big laugh, as though she can't believe she's said it.] That sounds interesting, huh? I want to dig up the first emperor's tomb in Xian—that's my goal in life. Or I would want to do business within the Pacific rim. Mainly I just want to help out the Asian community. If I would do Asian-American studies I would maybe set up community centers, or projects for kids.

Things are better than they were last summer—maybe because my parents realized that it's really the last year. I think they're sad, because they realize I'm growing up, and, like, it's all over. I'm kind of sad, too: I'm scared, 'cause I think this is such a big step, going from high school, leaving home. And how everyone stresses college—they put so much emphasis on college. And I'm kind of scared, 'cause I don't know where I'm heading. I say I want to go into this major or whatever, but in some ways I don't know. I feel lost compared to all these other people around me. A lot of people in my class know what they want to do—engineer, pediatrician, veterinarian, psychologist, whatever. And I'm all, "Oh, I don't know." [small voice] What if I don't know what I want to do in life? What if I don't find that spark within myself that says, "This is what I want to do?"

I think about my four years in high school, and just where'd it all go? I don't know. I guess I learned enough. I really don't know myself fully, but I'm closer to finding out more about myself. I wish I could be stronger in dealing with myself and other people, and the way they act toward me, and how they treat me . . .

I guess that goes back to what Sharon and Lydia said: what is my worth? [small laugh] I guess I don't know what I'm worth. They know what they're worth—they're always saying, "You're so beautiful, you're so nah-nah-nah." And I'm all, "Shut up." That's my own insecurity, 'cause my definition of beautiful is not that waif-like model in *Cosmopolitan*. It's . . . I don't know, beautiful. It's everybody, but I don't think that I fit the standard of it. Do I think it's everybody, but me? Yeah. [laughs] *Yeah.* I know that's not really healthy, the way I am thinking, and it's kind of like, *hello*, you're gonna have a big complex when you're older.

I don't think my parents feel this way, but I feel this way—that I'm like, a loser. [hurting laugh] I just feel like I'm a fuck-up. [softly, sadly] And I guess you can see that with the way I act, 'cause I'm really self-conscious. I don't want people to dislike me, so I do stuff for people, you know, just because they want me to do it. And I guess that's my problem—'cause I can't say, "Well, fuck what everyone thinks— you're here for *yourself.*"

Michael Huang

Chicago, Illinois

W*e meet at a public library in the multiethnic neighborhood of Uptown, an inland port for immigrants from Appalachia to Southeast Asia. The library also serves as the headquarters of* What's Uptown?, *a monthly newsletter put out by local high school kids, for which Michael is a columnist. He's wiry and edgy—twisting, swiveling, and sprawling on the carpeted floor as we talk. "I don't know about being a hyper person, I just like to move. I can't sit still for long. The only time I'm still is when I'm sleeping. Sitting still is, like, boring and a waste of time." He notes that in May he'll be sixteen, able to get his driver's permit. For now, he is fifteen.*

In Vietnamese culture being a teen really has no meaning, because you have like maybe an ounce more freedom than when you were two. The culture is very family oriented. You reach eighteen and start working—you still live with your parents. And then you start raising them, you know what I mean? They raise you, you raise them, and then your children raise you. You are not really an individual, so rebelling and being a teen has no meaning—there's no point in it. Actually, if you do rebel you're looked down upon, and every other teen thinks you're crazy.

I am half-Chinese, half-Vietnamese—both my parents are half-Vietnamese, half-Chinese. I have one sister, she's sixteen, but I have like two billion cousins and uncles and aunts—there's too many of them, actually. [laughs] I grew up in Vietnam, in a suburb of Saigon or

Ho Chi Minh City, whatever you want to call it. I don't remember how to read or write Vietnamese—I can speak it though. I guess my life in Vietnam was better than most, because on my mom's side we owned a little motel and pool hall, and a restaurant. On my dad's side we owned an herbal shop that's been in the family for a couple hundred years or something. I'm just waiting for my share of it. [laughs]

I had a bad heart—there was something wrong with my blood— and when I was younger I could walk but I couldn't really run. And then at four I couldn't move the muscles in my legs—I just couldn't do *anything*. My grandmother had that herbal shop and she used to put weird things on my legs, and do massages, and make me take a lot of herbs. [shivers] The fact that I can walk is all thanks to my grandma.

My parents attempted to leave Vietnam ever since I was born. When I was one year old we were one of the boat people, but we didn't make it. We attempted that maybe three times, but we ran out of money. We were kind of Americanized then, because we were living off their parents. [laughs] Then my mom's mother and her family left for America, 'cause she had a sister who was here already—like since the beginning of time. Well, for a while . . . [laughs] My grandmom got some kind of church sponsor, and so we got here on the plane. I was five.

We flew from Vietnam to Bangkok, and stayed in this camp—it was terrible, you go naked and they examine you. And the food that they served—the camps are *nasty*—so it's rice and soup, rice and soup every damn day, OK. After that we flew to Tokyo; then we flew to San Francisco; then we flew to Chicago. I was sitting by the window on the airplane coming here, and I looked down and saw lights, cause we came at night, and it was just beautiful. I was like, "Wow, I can't believe I'll be living here!" [laughs] But I ended up not living here—for two years I had to live in the suburbs, where my sponsor lived. She was really cool. Every day after school she came by with a coloring book, and was pointing things out. She picked out my English name—Michael.

A lot of immigrants who come to this country go directly to Uptown, and that's where their children go to school. The thing is, there are so many other immigrants, when you go to school you see someone who speaks your language—and you speak your language. You will *not* learn English that way! When there's no one like you around, you're forced to talk to people who are different. In the suburbs me and my sister were the only two minority at the school, so I learned English pretty quick.

When I was in third grade I moved into the city. We got an apartment right next to my grandma. In Vietnamese culture, in Vietnam, you live in an extended family; but here, of course, you can't do that, because the apartments are like twenty by twenty. So you try as hard as possible to keep this extended family thing going. Third, through sixth grade I was at a public school—there was a lot of Asian people there. I felt kind of weird around them at first because I'd been around all these white people all my life. [laughs] White people! I don't mean to make it sound bad.

Vietnamese culture is pretty strict: you go to school—that's your job —you go home; you do chores; you do homework; you go to bed. That's not how things work around here, and it's very hard for my parents to accept that. I know exactly where they're coming from, though; the problem is, they don't know what *I'm* talking about. My parents are Americanized, they're not that strict . . . but all these influences around them—my grandma, and her old kind of friends, and old aunts and stuff—mock on my parents: "Why are you letting your kid do this?" My mom, she knows that I'm smart enough to not get in trouble, and she trusts me, but she does not want to disappoint *her* mother.

In Asian culture disappointing your elders is a big taboo. If I do something bad, it's like my whole family has been cursed. I do something bad, my grandma thinks when she walks out in the street people are going to look at her. You are not an individual: your actions affect everyone else. Which is not like the American way: I am myself, so you can kiss my ass for all I care! [laughs] And sometimes I bring that attitude home to my parents, which is terribly wrong. You know, going outside and coming back home are two different worlds—*totally* different. When I'm at school, the American way, I'll talk back to anyone I feel like. Of course, I know better. When I am at home I do not talk back to my parents. But sometimes I forget that I'm at home, [laughs] and I *will* talk back to my mother. I start doing reasoning crap.

I go out a lot, you know, dating. *Big* taboo! Oh, they think dating is the most horrible thing you can do—after sex, which is the *worst* thing you can do in your whole life. I was dating people, and my parents found out . . . after, like, my fifteenth date. Of course, someone snitched on me, or maybe they had a spy following me around—they have like a network thing. And I had to explain to them, it's not like I'm going to marry this person, it's just I'm trying to build a friendship.

They're very heavy on marriages: they want marriages to work, and they don't believe in divorce. And my reasoning is, if you don't want that to happen, I think you've got to train for marriages, and by doing this thing, dating, you train. You learn how to interact with people, how to interact in a relationship; you know what to do and you know how to fight, how to resolve conflict. But they don't believe in reasoning. They're up there, I'm down here: people up there are right, people down here are wrong—that's it, that's all there is to it.

I try to reason with them, and sometimes they listen, but sometimes they act like there's someone over their shoulder saying, "Don't let him talk to you like that. You're the parents, you're in control here! Why are you so scared of your kid?" Culture dictates that a fifteen-year-old does not have a mind of his own, does not have his own ideas. I think it's a matter of control about the Vietnamese culture—I think the elders [claps hands officiously] want control, and once they're losing control they get frustrated. Like when a parent tells a kid to do something and a kid refuses, they feel they're losing control: they get frustrated, they start hitting. Not that hitting is bad, but they start hitting because they don't know what else to do. And if hitting doesn't work, then they just totally give up and they go in their room, and they close the door, and they cry. I guess all parents, not only the Vietnamese, are very good at guilt trips, especially mothers. Guilt trips are a universal method to discipline a kid.

As a teenager, you're in an in-between stage. Your parents are like, "You're grown up," but then, "You're still a kid." You get two contrasting things going. I like to think I know everything, but I really don't. Teenagers think they know everything, because they know much more than they did when they were like nine or ten years old, and that's a really big leap. Since it's such a big leap you think, "Oh, I've reached the pinnacle of knowledge, I can't be any smarter."

Some kids just rebel, because their parents are really strict and don't know how their life is. And there's no way, I mean *no way*, your parents will know what you're going through. You gotta really make the effort to let it be known what's going on with you. But some of these kids, they're frustrated and they don't know what to do. They go home and it's all strict; then they go outside and see how everyone else has freedom, how everyone else has the right to express themselves, and they don't—so they rebel. And that's where the gang thing comes in.

If you walk the other way down Broadway, you'll see by the video rental store so many of them standing there—in the summer outside, and in the winter inside—cause there's an arcade in there. After school, they'll spend like maybe from three to eight there. They don't know where they're going, no direction or anything. They're frustrated, and they feel a sense of hopelessness because they think they're not gonna make it through their teenage years. All those kids, they wear their low, big, baggy clothes and stuff, just to be like everyone else. A lot of parents object to that, but what can they do? My parents would *beat* me if I wore big clothes. [laughs] Not that I want to.

There was a period where I wanted to wear the big pants, and do what everyone else did, but I grew out of that. I was thirteen or fourteen. I saw these things when I was going to school, and I thought, "They're doing it, so why can't I?" Big pants, smoking, sex, and all that stuff. You know, "Everyone's doing it—so many people can't be wrong." People who follow the crowd are still developing their sense of self-worth. I guess I've developed a sense that I'm worth this much, and I will not lower my price by doing what everyone else does—because then I'll be just a duplicate, and not an original.

I was a pretty good child, pretty well disciplined. Third, fourth, fifth, and sixth grade I was around the neighborhood, but seventh and eighth grade I went to a private, rich, kind of snobby-people school. We weren't rich, and you see all these kids who were spending money like it was water, and were kind of ignorant about things, kind of insensitive, not aware that there are homeless people on earth. One time, we did this will thing, where if you die you're gonna leave something for your classmates. Back then I didn't have Nike shoes—I had generic kind of Payless shoes. And this one kid, Doug, wrote on his will, "If I die I'd leave Mike all my shoes because he couldn't get good ones." I wasn't insulted as much as I was shocked that someone can be so insensitive.

I felt kind of out of place. When I first went there I wasn't with the in-crowd, but I started hanging out with them. [softly] Sometimes I felt like a lesser person—because they're rich, they're smart, and they're beautiful people—physically beautiful. They're kind of like a clique, in-crowd thing. When you get to hang out with the in-crowd you get this sense of superiority over the rest, and I started getting into these snobby ways. I hung out with Doug a lot for some reason. I guess it kind of made me feel like I was climbing the social ladder. You know, "Oh, I'm hanging out at his high-rise condo over the Lake and swimming in his swimming pool." But then you feel like a phony.

I didn't invite any of those kids to my house. I was kind of embarrassed then, 'cause you go to these people's houses and they have antiques and handmade rugs and stuff. And they come to your house, you have an average kind of house, with average kind of things. And they probably don't notice, but you have that illusion. You do this "what if?" thing. "What if they come to my house and they see these things? Would they think less of me?" That school clouded my mind. I was kind of lost there for a while.

There was a period, thirteen, fourteen, when I did pickpocketing, and theft and stuff, shoplifting . . . The first thing I ever stole was baseball cards—which was really stupid—and then I started stealing bigger stuff, like packs of pens and pencils, binders, school-related things—for my education, of course! [laughs] I got caught stealing clothes once. I was taken to the station. My parents don't know. I'll tell them eventually, when I become a very successful person who turns out to be very moral and ethical. I'll say, "I did all these bad things, and in spite of all the bad things I did, I turned out good." I think you learn from your mistakes.

I guess friends do influence you a lot—I was hanging around with the rich white snobby kids; they were doing it for the thrill. I wasn't missing anything at home, and it's not like my parents didn't buy me clothes. I guess I just did it to rebel, and to belong; "Yeah, stealing is *good.*" [laughs] I knew it was wrong. It was kind of like a "so what, oh well" attitude that I had. A lot of people have this "so what" attitude.

Now I'm at a public high school where there's a lot of economic levels, and ethnicity. My school is really cool because they're hard on gangs and drugs, so we don't have that much trouble. The school is maybe fifty percent Hispanic, and then there's blacks and whites, and of course, Asians. All the races get along really well. I guess we've all been exposed to racism . . . Well, not the white people—they probably *do* it! [laughs] I have friends of all different ethnic backgrounds. I hope one day we've done so much melting, we've mixed together so much, you can't tell people apart. I know that I'm Chinese-Vietnamese, that's what I've been told—but am I *really* Chinese-Vietnamese? How would my parents know what happened two hundred years ago? People are, "I'm sure of my race." I don't think anyone is really sure.

Of course, like in every school, there's jerks who goof off and are generally mean to people. I have this curiosity: I'll look at people and wonder what's up with them. 'Cause it's high school, there's lots of people who don't know who they are and what they want to do with themselves. They just kind of go with the flow—"I'll do what you do" —so they don't have to think for themselves. And I wonder sometimes, like ten years from now, what some of the bullies are gonna be doing. While I sit in my nice little executive office looking down out the window, am I going to see them on the street begging?

But I guess school has a bad name to them; I guess their view of school is it's a strict institution where you can't do what you want, and you're there because people want to torture you. Which I thought—I used to . . . [laughs] The way I was brought up, education is important. I go to school as a job, not as a leisurely thing. School is kind of like doing laundry: if you want to wear clean clothes you have to do your laundry. If you want to have a good life afterwards, you've got to do your work now. So that's the bottom line for me. And I want to do it—not because I think school is great fun but because I want rewards after that.

We're Buddhists. We go to temple maybe two times a year. We have an altar and there's statuettes of Buddha and stuff like that. My parents talk a lot about Buddha, but they don't force it on us. They expose us to different religions—they talk about Jesus and all the other gods. I'm not religious; I don't believe that there are any superior beings or anything. I think I'm a superior being. [laughs] And I think it's a whole big mystery, how we came about. But I believe in reincarnation.

I could care less about the environment. Polluting is bad, and throwing trash on the street is not only bad for the environment, it makes the street look ugly—and the person I am, I care about looks.

[laughs] But I think this thing about conserving energy, and stuff like that, I don't believe so. The energy is there for you to use and you should make full uses of your resources. And when it runs out, you find another resource, or you don't—and if you can't live without it, you die. If my children blame me for using up their resources, then I think I've not done a good enough job of raising them. I believe in taking responsibility for yourself; I think an emphasis should be made on independence. Even kids should be told that they should start thinking for themselves, doing things for themselves, and worrying about themselves, because parents are not always there for you—they die eventually. They might even die when you're young. You can't always depend on someone.

To be an intelligent person, a good being, you need to learn how to deal with conflicts, and things that you don't expect—such as the deficit. You don't expect it, but it's here, so what are you gonna do? Sit here and blame your parents and ask them to make it all better? You can't. I think people should start learning to adapt to their environment, and the environment we're in is right now we're in deficit. We've got crime, we've got drugs, we've got people who dirty my streets. You've got to adapt to it. You can't reverse something, but you can make it better.

A definition of success to me—one of the most important things —is happiness. You can be living in a cardboard box, and if you're happy with it, you are successful. But I think success is enhanced with money. Money is just icing on the cake. I am materialistic—I admit that—but I care about community issues and stuff. If I can't help society, I'm not gonna make the problem worse by being bad myself.

I have a plan, I have a goal. I have several goals actually . . . [laughs] But I'm not sure about anything yet. Before, I thought of being something in the medical field—a pediatrician, a brain surgeon. [laughs] But I'm more of a brain donor. Well, now I'm looking at a more realistic goal, because I know I'm not going to be able to stay in school for, like, another ten years after college—I'm not a school person. I'm thinking of maybe journalism, broadcasting, radio, or maybe writing a book. But I know what I want to do, and that is to become successful —and *that* is to become happy.

Ramiro Rodriguez

Chicago, Illinois

He is the son of writer Luis Rodriquez, whose memoir Always Running *details his years in the gangs of east Los Angeles. We sit on their porch on a beautiful late spring day. Ramiro is built like a fireplug, with short-cropped hair, and intense black eyes. He speaks with great passion and much hand-to-fist emphasis. His eyes scan the street constantly. "I tend to look around, not just at girls. Where I live at, they always pass through here—gangs. Looking around, it's a habit." When I first tried reaching Ramiro, he was in jail. He has since been released on bail. He is nineteen.*

I'm from east L.A. I came to Chicago when I was thirteen. I live with my father, and my stepmother. They have two little boys, my brothers—six, and almost a year—and then I got my sister, she just turned eighteen. Me and my sister . . . oh, *forget it*—we used to always fight; we used to just trip out. They'd be, "Oh, there they go again, fighting, arguing." I love her a lot, but *man*, we used to go at it. My mother lives in Chicago now, too. My mother and my stepmother are like friends—they talk to each other a lot. People be telling me, "Man, *what?!* They *get along?* Man, for my mother to go see my step-mother, forget it, it would be boxing!" [laughs]

I was real small, probably two years old, when my parents got divorced. My father used to come visit, we'd stay with him on the weekends. I'd be happy to see my father, because my mother had boyfriends, and another husband for a while, that we didn't really get along too good with, my sister and me. We'd call my father up crying sometimes when we were little kids. We wanted to be close to him, but it was hard.

I think I was getting in trouble all my life—since I was a little kid. There was always those tendencies—you'd get those little urges, man. [laughs] One time I was fighting with my mother. She got a board with nails, and she's like, "*Yeah, you wanna hit somebody?!*" My grandmother intervened. It was good she did that, because I don't know what would've happened. We've had our problems, but because of my mother I'm who I am today, so I love her a lot.

My grandmother was *coyote*—they're the ones that bring the people from Mexico. Coyotes. We were living in east L.A., in the heart. I love my grandmother. She used to have all these schemes to find food, good things. Even though it was kind of like, *dang*, you're looking in the *garbage can* for food? But man, the supermarkets—I used to find *good* stuff. She had a van, so we would go all over in the city, looking for cardboard. The trick was, first you weigh the van with the cardboards, then they empty it out and weigh it again. You had to go from one block to another block to do that, so my grandmother would have me hiding in the van with the cardboard for the extra money.

I moved to Chicago because I had problems with my mother for a while—a lot of problems—so she sent me to my father. I don't really remember too much about all the frustration and anger I had, but my mother just couldn't deal with me anymore—I was getting too violent. I had friends here and there, just moving around from one place to another. I didn't go to school too much at that time. I hated homework; I would make up stories to say why I didn't do it. I used to be a little liar, sometimes—I just liked storytelling.

I'd been coming to Chicago since I was nine years old—me and my sister—in the summertime. I didn't really know my father, though, because he was always working. He tried . . . We'd go out together and stuff like that—but we never got a chance to see him too much. When I came here, me and father, we used to fight a lot. We got closer, but it took a lot of struggle, a lot of work. I love him a lot, too; I'm proud of a lot of things that he's accomplished. But at the time I didn't care too much about what happened to him.

He got me into a good school, and I messed that up with my grades.

I would hardly go, I cut all the time. I'd be like, "Man, all this *home-work* . . . " I wanted to go outside, 'cause I had a lot of friends on the block. I felt real bad—but at that time I just said like, "Oh well," and went to a public school. I used to get into trouble, sneak out of the house and stuff. He worried a lot, and I guess it got him more angrier. He never hit me, but he'd shake me 'cause he was so mad.

I had my friends, the people on my street. It was nothing like a gang thing. The older guys used to make money dealing drugs and stuff; we were kind of the peewees. We were just young kids, we'd go to the mall, the Lake—we used to go all over. We were just a bunch of kids hanging out together. That's what a gang is, really, you know? When I told the people on my block I was gonna join a gang, they were like, "*What?* Why you joining? Stay with us." But in high school the people that I started hanging with, they all joined, so it was like, "Alright, cool." I got beat in. I was fourteen, fifteen.

My father never thought I was gonna join in a gang, so he never really got into his past too much. Actually, he hid a lot about his life until I joined, and that's when everything hit the fan. I tried to hide it from him, but when he found out he got mad—he didn't want to see his son go through that. The way he came at me just made it worse: it made me want to be in even more. These guys are the ones there for me, and this man I hardly know is gonna try and tell me I can't be with these brothers? I was, "*Man, what are you talking about?*" I ran away, I stayed with my boys. As a matter of fact, one of my boys is the one that came to my father, and told him where I was at. I guess he figured I needed a father.

When I was fifteen I got sent to a mental home for three months 'cause of all the gang activities and all the problems. They put me there for depression and gang problems. I'm still a depressed person, and I'm still involved in the gang . . . I never really knew why I was depressed. I think too much, probably—but it's natural, you have to learn to accept it. I'm not always depressed. Am I now? I don't know. I used to be able to know, 'cause I used to change. Now, since this part of my life, sometimes I'll be with somebody, and I'll just stay real quiet—and I know I'm getting depressed then. I'll stay real quiet, I won't try to start up a conversation. And if you don't start one, then we'll just be two quiet people . . . [laughs]

The only thing that came out of being in the mental home was that me and my father, we got closer. Who put me in there? [laughs] My father. He was at his rope's end. He used to try and visit, but I was *mad,* man. I was in full leather restraints all the time, from fighting with the staff. What happens is you act up, you go to the Quiet Room. They had drugged me up. But they're so stupid, cause they would give me drugs that made me feel like I was getting high. It was funny—I used to walk around in circles. [mimes head down, fierce walking] I liked taking the drugs . . . [laughs]

When I went back to school I was in the ED/BD program—emotionally disturbed, behaviorally disturbed—'cause I was a punk. The whole school system should just crumble. It's good to know the basics, man, but I think the way the school curriculum now is, it has to go. We have to involve the kids, involve the youth. You know how they just want you to learn: they won't say what you need it for—you just have to be there. What we have to do is involve the youth, take them out, show them where things are happening. This is what you want to be? Show us, teach us something about it—don't just teach us everything *around* it. "Oh yeah, you want to be this? That's a good dream. Learn your math and science, and you'll get there." Which is not always true—they don't teach you what you want to be, that's the way I look at it. It's sad.

Me and all my boys, we made it to senior year. Every day we come out of school, fighting—beep, bop, boom. Then you go to the next class, do your work; come outside again, fight; go to the next class . . . We got kicked out of high school, because we were always fighting rival gangs. The chiefs of this other gang, they trained at the YMCA to help kids in gangs. They got into our school, said they're going to do a gang intervention program. OK, cool. What they didn't tell the school is that they were just gonna help their own: they told the teachers and the students that my gang, we're killers and murderers, we're always gonna cause trouble. So we got kicked out. They're the ones that killed one of our boys. I mean, we've done a lot of things through times of war, but nobody'd ever been killed. They wanted it to be, "Oh, OK, that's it, we'll freeze it now"—like try to stop the war. Our mentality was like, "What, you crazy? *You just killed one of our guys, man!* That's it—it's on for *life."*

The gang I'm in—we're Folks—we're having a lot of problems. We used to be four, five hundred members, and we're only twenty, thirty deep now. The thing is, from being so small, you're a family—and you know about those people. None of us are really related, but that's how close we are. Different mixtures: Mexicans, Puerto Ricans, two blacks. People think the gang wars are all racial, and that's true in different parts—but in Chicago a lot, everybody just fights for a name, what name you are. What makes us different from People? Actually, nothing. It's all the same. They don't know what they're really fighting—nobody has the knowledge.

I know a lot of political stuff from my father, but I'm naive too in a lot of things. At least in a gang you got something to fight for—at least you're not there, man, doing nothing. The way society and the system is, they already told you ahead of time you're gonna get locked up. There's barrios and neighborhoods, and they say: "We know when you're a baby, because you were born in this neighborhood, you're gonna be in a gang. We got you on record, and we're gonna lock you up every day. Because we already know where your home's gonna be: it's gonna be in a cage like an animal."

They got stereotypes for all of us. This is what we *is:* hanging around, being with a family, being with people you *know* and *trust.* It's true, the violence and the drugs, they have to go. But how you gonna go against gangs and say, "All they are is criminals, we don't want them" —lock them all up like animals—when they could be your own kid. Everybody's kid has friends. But if you don't want your kid to be in a gang, if he does join, don't turn your back on him because he did—try to *help* him. Be a part of his life, don't exclude him.

Man, *everybody's* involved one way or another, whether they like it or not: this is the future that's gonna be. All the young kids growing up, they're gonna end up doing the same things, and it's gonna be a worser time. Our parents who were gangbangers are saying, "Man, look at our kids, now *they're* joining gangs." Your kids' kids' are about to do the same thing. This is what's happening! *El futuro,* you know. You have to understand: gangs is a necessity, it's a part of what we are, a part of kids growing up. Not *all* communities, that's true. But there's gangs in a sense: Boy Scouts, boys clubs, college fraternities—all these clubs and stuff, that's like gangs too.

A year ago, we had a youth conference, Youth Struggling for Survival. The conference was to talk about the issues, about everything—sexism, racism, police brutality, gang violence. What we want to do is get together all the youth groups in Chicago, 'cause there's a lot of groups fighting. Even the politicians, they're fighting each other too: they're just like a gang—not working together. How can you tell us that we should work together, when you're fighting, invading other countries, and slaughtering people, mothers, children like it ain't nothing? It's just *messed up*. They're in a gang too, on a higher level: they got more money and more resources. Mayor Daley, his father and them, they were an Irish gang—that's how *they* got into politics. And now they're all against gangs. And gangs are spreading out of the city: American Indians, the Navajo Indians, they got gangs too. See, that's what you get from being Americanized. [laughs] That's democracy.

Proposition 187, I think it's stupid. Everybody's thinking all it's, gonna be are Mexicans, and yeah, send 'em back. But what's gonna happen is in the future it's gonna be all minorities, all immigrants, it's gonna be *everybody*—and that's the sad thing. Man, the guys, especially in Congress, are setting up laws to go against the minorities—cutting out welfare, cutting out everything—welfare, farewell. Prop 187, it's against my people, my family. They say, "Oh you got your own country, go back to it"—but *you* invaded my country, and took half the land away, and all of the resources.

In my community you got guns. But we're not the ones that bring the violence and the drugs here first, you know? They should legalize drugs and get programs that would help people stop using. But you have to go up higher than that: the only way you're gonna stop it is to stop the capitalists and the politicians—*they're* the ones sending in the stuff, *they're* making more money at it than anybody else. *We're* not the ones that be supplying it and flying the planes and dropping it off; *we're* not the ones that manufacture guns. They know where the most money they're gonna make is at—the place where there's not a lot going on.

You can live off dealing drugs as long as you don't get caught up. I was never really big into it, it was just money to have. Now I have a job. But it sucks, working at these cheap jobs. The job I have is straight—five-fifty an hour doing janitorial stuff, and you get raises. It's not hard, but I want to go to college—I don't want to be a manual laborer all my life. The day I registered to go to college, I got locked up. I'd just registered, I had my financial aid, I had everything set. I even went and got my school ID—I got it here, in my pocket. [He proudly shows it.] That day I was real happy, but I got locked up that night. I spent six weeks in the County.

I can tell you the charges: two charges of attempted first-degree murder, two counts of aggravated discharge of a firearm, and two counts of unlawful possession of a weapon. I don't know w*hy* people go trick. You're in a gang, why are *you* gonna go say, "Oh, they tried to kill me," when *you're* doing the same thing. My family, everybody, they try to be optimistic about it, but I'm just trying to be realistic, you know. I'll probably do some years. If worst comes to worst, I'll learn to deal with it. I'm gonna try to go to summer school, just for the experience of going to college—and all the girls! [laughs] If I do get locked up, at least I can say, "Man, I went through a couple of years of college, I had a chance to be part of jobs, the youth groups, whatever . . . " I just want to do what I can, now. I want to be able to be a part of something for a while, before I end up being part of the system.

People tell me, "Oh wow, man, great! Now you can get out of gangs." Hold up, man! Let me take my time—let me try and figure out for myself what I want to do, how I want to do things. Don't rush me . . . Because I started doing good, all of a sudden I have to be the kinda way *you* want me to be—just leave the life. But like I say, you live in a community, you feel *part of it.* How you just gonna turn your back on it?! I could get out, if I wanted to. But you know what? I ain't. The brothers are fighting—I'm fighting with them.

A lot of times, though, we tend to be by ourselves. 'Cause when some of those brothers turn their back on you, you learn to depend on yourself. Yeah, these brothers out here, you can't always trust 'em— some of them are dopies or thieves. But even though I'm gonna try and better myself, I ain't never gonna turn my back on the family that was there for me at first. All the years . . . They're my brothers—and I can't just turn my back on them. Even though we're still fighting and stuff, we're trying to figure things out—we know there's something out there, we just don't know how to get it.

I give my family a lot of credit—they bailed me out. They've been through a lot. I guess a lot of stuff I'm trying to do is for them, too—working, going to school—so they can be proud of me, so they can say I wasn't a bum all my life. [laughs] I want them to be proud of me for something, even if it's small.

My future? What I'd like to be doing in ten years? I really don't—I'm sorry, no, I can't, I can't really picture. I would like to, you know, it would be nice . . . But I look at the world as bleak and dreary . . . [little laugh] no. It's just the way it is. If I try and look into the future, the only thing I see is me doing time, so it's like, man, I'm *facing* it—why would I want to *look* at it?

I still got hopes, I'm still gonna go to college . . . My setbacks would be me getting locked up or me doing stupid things—or that someone kills me. Those are the things that I have to watch out for. I don't really know what I wanna be, I don't really know what's gonna happen to me five, ten years from now—I'm just looking at it from day to day. I want to go to college just for the fact that I'm gonna have a chance to learn. The only thing I really know is poetry.

I started writing poetry when I was thirteen—when I moved here. We had a chance to go to the Museum of Science and Industry on this field trip, and I really wanted to go. I didn't do the homework, so like the night before, man, I wrote all these poems, just at one time . . . Never done it before—it tripped me out! My father was like, *"Man! He's a poet too!"* And to see his son writing poetry . . . I think that's where my influence came from—it was just in his genes. [laughs]

I don't write every day—it comes out of nowhere, it just hits me. Poetry gives me a chance to express the way I feel, and how I look at things in this world. I do it for myself, not for fame or anything. You know how people say, "I want you to know what I'm feeling?" When I do my poetry, I don't do it just for that—I want people to read the poem and have their *own* feelings, and to think, and remember: "Man, *dang* . . . This poem—I remember when I went through this and that." I like for people to have their own meanings to it—like if *they* wrote it.

I wrote this poem when I was locked up. I'm trying to remember it. My poems are untitled. Titles are just . . . I don't know, yeah—for people yeah, cool . . . but that's not the poem—it's *extra*. I like to be right down on that and just *write it*. Alright, here goes:

The day the world took my life away
The day I took my life away from the world
I opened up my eyes to this world
That has chained me to this dying earth
My heart has been broken
Not for the love of someone else
But for the love I did not have for myself

Straightening Out

Bonnie Coyne

Watkins, Colorado

Bonnie is nervous, with good reason: the police have heard she was witness to an assault by two white supremacists against a black man. Under pressure, Bonnie has agreed to testify. Since then, for reasons of safety, she's had to transfer from her high school to an adjunct high school for kids who are having academic trouble. I had planned to interview her the day before, but she had had to catch a ride home: "I don't want to walk—I got a death threat yesterday. They told my sister they're coming after me." Bonnie is Italian-Irish, too thin, with light brown hair and glasses. Her voice is soft, uninflected. She is seventeen.

Where I live, my block, is alright. There's housing tracts all over. They mostly look alike—some of them are different sizes and colors. I live with my mom, and my sister, Kathleen—she's fifteen, and my younger brother, Jeffrey—he's twelve. My older brother is eighteen, and he lives with my dad in Kansas. Our dad got remarried, and he has two other kids now. My dad hasn't paid child support since . . . He left my mom just before my little brother was born.

The divorce was hard on me at first—I was only in kindergarten. And then my mom started seeing this guy, and I'm like, "Where's my dad, where's my dad? This guy isn't my dad!" He was very abusive, he used to beat us. He hit her too. I couldn't understand why she couldn't just tell him to leave. Even though I was young, I remember everything that happened. I never really did like him.

I used to hate my dad a lot because he'd never come and see us or anything. But when I went to stay with him for like a month—that's when me and my mom weren't getting along one time, and I was getting kicked out a lot—he told me that he *had* written us and called. He had receipts of how much money he sent us for our birthday and everything. But my mom would say, "Your dad never wrote, he never called you." I didn't know what to believe . . . [sighs] I was just like, "Well, I can't take either your or mom's side in this, so I'm just gonna leave it blank." 'Cause, I mean, I know who my father is, but I don't *really* know him . . .

My dad moved to Kansas recently; he used to live in Denver. My older brother went to my dad's 'cause he was getting in a lot of trouble for breaking and entering, and stealing, and getting in trouble at school. My mom thought maybe it would be better if he lived with his father for a while—that he needed a father figure. He's been with my dad for almost three years now, and he's changed a lot: he doesn't do drugs, he's out of trouble, he's getting straight As in school now.

Now I'm the oldest in the house so I gotta be, like, in charge. Which is alright, but my little brother, Jeff, gets out of hand. He has a disability problem. He was molested three years ago, so he's kind of troubled right now. It was one of my mom's ex-boyfriends . . . We're still going through a lot with that—we're trying to cope with his problems, make things easier with him.

He's in counseling, and takes medication. He's been in and out of the mental ward for his actions. When he gets angry he likes to hit and throw stuff at you. I love him to death and everything, and he knows that I'll always be there for him, even with the way he's treated me— he almost broke my nose. I was scared of him, but I've learned to live with my fear. Now I try and talk with him, instead of hitting him first. When he gets angry, I'm like, "Jeff, let's talk." He's pretty much calmed down—he hasn't been hitting as much as he used to.

Sometimes I'll get blamed for stuff. Like my mom was doing the dishes one day, and she took off her nice rings, and I guess Jeff bent them all up 'cause he got mad at her. She's all, "Well, if I found out either you or Jeff did that to my rings, you're gonna be in a lot of trouble." I said, "So you're accusing me of doing that, already? I ain't like that. Why would I do a thing like that?" And I go, "You know Jeff, he *would* do that." She compares me and Jeff, and I'm not like Jeff—I'm a totally different person than he is. My sister, she's just off in her own world. She's more active: she's into drill team, drama, and she's always gone—performing plays and stuff—and she's into modeling. She's out of the house, mostly with her friends.

I was sixteen when I went to live with my dad. He's a Jehovah's Witness—there was no TV, and every time we ate we had to pray, and I couldn't hang around with certain people. My mom doesn't make us go to church if we don't want to. I *had* to go to Jehovah's Witness church—and it was like, "I feel like you're forcing me to go into this religion, either if I like it or not." I didn't like it there, so I stopped eating. My dad would be like, "What's wrong with you?" I'd cry every night, "I want to go home—I want to go home. I don't like it here."

I went to my dad's 'cause I was getting into a lot of trouble, I was ditching school. When I started high school I was doing all right. I went every day, just about. And then I got this attitude: I don't want to go to school no more. I just didn't want to care about anything anymore, cause I felt like everything was going wrong. Every time I tried to show my mom that I'm improving and doing good, doing better than I was before, it wasn't good enough for her—that was the way I felt. It was like, if nothing's good enough for her, why even bother?

She used to talk about, "Oh, Kathleen is getting straight As. Why can't you be like her?" It was like, *"I'm not Kathleen*—I'm Bonnie. No one can be me, I can't be anybody else." And I'd try and show her I'd improved, and she was like, "Oh, well you can do better than that." And it was like, "This is the best that I can do." She was a little proud, but I just wanted, "Oh wow, you did good!" I hardly ever hear that from her. I sometimes wished that I could get that, so I'll feel more better about myself. And I don't get that . . .

I started getting into drugs, and I met this guy Gene, and got in a lot of trouble with him—got arrested for breaking and entering, stealing, stuff like that. Yeah, to get money for drugs. I was doing crack cocaine, speed, marijuana. I did that for a year—six to twelve lines a day. First I was doing speed, and then I was doing crack—and then I didn't do crack anymore, I just did speed. It gave me a feeling . . . I don't know, I just liked it a lot: speeding around, [laughs] talking a lot, and walking all over town, staying up late.

When I met Gene I already knew he was doing drugs, and I totally thought, "No, *I'll* never do drugs." And then we started going out, and he gave me my first line. I had doubts about it, and then I wanted to try it—because, I mean, it's a new experiment. So I tried it, and, *oh my God*, it was a weird experiment. I was scared, I cried—I couldn't feel my feet touching the ground. I tied my shoes supertight so I'd feel them. [laughs] But ever since that, I was doing it.

My mom kicked me out because I lost my virginity. Had she talked to me about sex? [laughs] She just told me never to do it. She found out 'cause my brother walked in on us. [laughs hard] Oh, I was *so* embarrassed. The next day Jeff was putting his feet in between my legs, and I was like, *"Knock it off!"* 'Cause he was pissing me off. He wouldn't stop, so I told my mom. He got pissed off 'cause mom got mad at him, and he goes, "Well, Bonnie had sex in her room last night!" I'm like, *no-o-o*.

My mom was so mad, we got in a big fight about that. She started screaming and said she was gonna press charges on Gene, and throw me in jail. I go, "Well, let me come back when we're calmer and we can talk about this." I took off for a week, and I called her, and said, "Are you calmed down yet?" She's all, "No I'm not—come get your stuff and get the hell out of my house." [sadly] So I went back, my stuff was right there in the street. I was like, "Fine, I'll go out on my own." And so I was on the street for almost a year. That was my first year doing drugs. I was fifteen.

I lived with friends, but I would call my mom and let her know that I was alright, and that I was still alive, you know. She never said, "Come home." But then I forced myself to go home, and I tried working things out, but she has to bring up the past. I'm like, "Mom, look, I'm trying to make a change here, from the past—start over." "I don't want you starting all over what you did, I'm embarrassed," blah-blah-blah. I said, "I'm sorry, I can't really deal with you." I got my stuff and left.

I lost a lot of things, being on my own—clothes and things, pictures . . . It's like, "God, what happened to all my stuff?" One of the pictures was of me and Brandy, my god-sister—I love her to death. She's been dead for three years now . . . [sighs] She was molested and raped at thirteen months, and she died. [sighs] The baby's mother, Rita, was seeing this guy . . . [She sounds sadder than she has about her own troubles.] I guess he was burning the baby—she had burn marks all over. We'd say, "How'd that happen to her?" "Oh, she knocked down a lamp and burned herself."

Rita used to live with us—she had a drug problem and stuff. My mom told her, "We can't have this in the house. If you like, the baby can stay with us, you can come and visit her. As soon as you get your own place, off of drugs, and making money, you can have the baby back." Rita didn't want to do that, so she took the baby and was on the street. She took Brandy away from us, and I just cried and cried. She'd still be alive to this day if she'd just given us the baby.

I moved back home like five times, but it was, "No, this isn't gonna work." I was staying with one friend for like six months—her parents knew the situation. And then I moved out of there, 'cause we were doing drugs and I didn't want her to get in trouble. I went with other friends for two months, and then with another girlfriend for like two weeks. Then I got busted.

When I got arrested it wasn't really me who was stealing, it was the other people—I was just there watching, standing on the porch: *"It's time to go, let's get outta here."* [nervous laugh] When you're high, you're not really scared. It was my boyfriend's mom's house that they were breaking into. We took fifteen hundred dollars and rented a limo. [blushing at the memory] Oh my God. And then we went to the restaurant, and ate food—spent like a hundred dollars on food. We came back, went to the mall and went shopping. Then we went and rented the hotel, and stayed there for two or three days.

We got caught like three days later when Gene's mother came home from vacation, wherever it was she went. Gene's brother's girlfriend, Shelley, was with us. She's an adult—she got us the hotel and all, and beer. I went back to her house with her, and Gene's mom calls her: we were like, *"Oh, shit!* Oh no . . . "* And she's all, *"Where's Gene?"* And Shelley's, "I dunno." *"I want to know where he's at. He took my money,"* and all this. Shelley just broke down in tears and told her everything. It was, "Oh, we're in *deep* shit now." The next day me and Gene and this other guy were arrested at the hotel. They arrested me. They asked if I was a runaway. I said, no, but they looked it up on the computer. They took the handcuffs, and handcuffed my hands behind my back, sat me in the car, and took me down to the police station.

That's when they called my mom. "Do you have a daughter named Bonnie Coyne?" "Yeah." "Well, she's down here at the police station, we need you to come and pick her up" [ranting] *"Well I ain't picking her up—I don't want her home,"* blah-blah-blah, all that stuff. Oh my God. They said, "Well, we're going to get you for child neglectment if you don't come get her." My mother said, "I don't have a car, so can you drop her off at the house?" When they dropped me off, my mom's all, "I want you *outta* here. I don't want you to stay here if you're gonna be doing drugs," and all this . . . So I left again.

I came back a couple days later and said, "Mom, I'm gonna change." I went to drug rehab. I got tired of being all sucked-up and skinny, and not being able to sleep. I came to the point where I was doing too much, and overdosed. I was gone to the point of killing myself—that's where I was heading. One time I was high and I was looking at my future, and I just saw myself dead. It was like, "I don't want to be there." I want to be the high class, making money, and driving around in a car, and going to college, and having all those things. Where am I going to go if I'm dead? So that made me change. I was having dreams about myself being dead—all the time . . . [pained laugh] Maybe it was my guardian angel telling me if I don't stop, something's gonna happen.

I've been trying to help my girlfriend get off drugs. I'll say, "Is it really worth it? Is it worth having to come down, and being a bitch about it, and not sleeping and not eating. Do you really want to put yourself through that?" She's like, "No." I said, "Well, why would you do that?" *"Because I'm depressed and upset."* I say, "Let's talk about it. You're just fighting it more with drugs." I don't want her to go downhill and be kicked out of her house, 'cause she's got a great mom who loves her and would do anything for her. She has low self-esteem, I think. She's trying to lose weight to be more attractive to guys and gain boyfriends. And I can understand that—but you don't need drugs to do that! I used to do that, too . . . [laughs] I was anorexic for a long time: I would only eat a snack, once a day—that was it for the whole day.

I went to drug rehab for a month or two, and then I stopped going for a while. But I've been sober for five months now. Sometimes I'll still have the craving for it, and I'll want to do it once in a great while . . . but then I'll remember, "God, I'll just blow it—five months sober." Sometimes I hang out with my friends who still do drugs. They'll put a line out in front of me, and it's like, "I can't do it—I'm sorry." I'm like, *"God,* I can't believe I just did that!" But then I turn around and say, "I don't want to do that." They think I've changed a lot and I'm just Mrs. Know-it-all now. But I don't really hang out with them no more, I got a new group of friends—they don't do drugs.

My mom's still stressful about everything, and she still can't get over my brother being molested . . . [softly] Plus, like, let's see, a year ago I told her that I was molested, too . . . I was thirteen, it was that same guy. That was when the fighting all started; the fighting, the running away, the doing drugs. I didn't tell her what happened for three years, 'cause I had a feeling that she'd just flip out and go ballistic about it. She was so upset about Jeff, she was totally gone—she almost killed herself over it. My dad put the blame on her: *"How come you didn't see the signs?"* That made her feel bad, she felt so guilty. So, I couldn't tell her.

When I finally told her, she *totally* flipped out. She went to the knife drawer—she was going to kill herself, I guess. I screamed and ran out the door. I was just, *"Don't do this to me!"* She was yelling at me, *"Why didn't you tell me? Why didn't you tell me?* I could've done something about it." I was like, "I didn't know what to do! I had nowhere to go, no one to talk to. I didn't know what to do . . . " And I told her, "I couldn't tell you, because I knew exactly what you were gonna do—and that is exactly what you're doing now!" That's when she said, *"No more boyfriends"* and all this, 'cause she was afraid that—I don't know . . . I was just like, "Mom, there's nothing *anybody* can do. Life goes on." And I've handled it pretty good—I'm not crazy or anything. It doesn't really bother me. It's in the past; I can't change the past.

See, my mom isn't getting over what happened . . . [sighs] If that's the way she wants to live her life, I can't do anything about it—I may as well just go on with mine. I try my best to do what she asks me to do, but I have my own opinions, and I'm seventeen—I gotta start learning things on my own. I'm like, "You gotta give me some space, to learn things on my own, find out the hard way." Sometimes she won't let me do that, and it makes me angry. But a lot of times, I'll stop and think, "Well, maybe she's right"—I'll see *her* side. I used to have a bad temper, now I pretty much handle it pretty good. I talk to myself, say, "I got to look at other ways. I gotta see the other person's side before mine, and compromise, and put the pieces together before I make a mistake."

The people I was doing drugs with were people that were on the streets. We'd meet new people, get free stuff. Most of my friends are white. I get along with blacks occasionally. Some of them I don't like because—not to put the blacks down or anything—but a lot of them are really rowdy and rude and obnoxious. The ones that think they're all bad, and go around, "Yeah, I could kick your ass, you're white." I'm not prejudiced against anybody. If you show to me that you have respect towards yourself and other people, then I'll give you the same respect back. But if you give me the uncourtesy of being rude to me, then you're gonna get the exact same thing back. That's the way I look at it: what comes around goes around.

My ex-friends, they believe in White Power, but I don't think they're skinheads; they're friends with the skinheads. I'm not really sure what White Power is. I believe that you have to get along with everybody. It doesn't matter what color you are. God put you on this earth whatever color he wanted you to be. The way I look at it, there's niggers, there's blacks; there's whites, and there's trash; there's Mexicans, and there's wetbacks. There's always a bad name for each race, and there's a lot of people that aren't really that bad.

The stupid thing is, when I saw what happened, the attack, I was frying—doing acid. [laughs] That's when I was first in drug rehab. I was, like, sober for a month and then I got the urge. I did acid that day—I've never done it since—it scared the shit out of me. One hell of a trip, that's all I remember! [laughs] People look at it that I narked on 'em, 'cause I said I'd testify—people are judging me. If they look at it my way, I had no choice—I would've gone to jail, risking my life, because of them, for something I didn't do. Because I saw too much, the cops needed me to testify, and they said if I didn't, I would go to jail. I was under a lot of stress, plus getting death threats, and people said they were gonna bomb my house, and hurt my family, and kill me, slice my throat, and all this . . . My old friends are after me now.

But *nobody's* not gonna stop me. A threat is a threat. Why should *I* have to stop going to school because of them. I should be able to go to school, go over to my friends', go to parties, stuff like that. And if I run into 'em, I run into 'em. My mom's all, "You're taking this too calmly—you gotta be more precautious about it." I'm just gonna keep living life the way I want, and if there's fear in me, there's fear . . . But if the cops hadn't known I saw something, I'd have just kept quiet, yeah . . . 'Cause, I mean, I wouldn't have all this problem. But actually I'm kinda glad it happened, because now I'm here at this school, so there's like a good part to it. If I was still at my old school, if I kept quiet about it, God, I'd still be ditching and getting in trouble. Probably back in drugs again. I love it here.

I've never done so good in my whole life. [Beaming with pride, she shows me her progress report. It is filled with positive comments.] I used to get Cs, Ds, and Fs—never As and Bs, hardly. [spirited] I hope to get a good reaction from my mom. Once in a great while she'll still bring up my past, and it makes me feel bad. But I understand the hard life that my mother went through and that she's trying to make it different and better for us. I *understand* that, and I love her for what she's done for me. I'll be like, "Mom, the past is away. Look at me *now*, look how good I'm doing." Sometimes it's hard for her to look at that, 'cause she's so used to me screwing up all the time, and I'm not. It's like a big difference for her . . . I think it's, like, hard for her. Like, "Wow, Bonnie's doing good, but I don't want to tell her," you know? It's like a secret. I know that she's proud of me, but it's that she doesn't want to tell me. I guess . . . I don't know. It's hard to tell with her. I think she's just waiting for the right moment.

Phil Carpenter
Chicago, Illinois

W*e meet at the Gateway Foundation, an organization for juveniles with substance abuse problems. Most participate at the behest of law enforcement officials. Security is tight—cameras monitor the entrance, there's no sneaking in or out. He's tall, and well built, with a take-no-prisoners attitude and a charmer's smile. He has short hair with long strands at the nape of his neck, and several tattoos: Jesus Christ, the Grim Reaper, a cross, his name, a skulled jester, and the Madre de Guadeloupe. Phil was released many months ago—he meets me there after getting off work. He is eighteen.*

I grew up in the city, and then I moved to the suburbs, when I was like eleven. I have two brothers, my mother—that's it. My older brother is twenty-one, and my other brother, he'll be twenty soon, and then there's me. My mother works in a plant. Yeah, she had her hands full—she still does . . . [smiles] I pay my own bills, but I still live there with her.

My father? I dunno. Just going about his business, I guess. They got divorced when I was about four years old. All they ever really did was fight anyway. I saw him when I was younger, but since I got older, no . . . It's hard, but I don't care. He must think the same way about me and my two brothers, 'cause he don't put forth no effort to call, or to come by the house. So why the fuck should we? It's sad, in a way. But, you know, you can't just not have somebody in your life for so many years and then here they come strolling along, talking about "Hey, you want to go to the zoo? You want to go to the show?" That shit just don't work. You can't just make your way into somebody's life, man. It don't work like that.

He ain't about shit anyway—he don't do nuthin with his life. He don't help me, so why should I help him? I don't know if he works, I don't know what he does. I ain't talked to him in a few years. He does what he does, and I don't like what he does. He smokes pot. That's all he does, and I don't care for it. I used to do it myself. Oh yeah, for a few years, four years, about that: PCP, cocaine, LSD, Xanax, Valiums, alcohol, reefer. Everything but rocks and heroin, man! [laughs] I started using probably when I got in the gang. That's when I got real bad on the stuff.

Where we used to live, now the neighborhood's bad. It's all gangs, man. That's all there is in this fucking town. Any town you go in there's gangs. When I was a little kid it was real nice. A lot of older folks, and lots of Polish people. I'm not Polish, I'm German—both sides. If I go there now it's a lot different, a lot more blacks, a lot more Mexicans, less white. And in my eyes, they're the ones who fucked up the neighborhood. They're dirt. They're dirty, they don't care about nuthin. That's just how they are. I just don't care for them.

My school was all black. It was rough sometimes. When you're a little kid, you don't know how to fight; my older brothers would always have to come and protect me from the black kids. They stabbed me with two lead pencils in the third grade. That's why I don't care for them. You know, they don't stop, they don't learn . . . They should learn how to value what they have, and just thank somebody that they have it. Leave other people's property alone. They steal your car, they steal everything. Walk down the street, they stick a knife in your back and take your wallet.

Am I a racist? Nah, I ain't . . . Well, I dunno—it's hard to say, cause sometimes I am, and sometimes I'm not. Skinheads? Skinheads are crazy. Well, they have strong beliefs, that's all. No way I'd join them, nuh-unh. But some of the things I do believe. See, there's a difference between a nigger and a black person. Some of them are a disgrace to society; same thing with Mexicans—even white people.

Skinheads, their beliefs are a lot stronger than mine. But they're fulla shit, just like any other gang. [He shakes his head] But a skinhead,

I just couldn't do it, man, 'cause if I had a bald head and big combat boots and I walked on the bus one day, and they was all black—your ass is grass. I couldn't do it, man . . . [laughs] 'Cause I wouldn't know what to do if I got on a bus with a bunch of blacks, and I had a bald head, and fucking swastikas here and here.

I joined the gang when I was thirteen or fourteen-years old. I was the first one to join the gang, and then my older brother did, and then the middle brother did. That's how it went. I was out of the city by then, I was over in the burbs, but I grew up around the gangs in Chicago. I grew up around People. I don't know if you know the difference between People and Folks—there ain't none. It's just dumb shit.

In the gang that I was in, there was white and about three or four Mexican. We had branches in the burbs, branches in the city. I really couldn't tell you how many, 'cause to this day I still don't know all of the gang members that are in the gang—I haven't had the chance to meet 'em. [laughs] I don't care to meet 'em now.

I don't know even know why I joined, to tell you the truth. To this day I still wonder sometimes. We were outside drinking beer, and we went through about two cases, and they asked me and I just said, "Alright." [laughs] I was *real* drunk. I mean, they didn't pressure me or nuthin like that. I just did it. Was I blessed in? Nah, I got my ass *whupped*, I didn't get *no* blessings. [laughs] I didn't feel a thing until the next morning. It's the truth. [laughs] I was sore. And then the next day it's like, *"Wow*—I'm in the gang." That's how it happened to me.

I didn't tell my family at first, but man—word gets around *fast*: that same day, they *all* knew I joined. My mom told me I was stupid, and I'm an idiot, and I'll regret it. Yeah, she was right. I didn't think that then, 'cause if I did, I woulda got out a long time ago. I was in for five years.

The people who I hung around with in the gang, we weren't into the dealing drugs, we were more into the running around, causing trouble, busting out peoples' windows and stuff like that . . . Wherever we find 'em, we get 'em—Folks, rival gangs. Teach 'em not to come back in your neighborhood. [laughs]

Somebody had to be looking over me once in a while, man, cause some of the stuff I did, I should be locked up. [laughs] I have been locked up; that's how I got here—through the system. What'd I get locked up for? None of your business! [laughs] Yeah, it was a pretty high felony. Yup. I was sixteen. I went to Audy Home [officially known as the Cook County Juvenile Detention Center] for three months. I was the only white guy in the section, and there was one Latino. And then as the days went on, a couple weeks before I got out, a couple white guys came on the section. But for a little while, *pshew* . . . I guess I was kinda lucky, 'cause they put me on a section that was all my kind, you know—it was all People. I had problems, but not as much as I woulda had if I went on a section with all oppositions.

Then I was in here for six months. How'd I get here? I didn't get here, the judge put me here. He said, *"Straighten your ass out."* [laughs] That's what he told me. If he hadn't put me here, it would've been two years in the Department of Corrections. That's a lot differ-ent—that's the joint. [laughs] Why'd he give me a break? [softly] Maybe he seen something good in me.

I was one of the first ones to come through here—the place had just started. When I first came there were seven people. We didn't do nuthin for the first two months. We sat on the couches, ate potato chips and smoked cigarettes, and watched TV all day. Then a month later, just *pshew*—*everybody* came in. There was like thirty people here.

This program is just to show you who your self is, I guess. They show you things about yourself that you can't see. Like just how you are. When I was here I learned a lot of stuff, I did real good in here. It sucks, man, but I had to do it. To tell you the truth, it's bullshit, but it is good for you—just the way the rules are around here, what you can and can't do. Like, you can't do whatever you want. [laughs] I mean you can't go home—you go home when they tell you go home; you shower when they tell you shower; you piss when they tell you piss; you eat when they tell you eat. When you're in jail it's a lot worse. This is a *lot better* than jail: you got a weight room here, you got three hots and a cot. They give you your shampoo, your soap, they give you everything you need here. I'd been through a place like this before. I was around fifteen years old, in for six months. But I still had some more rounds in me . . . Not no more—you only get so many chances. Three strikes, you're outta there. This is my second strike, so I just figured . . . [laughs]

I was the top of the house, the coordinator. He runs the house, calls the shots. Man, I used to hook a lot of people up in this place. [grins] "Hooking" means getting their ass in trouble. 'Cause, I mean, who are they gonna believe—him or the top of the house? I was kinda crooked in here, too, but they never found out. I never like did no drugs or nothing like that, but I used to sneak shit in my room that shouldn't be in there, smoke in my bedroom.

You don't buy nothing in this place: they give you everything, even cigarettes. So me, I would go in the storage room. I would take shit out of there and bring it in my room. But then when I'd catch other people doing it, I would snitch on 'em: I'd say, "Yeah, he got cigarettes in his room," when I'm sitting there, and I got a pack in my room too. [laughs] It's the name of the game: you gotta get them, before they get you, 'cause they *will* get you. That's just how this place is—they play a lot of shit in this place—bullshit, you know? They get each other in trouble and then they start fighting, getting in fistfights, and then they get kicked out and go back to jail. It's piddly stuff. It happens 'cause there's nothing else to do in the place besides your getting treatment. I mean, you gotta have some fun.

I never watch my mouth. If I have something to say, I'm gonna say it. I'm gonna say something to one of the guys when I walk outta here, 'cause he's fulla shit. He went through here with me, and now he's back in here. A black kid. He was alright, he did everything the right way, but look who's back here—not me. He bullshitted his way through this place. He's stupid. That, or he's hiding out from a gang in here. And in here the cops can't walk in and just grab you. This could be a lot of things for people: it could be a shelter for somebody that has nowhere to go; it could be a hideout; a runaway spot—whatever they make it out to be.

I think a lot differently since I got out. I ain't running around the streets no more. I value what's mine, and I respect other people's possessions and property. I was a punk before . . . I thought I'd whup everybody's ass that comes around. I don't feel that way anymore. I know somebody out there can whip my ass, you know? [laughs] It's been done before. This place straightened my head out a lot. I respect my mother a lot more than I did. Was I awful to her? Yeah, that was it. My mom didn't have no control over me. What is she gonna tell me? I'm bigger than her, I have a meaner attitude than her—what can she tell me? It ain't what I did, it's what I *didn't* do—'cause I never did *nuthin*. She would ask me to do this, do that—I wouldn't do it. *Clean the house:* I wouldn't do it. Eat, sleep, and there I go.

I always worked, my whole life. Always. I like working. Stocking, shipping, receiving. *Pshew*. Sales, what else? I tried selling drugs, and I couldn't do it, 'cause I kept smoking it, and I never made no money! [laughs] Now I play with cars. Shocks, struts, rag pins, tires, rims. I've been doing that for almost six months. I start a new job Wednesday, as a matter of fact: laborer—moving for a moving company, ten dollars an hour. Ten years from now? I just want to be rich, that's it. I'm sure that's everybody's fantasy.

I quit school when I was fifteen years old, 'cause of gangs, drugs, just carelessness. Nah, I never liked school, but I'm real sorry I quit. The GED . . . [softly] I took that test. I missed it by five points. Five points! [laughs] I gotta go back and take two more tests. I was pissed. Five fucking points, man! Five points ain't *nuthin*.

The way the world is going—it's gonna go the way it goes. I'll leave it up to the brains to decide what they want to do with it. It's already messed up. Law enforcement, that's like a *big* problem. I don't like cops: they're crooked, they're corrupt, they lie, they cheat, they steal, they're fucking assholes! I don't like 'em, and I never did like 'em. I don't just say that because I had a lot of run-ins with 'em either—it's just the way they are: they're the authority, they can do what they want. They can take off that badge and that *pistola*, and they can beat your ass, and bring you in, and say, "We picked him up in a fight." See, it's things like that they get away with.

And the *guns* are a bunch of shit. I mean, you can't even get out of your car and have a good fist fight with nobody no more. When I first started gang banging, once in a very great while, somebody would pull a pistol out—and this was a couple years ago. It's gotten a lot worse. I did carry a gun for other people, but never for myself. I would rather fight a man with my bare hands than pull a gun on him. Now if I can't kick his ass, you're damn right I'm gonna grab a weapon—just in my defense.

Welfare, put it this way: I work for my money, I don't deal drugs, I pay taxes. Why should I pay taxes for some fucking bum that's gonna sit on his ass on *welfare?* I just don't think there should be any of that shit. The welfare's supposed to be for their kids, and they sit there and use the money and the food stamps to go get drugs. And then their kids are sittin' there with nuthin. That disgusts me, man. If you're able to wake up, get out of bed, take a shower, and go to the store, why can't you wake up, take a shower, and go get a fucking job? If you're able to go sign that check and go buy drugs, then you're able to get up and look for a job. That is *sick*, man, that is *very sick*. Some people, they pay taxes, and just don't care where their money goes. I could fucking use that money that they take out of my checks—I wish *I* could have that money.

I don't care about affirmative action, as long as it ain't my job. If it is then that fucker's in trouble; that's all *I* gotta say. And illegal immigrants should go back where the fuck they came from. They should just stay where they're at—they shouldn't be here.

About abortion—it's everybody's right to do everything. See, I don't really talk about shit like this, 'cause it's my *opinion*, and people don't like my opinions. If I'm not financially fit to support myself and pay my own bills, how am I gonna support no one else? So if I had to, I would.

Do I want to get married and have kids? *No.* Maybe a kid. I really don't see marriages lasting. Fifteen, twenty years—eventually you're gonna get sick of that person. And then she'll get everything that I own. I ain't stupid! [laughs] But it would be nice to have a little Phil running around. If it's a girl? I don't know. I'd keep trying then.

Am I a sexist? *Yup, yup, yup.* No, I don't think women are inferior, but we do all the work, man. What do you guys do? We're the ones that bust our ass and bring home the money—all you guys do is spend it! [devilish grin] Yeah, I believe that, of course I believe that—it's the *truth*. They should get up and go to work too. Dinner? She'd get over at the stove and start cooking. And she'd clean the house the next morning or something. Laundry? Well, that comes along with it too! [laughs] Hey, that's just what I believe!

Me, I take care of the house, bring home the money. [laughs] And if she's working, we both bring home the money—it's fair. To me, it's fair. It is—based on nuthin. I think it's fair—I mean, it ain't a man's job to wash dishes and cook dinner; women have the talent to cook. I guess they're just born with it—they're gifted that way. But changing my baby's diaper, I'd do it, of course I would.

If I have a son, I wouldn't worry about nuthin—'cause I'd buy him a weight set, build him up, teach him self-defense. When he gets old enough, he'll do what he wants to do. As long as he don't do what I did, there won't be *no* problems. If he does what he wants to do, and it ain't what I like, then his ass is gonna get kicked. I won't whip his ass, but there ain't nuthin like a good old-fashioned spanking. Turn him over my knee and tan his ass. If it needs to be done, it needs to be done.

I'll teach him his values and his morals, man. That's one thing that this world probably lost, family morals and values. That's what I believe. Did I have 'em when I was in a gang? Sometimes. I know what I did was wrong—I never said it was right. Everything I did was wrong: I knew I was doing wrong, I just didn't care. But you gotta grow up sometime, man. And I know what's gonna happen if I do it again: I'm gone, *pshew*, up the river, no floats. Why throw away everything I have? It's senseless.

If I had to flee the house, like it was burning up, I'd just make sure my family was out . . . I'd take pictures. Gloves. The gloves that we carried my grandmother's casket with—my dad's mother. She was a nice lady . . . [sighs] She died four—three years ago. My grandma was real religious. I'm religious, I believe in God—I always did. But I don't argue my religion with nobody: everybody has their beliefs. I don't believe that I have to go to church every Sunday in order to talk to God. Yeah, it's nice to go to church when a person wants to go to church; it's nice to pray when a person wants to pray. But it's their prerogative. I don't argue the point, I don't stress it on nobody. If they believe, they have their belief, and I have mine.

Jason Hudgins

Eugene, Oregon

W*e meet at a center for home-less youth. Jason is a hand-some young man with intense blue eyes and shoulder-length hair. He grew up in Oregon. His father is an engineer. His mother has worked as a graphic artist. He is nineteen.*

The earliest I can remember is probably five years old. My mother was a really bad alcoholic. Basically, how I grew up is I was not to speak until spoken to or asked a question upon. I couldn't have been more than one and a half when my father left, and he stayed gone a long time. When I was five or six he started coming around and asking for visits, to see me . . . I didn't like it. I remember having a lot of anger towards him, wondering *why, why did my mother and father split up?* "Why would you get divorced? Don't you love me?" Just not understanding—*really* angry . . . I've learned that behind anger there's a lot of pain, but I was angry at this real early age.

When I was eight my mother told my father that she couldn't control me. I remember getting angry—really, *really* angry, and going in my room every time my mother told me to do something. I'd slam the door, punch on the walls, take silverware and throw them on the floor. Every time she tried to spank me I would hit her in the stomach or in the face. I remember being so out of control, disobeying . . . Everything that she told me to do, I defied her. A lot of the time she slapped me around—there were times that she point-blank hit me in the face with her fist, and pushed us down—both me and my sister. So it was difficult, it was really difficult. She asked my father if maybe he would take custody of me and see if that would work—if it would help me out any.

My dad was drinking also—he's an alcoholic. He slapped me around, but not as much as my mother did. He never closed-fist punched me, but he did slap me around, and he did threaten me. When he got drunk I was scared for my life a lot of the times—he was really intimidating . . . He's not really a big guy, he's medium-sized, but *really* intense. He's a real strict man—he served four years in the navy, and I think he brought that with his life, on and on down the road.

My sister came to Washington to live with me and my father. My mother was involved with a member of the Hell's Angels, and he, uh . . . wanted to have sex with my sister a couple times. When she told my mother, my mother didn't believe it—basically told my sister that she was lying. I think my sister began to tell the police that he *did* rape her, but I don't remember if it happened or not.

Then what happened was my father got sober. He found a spiritual experience . . . He had been seeing what was going on in his life, he wound up in some kind of hospital, detoxing. He got on his knees and said, "God, I surrender." And it was removed: he never drank again. He got real spiritual, real religious. For me, it sucked—I didn't like it. He forced me to go to church every Sunday, and he made me wear these *ridiculous* pants. [laughs] I couldn't stand it. They were brown, and I can't *stand* the color brown! You ain't gonna catch me wearing brown, no . . . He forced me to Boy Scouts even, but I was OK with that—I liked going; those were times when I wasn't with my father. We went camping, and I was given a chance to hang out with people around my age. Then there came a point in time where my father got involved, like wanting to be a scoutmaster and a director. I got really resentful, 'cause this was freedom—I felt freedom from anger. He never threatened me when he was sober, but I was still scared.

I was about twelve years old, and I started leaving. I was constantly running away, running the streets. Every time I'd run away, I'd be found and brought back to my house. I remember this one incident . . . In our town, there's a park with a big lake, and I went over there and started crying, 'cause I couldn't get across. It was really cold, and I'd been walking for at least five hours. I just remember crying, and that my father called somebody to check the park. I felt hunted. He was promising kind of rough treatment: "This is my way, this is the way it's gonna be"—this is law, basically.

I got molested between the time I was twelve and thirteen years old. I was living at a group home, and I remember being sick, and this foster parent coming to see me. I felt something weird about this guy, but I went ahead 'cause I wanted to be somewhere other than my father's house. He had this camp that he took the kids out to. In the beginning it was alright. I felt a little safe, and we'd sit around the camp fire and sing songs, eat marshmallows, all that stuff. He had between five to ten of us—him and his wife also.

What happened is, we wound up going out to the camp with another guy. The way the camper was, there was the big bed, and then an overhead drop-down thing. I got up there, and he says, "Well, why don't you come down here? I'm a cuddly guy," or something. You know, at that age, I didn't think nothing of it. He started to ask me questions like, "Have you ever gotten high?" And I said, "Yeah, I've gotten high." And he pulled me into this room and got me stoned—and it was really good weed. I was just, "*Whoa*, this is cool! I like it." And then we got into bed, and he started touching me, and touching me on the forehead, and I knew exactly what was going on. I knew that I was either going to get basically screwed up the ass, or . . . he was gonna molest me some way. I knew it. And I started praying to God, I said, you know, "I can't stand it."

The other guy was asleep, or he just blew it off, just didn't say anything. And so this guy started touching me, and the next thing I know, he was sucking on my penis. I was crying. I kept stuffing that pain deep down in me. I was very, *very* scared, you know? I thought in my mind all the things that a normal person would think: the conflicting, wondering, "Am I gay or straight? . . . It's my fault . . . All them feelings. It happened a second time, and again, I went through all them feelings. He told me, he says, "If you *ever* say anything to anyone, I'll make your life a living fucking hell." That's exactly what he said.

My mother came to visit and I told her the story, and she said, "You're staying with *me* tonight, and I'm calling your caseworker. He thought I was lying; my father thought I was lying. The next night I went and told the story to the police officers. Other kids came forward.

He pleaded guilty and got twenty-five years. Today I'm still dealing with the insecurities around men. I don't trust men.

When I was thirteen, that's where the drugs and alcohol came into the picture, and I found out what they were about. That opened a world, and I began to see where I wanted to be. I was doing marijuana and alcohol. I started drinking Jack Daniels, and Everclear—pure, a hundred percent alcohol, basically. [laughs] It *really* blows you away. I wasn't doing it every day at first, but by the time I was fifteen I was a full-blown alcoholic. I'd drink whenever I could, the more the better, the drunker the better. Every time I had a chance to get high I would, and I couldn't stop. Drugs and alcohol gave me freedom, gave me acceptance, which my father never gave me.

When I was fifteen years old, I'd been running away for two or three years. I'd been in foster homes, group homes, halfway houses, this and that. Most of the time he took me back. I remember going to different agencies, and they said, "Well, we can't help you—you're underage, and we're gonna call the police." So the police put me in a halfway house, because I didn't want to go back to my father. And then they'd say, "We'll get a hold of your father."

I saw my mother maybe four or five times a year. She was living with the Hell's Angel, and I noticed there was something going on. I went back and told my father, "I think there's something wrong"—it was an internal feeling. I found out later that he basically beat her over the head with a tennis racket, beat her up really bad, raped her three or four times, broke her ribs, broke most of her fingers. He did a lot of really hard manual labor, rebuilding Harley Davidson's—that's what his profession was—so he was *strong*. After she got better, that's when I was living on the streets. She left him and got in a program in Nebraska for battered women, and after that she met another guy.

I went to Nebraska—still was drinking . . . My sister got fed up with my father's shit too, and she came. My mother was drinking really heavily also, and she used to buy liquor for us all the time. One night I was doing a lot of marijuana, and the marijuana was laced with PCP, but I didn't know that. My sister told me to get out of her room, and I told her, *"I'm* the one that bought this beer, OK? *I'm* the one that bought this half ounce of weed, OK? This is mine, I'm taking it with me." And she told me, *"No, you're not. "* And we began to get in a physical confrontation. My family, that's how we handled situations, we were violent towards each other, physically and mentally.

Her boyfriend stepped in, and basically took my hair and slammed my head into the concrete about seven, eight, nine times, and I pushed this guy through a wooden door. I put my hand up to his neck and told him that if he *ever* touched me again, I'd kill him straight out. I started to run up the stairs, and he pulled my feet up from underneath me, and my chin hit the floor, and I wound up doing some kicks and I was flying-kicking and hitting him in the face. I ran upstairs, and I said, "You guys better leave, because, I mean, you're *dead,* D-E-A-D."

My mother came screaming out. *"What's going on?"* I said, "Mom, I'm gonna kill 'em." I was getting angry at her, 'cause she was pushing me around. I said, "I'll kill you too." She ran right in front of the knife drawer, 'cause I went for it. My sister kept pushing me, saying, *"If you want to fight me, let's go!"* I said, "I *don't* wanna hit you, I *don't* wanna hit you!" I was somehow trying to think of a way out: there was some little bit of sanity there. But I *snapped.* I wound up kicking my sister down two flights of stairs, and jumping over this eight-foot drop thing. I landed on my feet, and *ran.*

My mother called the cops. They didn't find me. But stupid me . . . [laughs] I walked right back into my mother's house. One cop came through the back door, one cop came through the front, and I was arrested. When I got locked up and I came back, I told my mother that I wasn't really meaning that I'd kill her, but she told me, "Jason, you *did* mean that." I didn't remember—it was one of the first blackouts I ever had.

I ended up a state ward of Nebraska. I'd gotten involved with the court system—for running away—and I had a couple of assault charges. I have a juvenile file this thick. [He holds his hands far apart] I went to court, and they demanded a thirty-day evaluation in the state mental institution. I wound up in the adolescent ward for youth in Lincoln . . . I spent a year there. It was a maximum locked security. More or less it was like prison: the doors would slam—there's no way of getting beyond the doors.

Once I accepted that I was going to be there for a long time, I started studying the evil powers of the mind. I asked Satan to help me be able to lick this program, help me manipulate my mind into doing exactly what I needed to do to show these people that I was OK, so they would let me go. You gotta learn the game—to say the right things, tell them what they want to hear. I studied looking at myself, and my eyes, and fronting. I always before had superlong hair, and always put my hair in front of my face. They looked at that and said, *"This* is a troubled kid." I'd always be looking away, never looking someone straight in the eye. I began to teach myself how to do that. I started pulling my hair back in a ponytail.

I was really mean. All the kids looked up to me but me and two other people in there were a clique, and we were setting people up. Like I would hit somebody in the face, and the two of them would stick up for me and say it never happened—that *he* hit *me* in the face. And I would have someone hit me, make a bruise on my face, and say, "Look what happened." I began to physically abuse myself a lot, to teach myself pain techniques. I began to closed-fist hit myself in the face . . . I was *really* sick—I was in a lot of pain. I was looking for an escape, and I couldn't find one. But my problem always lied within me: *I* was always my problem. Drugs and alcohol just intensified it. I became a person that I didn't like.

It was a good thing they locked me in there. It protected me from me, and protected others from me . . . [sadly] They told me that I was unfit in society—at fifteen years old. But I got a high out of that some-times—just, to be a troubled kid, I liked that. It gave me a certain "I'm a fuck-up, leave me alone" type of crazy power trip. It was fun.

They had doctors there, psychologists. I went through a year of relaxation tapes; I learned how to control my anger. Sometimes I get that rage, but that's part of life. I know that when I get angry what I'm really saying is, *"It hurts."* You know what? The anger control and all the relaxation stuff helped me. Those were the two best things that I loved about the treatment center. There is no doubt in my mind that if I did not do that treatment center that I would be locked up, I'd prob-ably be in prison.

When I got out I did start getting high again. I changed from drink-ing alcohol to doing speed a lot—was finally injecting methampheta-mine—and all the other drugs. I did LSD for two and a half years. I went insane, I tripped out, didn't know who I was, didn't know what planet I was on. Walking up to everybody on a main street, asking them if they thought they could kick my ass . . . Getting very violent. Walking into a blood bank where you give blood and assaulting three people at once—they couldn't get me down. And then I got arrested.

I didn't think I was in jail, I thought I was in some kind of Marine-ist army base. I thought I had a job, and I was at work in jail. I hallucinated that the walls started to turn into robots and they could communicate with me. There are so many things I saw out there—I believed that I was in some kind of spirit world. Just really far gone. I'm really lucky and grateful that I'm alive today. I wound up in a detox center, freaking out again. I couldn't stop my hands from shaking. I began to understand that, yeah, I am an alcoholic and I *am* a drug addict. I knew that there were two choices I had: I was either going to die—kill myself—or I was going to get on my knees and surrender. This guy I met though this program I'm in told me that if I ever was in his town, to come visit. He was a heroin addict, and he taught me that no matter what is going on in my life, I don't have to drink and I don't have to use ever again. One day at a time. I lived with him for about thirty days and began on my way to recovery.

I wound up back down here, on the streets, sober and clean. Actually living on the streets and not using drugs and alcohol was a big thing in my life, because when I wanted to get sober I didn't think I could even last a week. At first it was very painful, and then the more I stayed sober, and the more I kept coming back to this program, I was able to experience life as life, and get on, not run away from it . . .

In two days, I will be celebrating nine months. [joyfully] I have been *free*, completely *free!* It's really amazing! I'm proud of myself. I have totally surrendered my life to God and this program that I'm in. I'm not a saint, and I don't go to church every Sunday; I don't talk to ministers all the time, but I do have a very spiritual way of life. And it is so *cool:* I'm living in a recovery house now, waiting, trying to get into Job Corp—I'd take the electrician's trade. I want to be a certified electrician, and maybe some day get my own business; work towards owning a house, owning a car. And that is *all* possible. But if I allow drugs to get into there, none of that will happen. If I keep on hanging out with people that still use drugs, I'm not gonna make it nowhere.

One idea I have—I want to get a really big house open for kids. Kids that don't want to stay on the streets and get involved with drugs and alcohol. I'd allow them to have freedom to do what they want to do—beyond some limits: no violence—*some* rules. But not like, "I'm a parent and you do what I say." I want to give them a safe place. I want to be able to reach out to kids and tell them, "Man, I've been through this stuff, I *know* where you're at. If you ever need someone to talk to, I've been there." It's really time-consuming, not something I'm gonna jump into right away. I want to give myself some experience in learning how to help myself *before I help someone else!* [laughs]

I don't like my past history, what happened to me, but I appreciate it—you know what I mean? What makes me *me* is a lot of things that I did go through. [laughs] It's kind of weird to say that, but it's the truth. I respect the fact that my parents brought me into this world. I'm really grateful for that. And they did the best they could.

My father and I now are reunited. When I talk to my father, I have no anger towards him whatsoever. We've been talking about God and life, and he gives me information. It helps me out so much, and at the end of the conversation I tell my father I love him—we have that relationship. He reaches out to me, he lets me know that he cares, and I can feel that. There's another miracle: I never thought that I could ever, ever have a relationship with my father.

I broke off from my mother totally. I told her that if she ever got sober and clean, she could call me. But until that time I don't want to see her, and I will not talk to her on the phone. I don't hang around *anybody* that abuses me. I'm worth something today, and I will not tolerate *anybody* disrespecting me. I'll continue to write her letters explaining to her how my life is going, and maybe in something that I write to her God'll speak through me and get to her.

Today . . . I am a good person. And I am only the way I am because of the bad things that happened to me. But it grew me up faster than I was supposed to. My mother always essentially told me that I was nothing, from when I was just a little kid. But today when I look in the mirror, I don't say, "What a disgusting piece of shit you are"—I look in the mirror and I think to myself: "Look at the person that you're coming to be."

Faith

Shaila Kapp

Manhattan, New York

A *large Riverside Drive apart-*
ment. Shaila is a lanky, lik-
able, bounding sort of girl. We settle into a corner of the living room.
Soon after, I hear rustling from the next room: it is her mother,
preparing for Passover. The rustling permeates the entire interview—
she never leaves that room. Shaila is an Orthodox Jew. She is fifteen.

I've lived here all my life, in this exact apartment. I have an older
sister who is twenty, and she's in college. I have a brother who is
almost seventeen, and he is graduating high school and going to Israel
next year, for the year—most Orthodox Jewish teenagers do that.
Then I have myself, and my little brother is twelve, maybe. My parents
are only children, that's why my family is so big. There's not rivalry
that much, actually, because my parents, they believe that each person
is an individual.

My sister is a genius—she's *really* smart, she's a literary person, a
very good writer. And my older brother, he's just all-around knowledge.
My little brother is one of the best writers I've ever seen. Me and
schoolwork, eh, don't go that way . . . [laughs] I pass. I love my hands
—that's my speciality. I crochet kippahs, the skullcaps that boys wear. I
got a sewing machine for my birthday this year—I'm making a dress. I
do hems, I do buttons; I do clay, I do painting, I do sketching. I just
love to use my hands. My mom thinks I should be a brain surgeon.

My parents are consultants—they raise money. They don't want to,
like, talk about their work together, because they don't want to get in

fights or anything. My dad usually works in public schools, raising money, scholarships; and my mom works for Hebrew organizations. I'm happy to be Jewish, I love being Jewish—I'm really proud of my religion. My parents brought me up the right way: they gave me morals, and they said, "This is Judaism. You choose if you really believe in it." And I said, "I do." It gives me a better perspective on life. I have a lot of morals, and the belief that there's somebody watching over us, taking care of us. A big security. It tells us a lot of what to expect, what's due —it gives you advice on life. It is . . . it just *is.*

There's the Talmud, which is the laws of the Torah, explained. There are some laws that just aren't explained. Like, you go, "Why am I doing this?" and your parents just say, *"Do it"*—and you go, *"Why?"* It's frustrating. [She points to a wall of bookshelves.] That's the Talmud over there—that's our small collection: up there is the English, and that whole top shelf, that's *all* the Talmud—just different publications. [She gets up and goes over to the shelves.] This is *Shemot,* which is the story of God taking us out of Egypt. And here it exactly tells the story of what happened. [She kisses the book, then sets it on a coffee table.] We treat it as if it's a baby. So, like, you can't put it down right next to you, 'cause you don't want to be sitting on where a baby is. You give it the most respect you can.

I had my Bat Mitzvah when I was twelve. It's the time when the child reaches maturity, and they're going into the world, and learning more. In Judaism you're not responsible for your actions until you reach a certain age—I think it's eighteen—and this sort of brings you closer. I felt there was a change: I felt older, I felt better. It was really fun when it was over, because it was frustrating while it was going on—you're sitting there, and you're having a party for yourself, and it's not a pleasure.

I've been to Israel—it was my Bat Mitzvah present from my parents. I saw the *Kotel*—which is the Western Wall, or the Wailing Wall —and that was very moving for me. It's called the Wailing Wall because some people cry there, 'cause it's not their Temple anymore. That's a holiest spot of everywhere in the world—that's where the Temple was, and God was in the Temple. He had his place in what's called the *Kodesh Hakodeshin,* which is a little, little room—it's the "Holiest of Holiest," translated. And that's where God's *Shechinah* was, his soul, his presence. We now believe that God's *Shechinah* is everywhere, but that's where it was, and we're so sad that it's not there anymore. But we still believe, OK, God's there, that's where God is. So, everybody writes a little note, and sticks it in the wall. Like, "Please let there be peace in the world"; or, if somebody's sick, "Please heal my sickness"; or even the small things, like, "Oh, please give me a boyfriend."

When I got to the Wall I was like, "Oh, *this* is it?" And then I was like, "I'm so let down." I expected this, like, big thing, and all it was was bricks. But I went up anyway, and I touched the Wall, and I put in my note. It was time for the afternoon prayer, so I wanted to do it there. Once I started praying, I started crying, and I'm like, "This is it —this is the place."

I'm in a very protected community—Manhattan. There's very little anti-Semitism, unless you go to certain areas. My whole life, I've been surrounded by people who aren't . . . I've been very protected from that by my parents. I've heard people say stuff about blacks, and I say, "Stop—I don't want to hear it." It's just not right. It's immoral. "Oh, it was just a joke, just a joke." But it's not funny, and it's just not right. You don't do that—you don't want to hurt somebody.

I go to an Orthodox school. It's coed, except for gym classes, because of modesty. Personally, for me, I'm very religious, so I don't like to be seen in, like, unmodest positions—doing sports and stuff like that. It's like a public school because public schools have all different kinds of ethnic backgrounds in it, and we sort of have the same thing. There are two different parts of the Jews: Sephardim and Ashkenazim. After our exodus, one stayed near Israel—the Sephardim, and the other one got pushed all the way to Europe, the Ashkenazim. As time went by they got different practices and different customs, and also, Sephardim are much darker-skinned. Even though the school's quote-unquote Orthodox, they do have some Conservative.

The only difference I really know is that in Orthodox there's a minya, which is ten men put together to daven, to pray to God. And Orthodox believe the men are to sit on one side; the women on the other side. There's something called a mechitza, a barrier, that separates the two, so that when you pray to God, you're with God, you're not trying to, like, impress somebody else. Conservative people believe in egalitarian meetings, which is men and women together. There are laws for women, there are laws for men. The women are actually considered closer to God. Now that life has progressed, and women want equality, some women want to be rabbis. But in Jewish religion you can't, because it's the man's job, just like only women can light candles for Shabbos, to bring in the Shabbos. So the rabbi is always a man, but in Conservative, it could be a woman—they sort of bend the law. And then there are Reformed, which is not as religious. Some people think it's a starting point for Jews, other people think it's like a cop-out. Personally, [whispers] *I think it's a cop-out.* I mean, some people, they're trying: they start off Reform, they go "I want to learn about it," and they go higher and higher on the ladder. Some people don't really feel it in their heart, and some people really do. And I do. Reform people who do—those I respect.

At school there are the kids who are very religious, like me . . . there aren't so many of them nowadays. But I'm not supposed to say that, because the school won't admit to that. They represent themselves as such a religious school, and sometimes they're just not. So that's why I think it's like a public school—'cause there are people that have different appearances. Like just in clothing itself, you'll see someone dressed in a long skirt to the ankles, 'cause it's very modest, and you'll see other girls with higher skirts. The specific dress code is the skirt has to be to the knee, but I've seen a lot of skirts up to the thigh. If it goes high enough the teachers will say, "Come to the office, you're changing," and then they give you a hideous skirt. It's blue, and it has stripes. [laughs] I'd rather stay home than ever have to wear *that.*

I never really care about my appearance. When I was little, I didn't belong, I was ridiculed by my friends, 'cause I was a tomboy. They always have one of those, and I was it. I loved cars, I loved blocks, and I loved my short little haircut, which I didn't have to do anything with. In kindergarten these girls started saying, *"Ha ha,* you're a *boy!"* and I said, "No, I'm not." When I was five I got my ears pierced, and I grew out my hair. But I was still a tomboy at heart, so I didn't brush my hair: it was knotty, it was disgusting, but it was my long hair—to be a girl.

I wear these jeans every Sunday. To school I wear a long skirt. For me long skirt is ankle, short skirt is knees. I don't believe in mini, I don't want to wear them. My faith, it doesn't allow me to—but, I mean, I don't want to show *that*, it's mine. There's something called *beged ish*, which is clothing of a man. Some women believe that girls and women should not wear pants, because that's man's clothing; and then there are people who say, "But there are pants made for women." And that's what I believe: there are pants made for women, and that's OK. But I can't wear pants to school.

I have friends now who are not as religious as I am, and it's a difficulty sometimes, 'cause of my being kosher and stuff. Kosher in a nutshell is no milk and meat together. My best friend *doesn't* eat kosher cheese. Now that might sound stupid—I mean, it's cheese, what are you gonna do about it?—but knives touch it, forks touch it, and that makes me unable to use their forks and knives. So when I come over I have to eat on paper plates, and with plastic forks and knives. The family really respects it—they bought them for me.

Like I said, my school isn't the most Orthodox place in the world, so a lot of things go on. It just depends who you hang out with. I hang out with the religious kids, but there are other kids who do pot, and every year somebody gets caught and thrown out. We get sex ed in school—but first of all, you're not allowed to have sex unless you're married—it's frowned upon *big time*. I don't think I'm ever gonna have a kiss with a boy before I'm married. There's always a time when I'm, [longingly] oh . . . There's always—but I always say, "Stop."

I think birth control is prohibited. Abortion? A woman has a right to choose, but in Judaism, we sort of choose for them. I think it should be available, like if someone perhaps is raped. I would never want to carry that person's baby, ever. And there's also the abortion for a person who can't have a baby because the birth might kill them —I think that they should totally be able to get rid of it.

I have a plan; I know my future, pretty much. I want to be a doctor —I like helping people. When I was younger, I wanted to be an artist, but then I kind of grew out of that. I want to be a pediatrician, or an OB/GYN, maybe—or a specialist doctor, like a stomach doctor, something like that. I'm gonna go to high school, and then I'm going to go to Israel for a year, and then I'm gonna go to as many years as I need to of college, and then med school, and then I want to get a profession. And after—which is the strange thing—I want to find a husband in the United States, and then I want to move to Israel and have my profession there. I want to be going out, and maybe even be engaged, but I just want to finish school. I know a lot of people who got married in the middle: they found a husband, and then they wanted a kid—and then they just didn't exactly ever go back. I don't want that to happen.

I would like to live in Jerusalem, but there's a little problem. My family has this custom that you wear skirts in Jerusalem, 'cause the Wailing Wall is there, and it's very holy. I don't think I could live in skirts; I *need* my pants. And I also want to live somewhere that resembles Manhattan, 'cause I love living in the city. I'm very free: I want to go somewhere, I just get on a bus and I go—I'm not dependent on a car.

My parents are totally for whatever I want to do. I always wanted to live in Israel—it's where I'm supposed to be. It just is. My parents wanted to move there when they got married. My grandfather died two months after they got married, and both of my grandmothers said, "Oh, we're so old, just wait until we die." And of course, my mom on my mother's side is seventy-eight and healthy! My parents are like, "Just move to Israel with us," but she's deaf, and she figures there are a lot of people here who help her—it'll be too hard for her to leave. My other grandmother, she kind of thinks she's sicker than she really is. I don't know exactly why, 'cause I only hear bits and pieces of the story. Apparently what happened was in the Holocaust her family had the decision of sending one child away: she got to go, and her sister stayed, and died. And so she's always felt bad about that.

None of my grandparents were in the camps. As soon as they heard about the Holocaust starting, my mom's mother went to England and my grandfather said, "I'll meet you there." He ended up not being able to; and only hearing two postcards for eight years, my grandmother stayed loyal. She said, "He's gonna survive." He was always one step ahead of the Germans, and survived by just running. Along with being Jewish, he was deaf—and that put two strikes against him. One time he was caught, and he had all his papers, and they said, "So you're Jewish, huh?" And he said, "No, I'm not Jewish." And they said, "So you're deaf?" He said, "Yes." They said, "OK, we'll be right back." Went right behind his back and shot a gun. If he was not deaf, he would've flinched—they would've killed him on the spot.

I am so against the peace efforts. I think that the peace process is one of the worst things that Jews have ever agreed to. I understand that they want peace, but they have the ability to defend themselves— We saw that in the Six Days War, where they defeated *all* the Arab nations in six days. But what happens now that they want peace? They're taking so much of what little of Israel there is that there's nothing gonna be left! The Arabs think of it as their holy land, but *we* are God's chosen people, and they're not chosen, and we deserve it more, I think, sort of, in a way . . . What is the best solution? I think it would have to be the Messiah. So we just have to wait, and believe.

Christal-Lynn Devaux

Leona Valley, California

A tiny desert town about an hour northeast of Los Angeles. We first meet in the post office, which consists of the back half of a counter in the local market. Our conversation takes place later, on the patio of a friend's hillside home, from which we view a narrow valley and the gentle mounds of the San Angelos range. Christal-Lynn is tall and fine boned, with long blond hair and high cheekbones. She speaks in country time—without haste. She is sixteen.

My dad's of French-Norwegian background, my mom is Polish; my dad grew up here, and my mom in Chicago. I'm the only child at home. I'm from my mom's second marriage. My sister's almost thirty-three; we saw her last week in Florida—she's in the air force. I'm thinking of following her footsteps. She works on hydraulics, she flies into storms, the big storms. She rides *with*—she's not a pilot. They ride into the storms to see what they're doing. They travel all over, they're like weather trackers.

I want to travel—you get to meet new people, and see things. The weather fascinates me. Everybody says I'd be a good weatherman! [laughs] We used to live in Washington, and moved here when I was six. My dad worked on tractors, and when logging quit, the business just stopped, there was no work for him—so we came down here. [flatly] And here we are, in the desert.

When we were up in Washington, the skies were so dark blue it was unbelievable, and here they look like mud. The water is brown and gray, and the rivers are drying. Stuff will grow, but not what you want. [laughs] Weeds. [with passion] You want *flowers*, you don't want weeds. When it rains it smells good, it cleans the air. It doesn't rain a lot in the desert. The first couple days it was in the hundreds. We went from seventy, eighty, to a hundred and twelve. It was terrible, we all got sick.

Our horse, Sally, she transferred better than we did, 'cause she was in an air-conditioned horse trailer. We had her for almost fourteen years—she was part of the family. She was given to us from friends; they didn't want her because she crushed a guy's ribs. They said it's because he drank, and she didn't like drinkers. My dad drank back then, and she didn't like my dad, so it was a horse for me and my mom, and we were definitely attached. When she died, I found her. My dad said, "Go out and feed Sally." "Ah, dad, I was already out there, and I can't." He said, "Well, why?" I said, "Well, I think she's taking a nap, and it's for good this time." Cause she always lay down. I'd go out there and shake her. [laughs] Her eyes'd pop open. Her eyes didn't open this time. She was here for thirty-five years, and it was her time.

My mom works at the post office. It's a candy–dish type post office. [laughs] Little kids come in, "Can I have a piece of candy." "Take three!" I think she likes seeing everybody, she talks to everybody. We gave a lady a couple chickens—we didn't ask any money for them—and she was so thankful. She brought my mom flowers and chocolates. I said, "Who are these from, Mom?" She said, "Some chickens!" [laughs]

We don't sit and eat at the table, we flock around the TV. [laughs] "What's on tonight?" We don't normally talk about our problems. My dad talks about work, my mom talks about work; and sometimes she'll get mad because he talks about work too much, and vice versa. It's like, "Wait! I have a problem. I don't know how to do number seventeen in math." It's like their ears are plugged to me sometimes. I feel left out. I wish they'd squeeze a wedge of time for me.

We live on five acres. I have a walk-in cage for my rabbits. We have a big chicken house, and same for our ducks; we have three or four dozen chickens—same with the ducks. I got a baby duck yesterday— I saved it. He was crossing a street down here, and a fella picked him up, and didn't know what to do. He put him in a little blanket, and was calling everybody in the valley. I was the only one who had a pond and a brooder house for him, so we adopted him. We have dogs: seven shepherds, mixed; a Lhasa; and a Lhasa Terrier—little Benjie dogs.

We love animals. I'm in 4-H—it's an agricultural program for kids seven up until high school. I raise chickens. Chickens, sewing—I sew, and I can . . . and all sorts of stuff. I learned a lot with my mom and my grandma—when I was little I used to help them can. My 4-H leaders are trying to get me to be a junior leader, because I'm so good at what I do. I don't think I would have the patience. I like helping, but I can't sit down for a long time and say, "This is how you're gonna do it," because I'll get discouraged if they do it wrong.

When I was in school they had a home economics class, and my teacher had me make a jumper. It was my choice to make a jumper—everybody else was doing little pillows and stuff like that. I wasn't finished by the deadline, and she sent me home to finish it, put a hem on it. She said, "Do it whatever way you want." I did a shirttail hem, serged on the bottom and folded under—and she gave me a D, because she didn't like it. [indignant] If she didn't like it, that didn't mean *I* didn't like it! I entered it in the fair, I got *two* blue ribbons. There's no way people can discourage me.

I'm a Christian, and I go to the First Baptist Church twice a week. My mom used to go to church a lot, but not as much now. I help at a church group for little kids, preschool to eighth grade. They learn their sections from the Bible. My own church group is really supportive. We talk about different things, we ask questions, we ask advice—it's like another family. We break into smaller groups, and there's only four people in our group. It makes it really easy: we know everybody, and we trust everybody. There are people who go there who smoke—cigarettes, and other things [laughs]—and we say, "You don't need this, you can look in other directions." People say, "There are none"—and I just don't understand why. I have a lot of faith in who I am and what I stand for.

The church is mostly white. We get a couple other races once in a while, but they won't stick all the time. I think maybe it's uncomfortable for them . . . I mean, it probably would bother me if I went to an all-black church. People put blacks down, or anybody—the opposite. We all put each other down, I guess.

I go to a public high school in the Antelope Valley. Every walk of life goes there. We have Mexican, white, black, some Asian, and we have a few foreign exchange students. People nitpick about different religions, and what you are and how you dress. Most of my friends are white. I have a few colored friends, and I know a couple Mexican people. It doesn't bother me, you know—we're all human. We were talking in English, and this one girl said, "The French people act rude." My English teacher was trying to explain, that's the way they talk—bold, fast. We're a slow-speaking country, I guess; they're from a different country, they're different from us. It's not how you speak, it's how you act towards others. I don't think anybody should be put down for who they are. The reason people say things and don't care about others is because they aren't being cared about themselves; they hurt, and they're getting their anger out.

I glided into being a teenager. Somewhere around thirteen, fourteen, I figured, "Oh wow! I'm a teenager—I need cool clothes"—but that definitely blew over. It was like, "This is stupid—this isn't me." I wear what I'm comfortable in. People say, "Why are you wearing *that?*" I wear guy's shoes—they're the only kind that fit! [laughs] I have *huge* boat feet, and they don't make tennis shoes in girls sizes that fit. "Why do you wear guy's shoes?" "*They fit.*" "But they don't look good." "*So?*" Gosh—I don't understand why people wear some of the things *they* wear, but I don't say anything. You never know—they might end up beating you up or something . . . [laughs nervously]

We have seven security guards at school, and there are almost four thousand kids. There are two deans, four or five counselors, and a couple sheriffs who are at the school all day. Nothing extreme happens, but there are days that, *whoa,* somebody did something . . . I come back after my vacation and I ask, "Where's so-and-so?" And they say, "She's suspended." I'm like, "For what this time?" I'm like, "This is great, she does pot, you do speed, somebody else does acid—I don't need to put up with you people." The security guards watch certain people that they suspect, but we're not searched or anything.

School's a struggle, but it's OK. I could be doing better. I show up every day, whether I want to or not. People cut. I say, "You won't learn anything—you'll be back here next year." "*I don't care,*" they say. I say, "You don't think your parents care. I feel sometimes my parents don't care, but they do. We just can't see it."

I tell my parents about interesting and strange things that happen at school. One day this friend said, "OK, I'm going to do eight lines of speed in my next class"—which was the beginning of the day. I'm sitting there: "You're telling me this, and you *know* I'm against it." [angrily] It's upsetting, very upsetting. She didn't care. She was saying, "I'm doing this, and you don't have the guts to." She did this stuff in her class. The teacher didn't see. I'm like, "Is this teacher *blind?*"

She was so high she couldn't *walk.* She was being helped to all her classes by other kids, and nobody said a word. The security guards and police officers didn't notice. I felt I had to tell an adult, but I don't know what stopped me . . . Nobody told on her. I think they felt they were too good a friend to betray her. I told her if she does drugs not to tell me, and she said she was gonna lay off it for a while. A friend at school gave me advice: "Always wear a smile: It makes people wonder what you're thinking." And with the people doing their drugs, it's *really* hard to keep up to that phrase. [quietly] Because it hurts inside that they're turning somewhere else . . .[She looks off in the distance intently.] Guinea hens. That noise.

I've been through a few relationships at school, and it was like a trap sometimes. You hang out all the time. You can't talk to your friends, because he's somewhere with his, and you're always like [She twines her fingers to demonstrate.] the thumb and nail. I have a few great guy friends who listen and are there, and understand, but you know it would be different after you went out, and after you broke up. They wouldn't be as good friends, I guess. Boys are always thinking about sex. I don't care who the guy is, that's what's on his mind, twenty-four-seven. *That's it*: twenty-four hours, seven days a week! [laughs] It was probably a problem for my boyfriends, but I thought about how I felt more than about them. There's always time—there's plenty of it. I'm only sixteen, I have a whole life to live yet.

My family and people around here lost a really good friend to AIDS. He was in his thirties. When he died, it made me feel, "Why does he have to go?" You never think it's gonna be somebody you know until it happens. I worry about violence, and the way the world may change. When they had the L.A. riots I wondered why the cops beat that guy, and why the blacks beat Reginald Denny. I just wonder why. Earthquakes I'm getting used to . . . [laughs] I find out I'm sleeping through half of them, which is fine. I don't know . . . Nature is nature, but the other stuff—why?

When we go to Palmdale we lock our doors. I see strange people, and my mom, she's got this thing about locking the doors—even up here. We've had so many break-ins it's *unbelievable*. It's kind of strange, because most of the people that live up here are retired cops and firemen . . . But I guess it's easy to explain: they have money, and people know. I was in San Francisco, and I saw a man standing on the road, holding a cardboard sign: "Older guy, will work for food." It made me really sad. I don't understand: Where's his family? Where are people to take care of this old guy? In one of the richest cities in the world, you know, and this guy's walking around . . . You don't see much of that out here, in this little rural area. I just think: help the people who are down, and you'll always be helped when you're down.

I worry about the environment, and how the vegetation may *die*—there may not be enough. I was watching the movie, *The Seventh Sign*, and a few of the things happened, and there's a few more things that are going to. The first sign is the water in the sea boils, and all the fish float up, are washed up on the beach dead. This little kid bends down to touch the water, and it burns him, 'cause it's hot. There's seven signs, and when you get to the seventh the world will come to an end, and we all die, I guess . . . It's something you really have to pay attention to, and wonder what's happening. Like pollution. We didn't have this brown sky a long time ago. There's big environmental changes—earthquakes, and fires, floods.

Do I worry about the world ending? Yes and no, but it won't be in my lifetime—*I hope!* [laughs] When we die I believe we walk on a big fluffy cloud. I always thought we'd get to ride on a flying horse, we'd get to ride Pegasus. Like when Sally went, I believe all the horses get pretty white wings, and we all get to ride on one. When I was little I was always saying, "I want to see the Pegasus." My mom's like, "No—not now." [laughs]

Nicholas Kristinsson

Chicago, Illinois

W*e talk in Nick's room, which his mother has made him clean extensively. He is close to six feet, with an air of being newly tall, not yet used to the world from that height. He has very curly hair, hazel eyes, and a pierced nose. He is fourteen.*

I live with my mom and my dad. My dad's a carpenter, and an artist on his own time; my mom's a teacher. I have an older half-brother— he's ten years older, and moved away—and a little sister, who's ten. Do she and her friends act goofy around me? They act goofy all the time, not that I pay attention. There are other things I concentrate more on, like my spirituality, my art, my . . . I guess you'd call it poetry, even though I like to call it song-writing. I like drawing. [He points to several figures drawn directly on his wall—superheroes in dynamic poses.] I did those a while ago . . . The level I'm at now is this kind of stuff. [He pulls out a more detailed drawing of a woman—with much cleavage.]

I'm a freshman at a big public school, and there's so many segregated groups. One of the main things I like about Hackeysack is that when we're playing a game there doesn't seem to be any discrimination between people or music types. You don't have to hate a person because he listens to music you hate. When we're playing Hack, we're all joking around; for that little while everybody's kind of like one. But I also enjoy hanging out with people who like the same kind of music and have similar views, so I can be myself without having to worry about what I say. There's always this worry—for me at least—

that, well, they don't have the same views as me, so if I say what I think or what I feel, they're gonna be like, "What the hell is your problem?"

Ignorance that's just kind of the way that society thinks is really a shame. The whole homophobia, bisexual-phobia thing really bothers me—judging someone when you don't know them. The leader of this band I like is bisexual, and there's nothing wrong with that. I have a greater respect for him. I could be bisexual. I'm not sure I could do it, but I don't see anything wrong with it—I wouldn't be afraid of doing it. But then everybody looks at it like, "*Oh my God.*" Anything different is just so scary for some people. When I hear someone say something about a gay person, and it really makes me angry, I'll tell them, "What the hell? Do you *know* a gay person?"

I'm interested in Wicca witchery. I've always really been interested in fantasy and magic and sorcery stuff. It's partly from my heritage, because I'm Norwegian, Scottish, Irish, and British—so there's this Celtic, Viking thing. Wicca are modern witches, which are completely different from what stories have told you about witches. They're similar to the Indians about how to be one with the earth, and to be careful about all living things. Even though it's not magic, it's something out of the ordinary, something that's not quite so Christianity—God-is-right. The Catholic Church I really disagree with on a lot of points. I think perhaps what the Bible says is true—but not the current Bible, maybe the original Bible. See, it had so many chances to be translated, and it had so many chances to be changed during translation, that you can't be sure.

My grandfather was a Methodist preacher. I understand the need for belief. But you can't decide for yourself what God would say to you, what God would forgive or get mad at you for—you have to have a priest tell you. The whole, "you have to go talk to a priest so he can talk to God" thing really bothers me. Why can't you do this yourself? The churches are made rich—you're donating to God. But what's God need this money for? You see these priests coming out with the gold staffs and ornate things—I don't think a person needs all that to tell you what God wants done. He doesn't need clothes *period*. He could be the most hippy, naked person you ever saw, and still give you God's supposed truth.

I try and look at everything from more than one side. That's why even though I disagree with a lot of what Christianity says, I don't think it should be abolished—because there are people who research Christianity and find that it *is* the support system for them. But you should think, you should look around, and not just choose it 'cause it's what everyone else is doing, or it's what you were raised into.

The only person who believes the things I do is my friend Eddie. We've been friends since third grade. We go to the same school, and believe in the same things, even though we like some different things. You can't have friendship where you're so alike—there's gotta be friction here and there, otherwise it's kind of unbearable. Eventually maybe I can live that kind of life, but maybe not in *this* life. I believe the point of reincarnation is maybe to find spiritual perfection. I mean, if God just gave people one chance—*come on* . . . The whole point of reincarnation is learning new lessons.

From what I understand, my dad's really lived a hard life, and I don't think he has a lot of faith in anything. My mom believes in reincarnation. I can talk to her about that kind of thing, even though I can't talk to her about all of it. You can never talk to your parents about everything, just because they're your parents. If I could talk to my mom about all of it, I would have no reason to have friends, I could just hang out with her all the time. I'm actually glad my parents are mine.

I got my nose pierced six weeks ago today. I was with this girl who wanted to get her ear pierced up here, [high on lobe] and I figured as long as we were there . . . [laughs] My parents hadn't the slightest idea until I got home. I had mentioned it once several months before, and my dad said, *"Not in this house, you don't!"* This is my dad who was an older hippy during the hippy period, and lived on a mountain. I came home, and my mom was, "How was your day? Did you have fun?" and then she realized . . . [He mimics a double-take.] And it was, [inhales and says with wonder] "You got your nose pierced!" She kind of had this grin . . . I was like, *"Oh my God*—she's not gonna kill me."

The nose-piercing thing was partly testing my limits. But they were both really cool about it. For a long time my sister would answer the phone, "Oh hi—Nick got his nose pierced." [laughs] She told everybody at school. My half-brother was like, "Did it hurt?" I said, "*Hell yeah*, it hurt—a *lot.*" He was like, "Well, was that girl impressed?" Which wasn't the case at all—I really wanted to do it. Maybe it was, in some little way, a way to impress her, but that wasn't the whole thing . . .

When I got my nose pierced that *might* be considered a date, because we went to a coffee shop, and then to a movie, and then to this mall. My parents were like . . . [He cups his face in his hands, eyes wide.] I don't tell them *anything* they don't need to know—I don't like volunteering information. If they ask, then I'll tell them. When I was younger I used to tell my mom, "I like this girl," but I don't do that anymore. My mom would be like, "Oh, she's cute—I like her." Now, there are genuine emotions involved if I like somebody. I'm at the age that I have to tell *myself* about this, not my mom; I have to tell *my friends* about this, not my mom. When I'm eighty years old, I'm not gonna be like, "Oh damn, I wish mom was here. I think this one girl is really cute." [laughs] It's just part of breaking loose from your parents.

They haven't had a safe sex talk or anything; I think they let the school take care of that. I've never considered otherwise. Well actually, I never really considered it. Now, when sex is a thing to be considered, I'm always worried. Will I have a condom with me? It's not only that I might catch a disease, but she might catch a disease that I didn't know I had, or I might make her pregnant. If I get someone pregnant I'm not gonna abandon them—I will be there. But that means giving up a lot of things that I'm not ready to give up yet; and that means making her give up things that she really wants. So I'll try my best to take all these factors into consideration when the time comes.

In gym class there's that macho, testosterone, guy thing, and that's just so rednecky. I don't think you have to be so macho to be a guy, or so feminine to be a woman. In school you can pick either PE or ROTC. I didn't want to swim in public, because I do have a stomach, a belly. [He pats his stomach.] I get really self-conscious because I got teased a lot in elementary school. No one seems to notice in high school, but that's 'cause there's not sixty kids in our grade—there's, like, thousands. That's the reason I picked ROTC. My ideals have changed somewhat, but actually I was considering joining the marines up until pretty late this year.

My ROTC class leader would be yelling, [drill sergeant voice] *"Take care of this uniform, because it represents your school, your country, and God himself."* That was just so medieval sounding to me. If you look at it, all military does this, and the military does kind of really control this country. Maybe *controls* is not such a good word, but *influences.* Yeah, we're trying to work for world peace—but we're spending umpteen million dollars a year building new, bigger, better weapons. And so other countries are, "Well, we're doing it because they're doing it."

I have to admit, ROTC does bring a kind of discipline, and it does try to install an honesty trait, which I needed. One of the reasons I'm somewhat grounded is 'cause I'm probably failing algebra. Half the time I'm not even there. Ask any teenager: they've cut classes once or twice, and I just happen to do it a lot. In general, I've always never been a straight-A student. I mean, that'd be good—you can get scholarships to college—but, uh, I'm not an A, B student. I don't want to brag, but I know I'm smart. But part of my spirituality is: knowledge only gets you so far—it doesn't do a damn thing for you in the spiritual life.

My parents give me this speech every time I get somewhat of a low grade: "I know you're smarter than this," and "If you need help, we'll get you help." They don't realize: you can give me all the help you want, that's not gonna make me do the work. What will? Me *wanting* to—me realizing that I *need* to and want to. Disappointment works. Not so much with my mom, 'cause she can get disappointed and go ballistic over the littlest things; but my dad, when he gets disappointed he doesn't say anything to me, he just gives me this "well, uh, that's too bad" kind of walk-away thing. "I'm gonna go work out in the garage," in this quiet voice . . . And that really bothers me. I have this sadness, 'cause a lot of the reasons he does that are cause I'm doing the same things that he did, and that my brother did. And because he might feel that it's somewhat his fault.

They tell you all through grade school, "When you get to high school, you're gonna be confronted with drugs and all these things, and there are gonna be real big punks, and they're gonna use peer pressure: *'Do it, man, do it man! Everybody's doing it, it's just so cool, man.'"* There *is* some amount of peer pressure, but no one pushes it on you. Personally, I don't want to do drugs, because I know what that does to you physically from what I've *seen*. There *is* a certain amount of truth in what they tell you about drugs. Even though it doesn't happen in, like, three seconds, like everybody says—it happens in, like, twenty years. But, still, I just know what I don't want to do, and I don't want to do drugs.

It's everywhere at school—drugs are just full frontal in your face every day. I don't know how, but the school seems so oblivious to it: they pass out pins that say, A DRUG-FREE SUCCESS. Oh, *puh-lease*. You walk into the bathroom and you can smell the marijuana—it smells like burnt Eggos. There's kids, I know they come to school high—you can see it in their eyes—but they handle it really well. They still seem to be somewhat, you know, aware . . . . Another reason I don't want to do drugs is I don't know if I could have that much control over myself—I don't know if I'd be able to walk. I mean, I'm just that kind of person.

I have one friend who's *really* weird—he has to go to counseling before school. It's like he wants to be suicidal. I'm not gonna say, "Oh man, you shouldn't do drugs, you shouldn't do any of that," 'cause he *wants* to be self-destructive. Self-destruction is somewhat of an attractive thing, because there is kind of a "I'm depressed, feel sorry for me" thing. And being self-destructive means you can be really, really great fun at parties, 'cause you'll really get into it. And that attracts some people to self-destructive people—that they can have fun with them, and it's someone to feel sorry for.

My friends have all mentioned thinking about suicide. We've all thought: "What if I kill myself right now?" It's the idea that I can. I've looked and said, "I could jump right now. I could shoot myself. I could slit my wrists." And I have brought myself to the point—just to see if I could do it—where I'm holding a razor [holds wrist out under his other hand] like that. Or I'm taking my neck and twisting it as far as I can, just to see if I really would go through with it. And then I stop because I don't want to. I know I could though. The spirituality I'm heading for is, you take that giving-up with you. If you want to make yourself spiritually whole, you need to try your damn best to stick it out; you can't just give up if something goes wrong.

I have this problem of being melodramatic, and trying to make my whole life really dramatic. What I try and do now is say to myself, "It's not like that, Nick—even if it *is*, then let it be like that, but don't try and make it like that." Being depressed is depressing.[laughs]

With every generation teens are learning more at a younger age, and they're losing their innocence—I mean kids, *all* young people. Everything in this world seems to be faster, quicker: *do it the fast way, we've gotta get this done quickly.* People are losing patience. If a person from twenty years in the future had to live here, he'd go insane; if I had to live twenty years in the past, I'd go insane. There wasn't even video game systems twenty years ago, or computers, CD players. There are so many advantages.

I can see, "Well, I had to do things this and that way—*now* teens have it so easy." But they have it harder in other ways. The fact that six-year-olds have to get used to their best friend getting shot is a shame, and it's not completely the teenagers' fault, it's not completely the gangbangers' fault: it's because each generation has this need to learn more, faster. Greed has a lot to do with it also. You have to admit, if the government wanted to, they could completely eliminate drugs from this country. They have the power to do that. But they don't do that, because you know how much money would be lost? The government isn't so innocent as it seems to be. I don't trust any government, no matter how great it is. I might vote, if there's someone I like. If I get to a point where I don't see someone representing what I think should be represented, I might even run for an office myself. You don't have to have this huge, great education; you just have to live in this world, and see what's wrong.

Some day I want to get married and have children. I think I'd like my wife to have a job—the housewife role just doesn't seem very fitting to women any more. [laughs] Since I've grown up that way, I'm used to it. After I get married, I don't want to have kids right away. I want to go to Europe, and I want to explore my roots a bit more before I have kids, so I have something to pass on to them, something to tell them.

Teenagers do have this tendency to not listen to adults: "Hey, I'm a teenager, this is how I feel . . . " They *do* have a tendency to be completely to one side of the matter—and I do that too, I know I do. But that's part of growing up. You're always gonna have that, and you're always gonna have to learn to be your own self, unless you're the biggest blind follower ever.

But you start to realize that your parents are people also, even though they're never *not* gonna be your parents. And it's better not to deny that they are people, that they do have a life, that their whole life doesn't revolve around being the most perfect—or being the worst—parents they could possibly be for you . . . that no matter how much you guys love each other and stuff, their whole life isn't for *you*. And it is hard to realize that, it is hard to see your parents as people. But as you get older, you do.

You can get in a situation where you are forty-five years old and still angry at your parents. That is their fault to some extent, but it's also your fault. That doesn't necessarily mean you ever resolve it. To resolve it you have to let go of some things, you have to forgive—not necessarily forget. But there is a time when you just have to resolve, and it is better to do it when you're younger: the faster you do it, the more time you have to, like, see them as *people*. And you do have to demand of your parents, or whoever you're trying to resolve something with, that they do the same: let go, forgive, try to understand, listen. Because that's what you're trying to do.

Jolene Watson

Chicago, Illinois

W*e meet at the offices of* New Expression, *where Jolene works part time. She is African-American, pretty, and willow thin. On this afternoon she wears an old-fashioned print dress. She laughs a dove-like, cooing laugh—a hint of a laugh, rather than the real thing. She is seventeen.*

I live with my parents. I have one brother, he's twenty-four now—he's married. We moved into a house, a regular-size bungalow on the South Side, when I was nine, and we've been there ever since. Basically, the part I'm at, it's not very bad. I wouldn't say it's all peaceful, though—there are still drugs and violence, like most neighborhoods. But I'm not usually around on my street that much to see that.

My family, we have a very busy schedule. We're Jehovah's Witnesses, so we're always going to our meetings or in the ministry. My father, he works on the computer, and orders things for a car company in Indiana. He's been there over twenty years. My mother, she may do cleaning services from time to time, but mostly she's involved in her ministry. You know how you see the Witnesses going door to door? She does that a lot, and I do also, and my father. We go in the evenings or on the weekends.

Some kids, some people, think that the Witnesses worldwide are a cult. But when you see cults, they're usually isolated in one territory, and they have a human leader, and the leader claims to be from God: they do everything he says, and they do things in secret. But the

Witnesses, we're not a cult—we don't have a human leader. We believe that Christ should be the head of the Christian congregation, like the Bible says. And we don't do activities in secret—all our meetings are public.

I was baptized as a Jehovah's Witness when I was ten. We're basically a religion that's involved in a worldwide preaching: there's over 407 million Witnesses all over the world. And no matter which Kingdom Hall you go to, it may be in another language, but they *all* do the same thing. What we believe is that we are responsible to God to be like his son, Jesus Christ, who taught his disciples to preach door to door about God's Kingdom. I spend a thousand hours a year, or about ninety hours a month, doing that—that's about three hours a day. Yeah, you get tired, but one thing that helps is praying, and thinking "I'm not the only one that's going out." It's not like I'm doing it on my own.

It was hard when I first started. When I was little I used to get upset when people would close the door on us. My parents told me that you really shouldn't. Of course, you ain't gonna feel *good* after it happens, but it's not about being offended. The same thing happened to Jesus when he was on earth—they wouldn't accept him as God's son. I was a baby when I started, but when I got older my mother would let me talk to people at the door. My mother said when I was three, she was talking with someone, and my foot happened to touch the man's grass. He said, "You better tell your baby to get her foot off my grass before I spray her with my water hose." She was like, "You ain't spraying my child with no water hose," and walked away. People can be rude, but there's no need to argue about the Bible—we just leave. [laughs]

My parents never pushed me into believing what they said. They gave me a choice: they always said, "It's up to you to do what you wanna do." And one thing that made me want to is, I would look at other kids my age, and they were claiming to be a certain religion, but they couldn't tell you a lot about it; and then at school they wouldn't act like they were. They would curse a lot and get smart with the teacher.

I go to a business school where they teach you different skills, like typing and how to communicate on the job. It's basically minority—blacks and Hispanics—at this school. It tries to train them, and get them ready for interviews in the workplace. It's so hard to get jobs . . . My major is in accounting, and I do well, but to tell you the truth, it's not my favorite. I'd rather be working as an architect or a landscaper. There's so many Witnesses in my school that we're basically just accepted. There's a lot of Witness kids that are Spanish, and when I see them talking in Spanish about the truth, that encourages me—and even encourages me to learn that language. Kids that aren't Witnesses like to ask me questions, and I'm more than happy to tell them about it. So many people, they believe what *anybody* says, and they don't really ask for themselves.

A lot of people think that all kids are just *bad*. But what they don't realize is that not all the time—but *most* of the time—if you look at the kids that's in the gangs, and then look at they parents, you see *why*. Most of those parents haven't trained them right, or don't spend enough time with them, or give them freedom at such a young age that they just go the wrong way with it. When you're young, that affects what you do for the rest of your life. It's impossible to be born bad, unless you got mental problems where it's gonna make you act a certain way, and you can't help it . . . If the parents set a good example, at least you know it wasn't because of the parents that they turned out that way.

I was reading this article about a man—he's a Jehovah's Witness now, but when he was younger he wasn't. He talks about how as a child he never remembers crying or having feelings. He said he didn't know how to feel: it was like he was just there. He didn't know why, till he read this book that talked about child abuse, and he realized all the stuff he went through as a child, and how that may affect your emotions even when you grow up.

A lot of kids today, their parents don't really teach them how to show love to each other. They let them play any type of video game, or watch any show—and most of *them* deal with violence. So, it's like they have no feelings when it comes to caring for people. They think they can hurt somebody and the person won't get hurt; or they can shoot somebody, and they won't die, they'll just fall on the ground. A lot of kids, they're encouraged to be violent. And when they grow up, that's how they act. I feel sorry for them . . . Well, not so much sorry that you feel *sad*, but sorry that you want to *help*—which is why we keep going door to door. [laughs]

I like school, I do well in school—I'm an honor roll school student

—but I get bored *bad*. I want to *graduate* . . . [smiles] When you're a senior, you have to work. I go to school half day, and then I come to work. You get paid and you get credit. It's a real good experience. It helps me to see how much responsibility my parents have, because I didn't really realize. I used to think, "Well, when I get to be eighteen or nineteen I'll be able to do this or that." But now that I'm working, and I'm so close to being eighteen, I still see—that's a *young* age.

Most of the Witness kids, they don't act like a lot of the kids in the world today, 'cause they're encouraged. For instance, we're encouraged not to date till we're ready to get married. If you're dating at a young age, that may lead to you having sex before you're married. And that's one thing that helped me—'cause I saw other girls my age claim they like somebody one minute, then the next minute they *don't*. Personally, I don't want to get involved yet. Most of the kids in my Kingdom Hall, we all grew up around each other, so we act like brothers and sisters mostly.

Ever since I was very young my parents taught me about sex. They didn't lie to me or try to keep anything secret. My mother has said, "I trust you, but I *don't* trust the people in the world"—so of course they're gonna be cautious about where I go. But they basically trust, because I wouldn't do anything that'd make 'em not trust. [laughs] A lot of kids don't like to talk with their parents; but one thing I appreciate now that I'm getting older is that they have a lot of answers for things I have questions to. A lot of kids rebel when they're still young, 'cause they think their parents can't tell them nuthin after they get legal. [laughs] But if they still living in their house, then they still have to be obedient, give respect. They think, "If I get out the house, all my problems will be solved"—and they *go*. A lot of girls will turn to prostitution because they don't have anybody else to give them money or they can't get a job. I wouldn't never wanna leave home without knowing what I'm about to do. I would never want to leave and have a bad relationship with my parents.

My father, he encourages me to pay attention to the news, 'cause being out with the public—we *can't* be dummies when it comes to society. I try to pay attention, even with the political stuff. You can see the stuff people in Bible times said would be happening in what's called the Last Days before God cures all this. So it's almost like studying to watch the news. A lot of people don't want to watch, 'cause of all the bad news—but they should keep in touch with it, 'cause how can you know how to control things in your own life if you don't? We can learn from the mistakes other people make.

Basically, the reason the Witnesses seem so dedicated is they know things won't always be this way. The Bible promises that soon God will destroy all wickedness, and the earth will be a peaceful place. According to the Bible, the people that will go to heaven, they're going to rule with Christ over the people in peace on earth, where everybody will be united. I know that this system won't last very long the way it's going. A lot of kids are scared about the future, but personally I look forward to living on earth in peace. And basically, that's why I'm not really afraid of my future—because I know that it won't be like this. I have hope.

Emma Slavsky

Oak Park, Illinois

E*mma is slim, and earnest,
with large brown eyes—an
old soul in a young spirit. Poised as she is, when her mother makes
her laugh mid-sip, she rushes to bury her face in her mother's neck.
Her mother murmers, "Oh, did I make orange juice come up through
your nose?" And over Emma's shoulder says, "When I'm really good,
I can make her pee in her pants, but, of course, I wouldn't do that
now." Emma is fifteen.*

I have two parents; my big sister is twenty-five, and my little sister is
ten, and then there's a bunch of other, like, Martians sort of roaming
around—we have a big extended group of people that call me their
niece or whatever. All the adults around me are education people, and
work in schools, and try to change them, like my parents do, and so
they all have the same orientation. Or else they're old civil rights people. I have a very strong sense of what needs to be done, because I'm
surrounded by people who also have a very strong sense of what needs
to be done.

My grandfather, he'll say, "Schools? Why do you guys care about
schools? It's not schools, it's *jobs*, don't you understand? What's
wrong with you people?" [laughs] He's stuck in this labor union thing,
no matter what era it is. He's sort of seen everything he's ever believed
in completely fall apart at this point, so I can understand being a little
bit insane. It's sad in a certain way . . . I can imagine all those people,
those old communists and old socialists—from what I see as the old,

old days—being really forlorn. You know, you're sitting around and watching the Berlin Wall come down, and we're all going,—Yes! Thank God." And they're going, "Was I doing something *bad* all this time, thinking that I was struggling for good?"

When I look back as an adult, I'm not sure that I'm doing things that I'll always be proud of. But the most important thing is that I'm not doing something with rules, like they were, where they're so dogmatic they can't change their ideas. If they hadn't been so dogmatic, and they had been more open-minded, then maybe they'd be more satisfied with themselves. I would *never*, like, have a book that I thought was the end-all and be-all—a manifesto.

I think, in general, it's about what's making you happy, and not whether it's really changing the entire world or not. The point is that if you think that you're doing something good, you probably are, and whether it really changes everything or not is sort of secondary—you can't know. But my self is sort of a big thing, [laughs] and I'm not very good at keeping things in perspective. I'm really a passionate, emotional person. So if I'm doing something that I believe in, I get really emotionally tied up in it, and that's not always good. There are certain times where you shouldn't let them see your emotional side, your humanness, because it shows your enemies that they're getting to you. But it's also the thing that makes me do what I do—so if I cut out my emotions, I think I would stop being so driven.

The people that I hang out with, we talk about the problems we face as a society, and what we need to be doing as individuals; we talk about organizing. A lot of social things have changed just in the last thirty years. But, you know, I'm still dealing with racism every single day. And people are so cynical now: they think that the way you solve things is by being selfish—that you just take everything you can get and hoard it—and that everyone else is the enemy. When I talk to people I don't know if I'm really making them think—if they come away struggling with the ideas that I'm presenting—or if they're just going, "God, who cares?" or if they come away more tolerant or what . . . Little things might not change anything, and maybe they change everything. You just can't know.

We moved here last year from Chicago and [wryly] I was really happy about that move. [laughs] I didn't want to move *at all*, but we couldn't live where we were living anymore—on the West Side of Chicago. It was just too dangerous. Somebody shot through our front window—it was getting *crazy*. I wasn't scared, but I was also sort of oblivious . . . [laughs] So we went from completely bad apartment poverty, to a really nice house in the suburbs, all in my lifetime, which is cool. [laughs] I'm receiving the benefits of capitalism. I don't mind at all—I think *everyone* should have a big house in the suburbs.

A lot of my friends think that people should move to the West Side of Chicago—that by moving to the suburbs we're abandoning the city, and that's going to be its downfall. But I disagree. Yes, it causes the ghetto to be even more of a ghetto, and Mayor Daley is even less likely to pave the streets now that my parents are not there to whine and complain. But *I* can't go into the West Side of Chicago, this fifteen-year-old white girl, and organize the masses. That change has to come from the people there. *They* have to struggle and come together, and until people decide that they're gonna do it, it's not gonna happen.

High school is basically high school, and so this school was really not that different. I complain a lot about school, because school is not built for me. [laughs] I went to a magnet school before, and the reason I liked it was because I had so many friends there. That's basically what makes or breaks it, I think, because high school is so horrible—it's just a bad place. And it's not meant for anything but being bad to teenagers. When I talk about high school it's not about my high school, it's about *all* high schools—my old school has the same problems, except it's very diverse.

In my new school they have this big facade of being very liberal. The school is supposed to be this incredibly diverse place, which is the biggest load of BS I've ever heard in my *life*. Thirty percent minority, maybe thirty percent black, I don't know. The point is, there's all these kids that come here from Chicago—like me—except they're black . . . [sighs] They're taking kids and sticking them in regular classes—which are horrible—and not dealing with what they bring to school, and what they lack. They see them as a deficit; they see all of us as a deficit.

It's the whole issue of how high schools treat students, that we play no parts in the decision making processes of how school works, we're just looked at as the end product. We're not part of school, except that we are what they're making.

When I got here they put me in all these honors classes immediately, just seeing me—without my transcripts or anything—and I couldn't handle it all. I was so shocked by the fact that there was like one minority in each of my honors classes—the token minority. It was just very weird to me: it was hard for me to be comfortable. When I went from honors to regular algebra, the racial makeup of the class completely changed. There I was, one of five white people in my algebra class going, *"This* is where they put everyone." [laughs]

People are passive, but I think it's because they're confused, and they don't know why they're angry. In the lunchroom, people get into race fights—a lot of times it's blacks throwing Skittles at whites, and then people yelling at each other and getting into a fight. Somebody breaks it up, and then everybody starts eating again. It's not that uncommon of a thing. People don't understand why they're angry; they can't place what's making them angry, why they feel alienated, and so they take it out in that way. But that anger is coming from somewhere, and they *should* be expressing it—they're expressing it in the wrong way, but it needs to be expressed. Everybody needs to be angry, because it's not about just sitting around loving each other— change doesn't happen that way.

We are in a society where I'm of a privileged race and class. I get it even concretely—I see it *all* the time. And there are minority kids who go to school with me that see it the other way, who get the other side of the coin: while I'm getting put in all honors classes, they're getting put in all regulars classes without question. It's a sorting process. So that anger is justifiable, and necessary for anything to change. And instead of saying, "Why are you fighting?" We should be saying, "Yes, take that anger and *do* something with it"—go and get in the face of an administration, and fight for change, and *change* the way that this school works, and let's stop this from happening.

I'll go to school board meetings about the discipline problem. They had this big discussion about how it was something like 55 percent of all discipline cases were taken towards African-American students, yet they're only 30 percent of the school. The board didn't deal with that issue at all. They said, "Well, it's a class thing, not a race thing."

We go around and around—and it *is* a race thing. It's a race thing because we don't talk about race at school—that, *yes*, people of different races *exist*. And it's not that you should sit there and treat everyone the same. We're *not* all the same, we're all *different*—all of us—and we should be taking those different things that we bring to school and utilizing them, using them. And, instead, we just glaze them over: you're all the same, we're treating you all equal—just stay in your seats and listen! [laughs]

Places like my high school need to stop happening, because they just turn people off. It's this huge place—it's like two thousand eight hundred—and *nobody* can know each other. You can't know what experiences I've already had or what I know or what I'm interested in if you have to deal with a hundred other students every day. It's impossible, physically impossible. It doesn't matter how well intentioned you are—and most of the teachers aren't very well intentioned [laughs]—but if they are, they don't have time. Some people thrive on the bigness and the lack of community, but I think that in general people don't. And maybe you thrive on it, but that's not how it is in the world in general. Like, I live in this place, I have my family, we have our community, we have our niche, and we work like that—we all tie together with our common interests, and struggle together, and help each other out. We couldn't do that if we didn't have any base, and if we didn't have any friends—we couldn't be happy. And so it doesn't seem the right thing to teach kids, that we should be just one in two thousand eight hundred.

I got involved with this group of students who were organizing to protest, and out of that came Generation Y, which is our student organization. It's Generation Y, with the letter, but the "why" is implied. Last meeting we talked about restructuring the school board. People are really interested in small, liberal changes, like just adjusting things a little bit. I'm more outrageous a lot of the time, like "I want to completely restructure everything, why are we stopping? I don't *want* a school board, so why are we putting students on it?" [laughs]

In September they're going to fire sixty teachers or whatever because they need more money. Nobody is gonna pay not even a dime more property taxes, and they don't care how many music departments are gonna get cut. If those classes are cut—the only ones that I even vaguely like—then I'm gonna hate it even more. That's gonna be opportunity for struggle and change, because with big bad changes come big good changes, hopefully. I'm looking forward to next year: that's a reason to get up, because bad things are happening. I think that people can change things if they struggle and come together. I feel if you're gonna be alive, and you believe that you can change things, then by nature you want to be where the bad things are happening, because you *thrive*. I thrive off of that, I feel as though I need it. It doesn't mean I'm going to, like, move to Chile! [laughs] *This* is the war zone for me.

But the thing about being in an organization is that you don't just get to act when you want to act. [laughs] You have to think about building the organization and getting people active and blah-blah-blah-blah-blah. So we're organizing a rally and campaigning, and trying to get people to vote for the referendum [which would raise property taxes in order to increase funding for the high school] and having a write-in campaign on the ballots telling people, at least symbolically, *no class cuts*. I don't know how long Generation Y will last . . . There's always a struggle. Like, there's a fine line between being co-opted and working within the system. People think, "Oh, I'm not radical enough to be in there." We have people whose parents would just like *flip* if they found out what we were doing. We need to be doing stuff that peoples' parents think is good—we need to show them that this is good.

Most people's parents don't know where their kids are, and they don't know how to find them if they did want to know—and I think that's scary. I spent the whole summer with my friend Edie: we would go out every Saturday night, and we would tell her mom that we were going to see the same movie, *Reality Bites*. [laughs] We were just waiting to see when she would say, "What, didn't you see that last week?" *And she had no idea!* [laughs] It was just ridiculous. There's times when people have, not too much freedom, but not enough concern.

The difference between me and most teenagers, like in terms of parents relationship, is that I am *really* honest with my parents. They know what I'm doing, and if they have anxiety it's *because they know* what I'm doing. [laughs] If I lie to my parents, it's not because I have to. We talk about stuff all the time. It blows my mind to hear people, like my friends, who are just *so* uneducated about their bodies and their health. It's ridiculous that's it's taboo. And people wonder why we have a whole section in my school for pregnant girls. My parents, we talk about life, and what my friends are doing. I'm with a guy who's going, "Yeah, it's this great mind-expander—you need to do this with me." And my dad's going, "*Yeah,* I gave somebody that line—don't believe it" . . . [laughs] It's never been like, "Oh God, we need to lock her in her room," because they *trust* me. They know that I'm not being stupid; and I'm not being stupid—because they think I'm not, to a certain extent, you know?

People don't tend to talk to their parents, and parents don't tend to talk to their kids—it just doesn't happen. How can you teach your kids if you can't talk to them? I know a lot of people who can't even sit down in the same room with their kid without screaming at them— because they're so *angry*—and there's *no* reason for it. People react to teenagers like, just, you know . . . they're terrified, and there's no logical explanation for it—except maybe *they* were horrible when they were a teenager or something.

One of my friend's girlfriends is very self-destructive—does a lot of drugs and goes out with really bad people—and I think a lot of it is a reaction to her parents rigidness. When I first met her I was like, "Wow, look, she has all this money, she lives in this great big house, has a seemingly *cool* family, and a car, and goes to private school. Wow—she's got it all." But she doesn't have it all, because with all of that comes, like, these expectations. Everybody has expectations of their kids that maybe their kids have no intentions of fulfilling, or don't like—or they don't want to be what their parents want them to be. So it makes all this tension . . . Or their parents are just crazy and let them go to the same movie five weekends in a row . . . [laughs]

When people are doing bad things to themselves, I have a tendency to just say, "God, you're really self-destructive. Why are you doing this?" Pointing it out to people oftentimes blows their minds: "You're telling me I'm self-destructive?! You're a teenage girl, you should be doing this too. Why aren't you? What's wrong with you?" [laughs] I've always felt kind of outcast and weird in that sense. If I'm doing self-destructive things, it's taking all my stress and making myself sick with it. It's not going out and doing cocaine or dropping acid. That's not me.

I watched a talk show last night and there was this seventeen-year-old girl with a three-year-old kid arguing with her parents about marrying the sleaze that got her pregnant. [She stretches her face into a look of mock terror] I was like—I'm fifteen! That means in two years I could be *her!* But I'm *nowhere near* being her, I couldn't *possibly* be her. I want to travel around the world, and go to China and Africa, and do all these things. *We're just on completely different planets.* The idea that you would be pregnant at seventeen means that you didn't know anything about birth control, or you were sort of self-destructive, and you were sort of unsure of what it means to be treated right by men. It means you're just completely doing bad things to yourself. Maybe you don't know you are, but you *are.*

I have goals. I'm really interested in art, and I could easily say I want to do art for the rest of my life and feel perfectly content, but I don't think that's what I'll end up doing. I'm really interested in broadcasting and communications. I work on my school television show—it's a high-pressure thing, but I like doing it. I'm a reporter-anchor-person. I think that I would like to do that, but talking about eight years from now—by that time who even knows? Will they still have televisions? [laughs] Will people still communicate the same way?

I do want kids, 'cause I like them. I think that kids complete a cycle. There's something really nice about seeing your face in somebody else. I would assume that I'll fall in love with someone and get married, but who knows? It's scary to think about, because it's far away. [laughs] The year two thousand and nine I'll be a senior in college. There's something very mystical about the way people say, "the year two thousand," like it's all of a sudden a year of jubilee, everything's going to change. It doesn't worry me. I feel like it's an adventure, that things are gonna be different, and there's no point in saying, "Yes, I'm going to do this, and I will never do that," because who the hell knows? [laughs] The reason that it doesn't scare me is because I know that it can't be *that* different: it's still the world, and if it still exists at that point, then no matter how much technology they come up with—unless it destroys the earth—it can't change it that much.

People look for answers. They're looking for this one thing that will solve everything, because they don't want the world to be complex—they don't want it to be so chaotic; and it is. We need to believe that things can be good, and we need to . . . *especially* we need to teach kids that things can be good, and show them. And to teach them that struggle is important. If I were going to start a religion—which I'm actually discussing with one of my friends [laughs]—it would be about celebrating the energy not of a person but of *all* of us. *We* can make things better if we come together.

If you take religion as this set of values that you believe in, then what I think, and what I would want to make sacred for my kids—and what I would want people to come together and worship, and sing and dance about—is believing that people make things happen, and that people's energy is what you should be worshipping and valuing. And *that* would be something worth celebrating.

Secrets

Rachel Ghorbanian

Manhattan, New York

W*e meet at the Hetrick Martin Institute, an organization that provides services for gay, lesbian, bisexual, and transgenderal youth. Rachel is training to be a peer educator on AIDS. She has long, dark wavy hair, intense black eyes, and a breathlessly energetic, dramatic quality. She is seventeen.*

I was born and raised in New York, and I'm living with my father and my older sister—she's going to college. My mother passed away when I was thirteen. She had cancer for a long time, a very long time —she was sick for about five years. She was diagnosed, I think, when I was in the first grade. They never told me that it was cancer until her death; of course, even when you're a little kid you have your suspicions, but nothing was really said outright. It was very obvious that she was sick, but it wasn't spoken about—so it wasn't like covered or closeted or whatever, it was just not discussed.

It happened very fast: one day she's working, she's doing this and that, and then the next she's at the doctor's, and he says, "You have to go to the hospital today and get the surgery done." I remember the day she was taken to the hospital—I was in the third grade or something. My father picked us up from school, and they wouldn't let us into the hospital because you have to be over sixteen. Sometimes we wouldn't actually interact with my mother for a long time—what we would do is stand in front of her hospital, where her window was. [laughs] My dad would be like, "Stand right here," and she would wave from the window. Sometimes my sister would be with me, and so we'd stand and wave, and do whatever sign language we could.

My mother died in August. We used to go for the summer over to my aunt's place in Connecticut. The night before, I was lying in bed, trying to fall asleep. I owed sixty-three dollars on my library card—I had this big project that had, like, eight books, and I forgot about returning them—and I was so worried about sixty-three dollars. And then, the next day, we were all sitting around. I was so oblivious, I was just, like, flipping through a magazine—I wasn't even paying attention to the discussion. All of a sudden I look up, and I see my sister crying, and I see my aunt running to her, and I don't know . . . I didn't hear it, but I *knew*. And then I started to cry. She was very, very sick—but, it's funny . . . I wasn't expecting it. And that night, I was lying in bed and thinking, "Last night I was worried about this library card, you know—and look at that . . . look what happened *now*."

I was in elementary school and I was always a pretty good student, no matter what. It's just in my character to keep everything in proportion, to keep everything steady, and rationalize. My mother's death— it put everything in proportion, it put life in proportion. You know, to worry over this library card, and to worry over this and that. I've become more carefree in a way, and more relaxed, and more sensible at balancing everything out. So I didn't really have, like, school problems. My sister did—she almost got left back a year because she was missing so much school—'cause she was upset.

Me and my sister are the closest, the *closest*. It can't get any closer. I'd say about seventy-five percent of my morals, and values, and even qualities, came from my mother. I would say that her life was a sacrifice for her children. *Everything* she did was for us, and everything she thought of was for us, and to benefit us. Even when she was so sick, her thoughts would be about her children. We were very close, me and my mother—*very*. And she always stressed, "Be close with your sister—just know you can't depend on anybody else as much." We're close in age but we're not competitive. I think because our characters are so different, there isn't anything to compete over. We're like day and night.

My mother was in the hospital for so long that coming home to an empty house was not unusual. So, after she died, you know, there was just the thought: "I'm never going to see this person again." And I notice, especially since I'm a senior in high school now, [feigning melodrama] "I'm never going to see this friend again, they're going to go away, across the country," and whatever . . . I'm very sentimental to begin with, and I loved my mother so much. There was this, I guess . . . whatever—mourning period. But, you know, the sun will rise tomorrow, and every day in your life you still have to just go on.

My sister dealt with it very differently. To this day she has, like, such trouble—*such* trouble. Sometimes she'll just break down and cry. She's still very, very shaken. So much of her life revolved around her mother; and, also, she's not very independent. [laughs] She's not independent *at all*, actually. At times I feel older than her. Sometimes I even joke, you know, because we look very much alike, and you can't tell who's older—so if somebody asks, I'll say, "Yeah, she's older in age, but that's about it." [laughs] Especially at that point, especially when I was thirteen, I felt that: my mother's family used to come to me and say, "Look, you're the stronger one, you have to take care of her, you have to take care of things." And, also, we had a lot of battles at home with my father.

He was a very difficult man. He's very stubborn, and he would go out a lot, and sometimes we would be left home alone for long periods of time; he would just *not* be home. I guess he hated being home because it was a crazy household at that point. [laughs] For like a year after my mother died it was *terrible*. So just dealing with his character . . . It's so intense. He would come home and yell for no reason, and this and that. And my sister would just take it and absorb it, and I would be like, "No—this isn't just!" [laughs] "This is *wrong.*" And they would tell me, "Defend your sister. You're the one, you're the speaker—you *have to* say these things, you *have to* speak."

My dad was a machinist, but because my mother was very sick, he had to take off a lot, and he got laid off. That was a really bad time. He hasn't really worked since; he's, like, just doing things here and there. I'm happy for him now, because he's getting this dream: he bought a house with whatever little money he had. He goes there frequently—it's outside of the city. But it's still in the process of renovation, so it's not a place to stay yet. Both of my parents had immigrated, and to own land in America for him was a big thing.

We're Armenian, and a *lot* of strings come along with being Armenian . . . [laughs]

We don't live in the house, we live in an apartment in New York. See, it's this whole complicated thing: my father remarried, but she's not living with us. You see—he got married like two months after my mom died, and didn't tell us! [laughs] We just, like, stumbled onto the marriage certificate. And of course we reacted violently—we totally went *nuts*. We were like, "*No!* We don't want this woman living with us!" [laughs] And, "Who is this woman?!" and whatever.

It was just terrible. We thought of it as respect: it wasn't respectful to my mother, what he did. And I starting saying, "What are your *values?* What do you value if you're acting this way?" He was very harsh at that point, too. You see, in arguments, he doesn't make much sense —at least not to me . . . [laughs] He goes around in circles, and he's *yelling.* If somebody's yelling at you, and it makes no sense what they're saying, it's still intense, whatever they're saying, because they're yelling. And then, my mother's side of the family got really involved, being very conservative Armenians, very overprotective. At one point we even had to go to family court 'cause there was such a big argument. But everything was dropped, and smoothed out.

I had met this woman before they got married. She was an immigrant, and she didn't speak very much English, which also made it very difficult: she spoke Greek, and I speak English and Armenian, and communication was terrible. The Armenian culture, you have to be hospitable and polite, so I would go out of my way to make her feel at home. But once we found out that she was married to my father, it was like, [mock yelling] "*What is this?! What's going on?*"

She lives in her own apartment, we live in our apartment, and he bought that house. At this point we talk to her, and sometimes she'll come over—but very rarely; it's very rarely. But my father has gotten more understanding, and he seems more tame now, more rational. Before, once he stepped through the door he would go off about this or that. And now, because in conversation we're less hostile, too, everything is much better. We've both grown.

Everybody's like, "You know, adolescence—it's *such* a rough period"—and I don't see it as such a rough period. [laughs] It's a stage of life, and as in any other stage of life, it has its problems . . . but, if anything, adolescence for me was great. I had such a great childhood, I had so much fun. I was always independent, and going here and there. I think that at this point, being seventeen, I'm discovering who I am more than I was when I was thirteen. It's just a different level, and I don't think of it as any more rough.

I feel like this is the beginning, you know? And it really is, because once you get your independence, that is the beginning. And I do feel very young. But, then again, in comparison to what? To the world? *Yes!* [laughs] But to my peers, sometimes I feel more mature. I go to a public high school—I'm a senior. It's the scariest thing. This is the beginning: if I step *this* way, it's a path; if I step *that* way, it's a different path, and it's going to branch out to other roads. It's like, "Oh, well—I'm going to go to college; maybe I'll meet somebody at this college." Or, "What if I don't go to that college, maybe I'll miss the love of my life." [laughs] And then if I go to this college, maybe I'll decide to go into this field at college, and whatever. It's like this whole web, and this is the beginning of the web. Which way are you going to go? [laughs] I don't know . . . it really drives me crazy.

I'm *definitely* going to college. I always said to myself, "I'm going to be big!" [laughs] You know? I'm going to be *big*—you're going to see my name in lights! If anybody has ambition, it's me. I really want to go into the arts: I want to be a writer so badly—ever since I was little. But my family—like my dad especially, being an immigrant, and coming here and struggling, he always says, in Armenian—*"You have to win money."* And being a writer just doesn't *win* money, so they're always pushing me to be a lawyer. One cousin says, "Be a lawyer," another says, "Go into computer science." They think that I'm perfectly capable of going far in these fields—and I think I can also, you know. Why not? If anybody can do it, sure, why not *me?* [laughs] But, I want to be happy: I want to be content with my job.

You know what my cousin said to me once? One time we were sitting outside in front of the garage in Connecticut. And he goes, "Don't worry, Rachel. When the time comes, I'll find you a good man to marry." I was like, "*Yeah*—OK . . . " [laughs] But that's the way they *see* it. It's a *crazy* culture! [She flings her hand out as though pushing something away.] It's so tight, it's so intense, it's so conservative, it's so confining . . . I'm my own person, I can choose whatever I want. When

I was younger, I had *so* much pride in my culture also, because I was surrounded by it much more. And whatever I believe in, I believe in a hundred percent. Everything in my life is extremes. [laughs]

I still have that pride, because that made me who I am; but I'm not very fond of the culture. This is the point of realization: everything starts to become real, and you start to think for yourself. I used to be religious; I used to be . . . Christianity . . . But, no, now I'm learning to think for myself and see for myself. I'm questioning. I guess I've become more cynical, or I just see it as being fake. It's something that man made up. And nobody has to tell me how to behave, and what to do. I live by the Rachel religion, you know? [laughs] By what *Rachel* thinks is right. And I *do* have morals—I don't need somebody telling me what they should be.

A year ago I just really started to question it. I had a very close friend, and we used to have these amazing conversations, and it really brought out a lot. Sometimes it takes a conversation to bring out your thoughts, to bring out your beliefs. Sometimes you're very firm in them, but you don't even realize that you have them until you have to defend them.

I still love the Church, but I think the reason that I loved it so much more when I was younger was because of the belonging to Church: the incense, the tradition . . . I *love* tradition, I think it's beautiful—but I don't want to *live* by it. That's what got me before, but now it seems very cold and laid out; and the core of it—I just don't believe. There's this saying in Armenian—excuse me for the language—but it's "Everybody's shit smells." Even the people who go to church. And everybody there, they seem so conservative in their nice clothes, and they're acting all proper. Everybody has their flaws—but they're so *critical* of everybody else. I really feel the tension in church.

Last year, on my sixteenth birthday, I started to think to myself: "Oh my God, sixteen years passed—sixteen years is *such* a long time, I could've done so much. This sixteen-year-old did this, and this sixteen-year-old did that, and OK, what do *I* do? I go to school, OK . . . " So then I'm like, "I have to go out there, I have to start *doing* something." So the first thing I did was I picked up the phone and called up hospitals, and I'm like, "I'd really like to volunteer"—because, I thought, "I could do this, I could go in there and cheer people up—I'm familiar with hospitals." I wanted to work with elderly people. And *seven* hospitals, they gave me this whole runaround . . . I'm like, "Look—I just want to work for *free!*" [laughs] And then I'm like, "OK, what else? Amnesty International. Yeah! That's a great cause, I wanna do *that.*" So I called them up, and I'm like, "Look, I will work for free"—and again they're like, "We don't need your help." Then one day an AIDS organization came to my school, and they did a presentation, and said, "We're looking for peer educators." I ran up there, I was like, "*I want to do this, I want to do this!*" As much as I'm doing it for the community, I'm doing it for myself. Because you're doing something valuable, you're doing something instead of just hanging out, or watching TV, or wasting time. I think time is so precious, and to just, like, do nothing—it's *such* a waste. I consider sleep a waste a time. You're doing nothing, go out there and do something. So I got involved with that group.

I met this girl through the group. She was bisexual, and we were very, very good friends. This is the friend that I was talking about before. So we became intensely close in, like, a short amount of time. Every day we would talk on the phone for hours, and she would always be over my place—she practically lived there at one point. We were *such* good friends. And then I noticed feelings developing, and I'm like, "Oh my God, *what* is this?" Da-da-da-da. At first I had a really, really hard time with coming out, to myself. And at the same time the feelings were reciprocated. But we didn't say anything to each other until, like, she couldn't stand it anymore. [laughs] See, she was out and I was like—seriously, this was my first love, you know? I was really in love. So she wrote me this huge letter about love this, this and that. So we had our . . . It was a beautiful relationship, it was a beautiful thing. It was the best and the worst combined in one, because we had our problems. [laughs] That relationship is over now, but it was the best time and the worst time in my life. It was a great experience.

Then I stumbled onto this Collaborative Campaign Project—that's a collaboration of organizations that target gay, lesbian, bisexual, transgender, questioning youth and deal with their issues. So I went as a representative of my peer education group and met *so* many people from so many different organizations. That really pushed up my pride, you know? Right now I feel so much more powerful, and I'm so happy with who I am. So it's like *really* a big difference.

I told my sister, and that was the only bad reaction I ever got. I would test people—I would be like, "So, what do you think about Clinton's health care plan? What do you think about gays in the military?" One time I asked my sister, "What would you do if your child was gay?" It was relative to the conversation, so I slipped it in . . . And she said, "Well, I don't think I would like it, but I would accept it— it's my child." So I thought, "OK, green light!" But then it was *such* a bad reaction! [laughs]

Whenever I get really nervous I start to laugh, so I was laughing, and I said, "I have something to tell you." I picked a day when she didn't have to go to work and I didn't have to go anywhere—we had to clean the house. So it wouldn't have to be, "Oh, by the way, I'm gay," and then run out. At the time I was seeing that girl; and I was like, "You know Alicia—she's a really good friend of mine, and she kind of likes me, and I kind of like her too." And she was like, "No, I don't believe you—I think you're going through a stage. I don't believe you —I think Alicia did this to you."

And so she called up Alicia, and they spoke on the phone for an hour or something *about my life!* [humorously outraged] I'm like, "Oh my God, I can't believe this. This is *my life.*" And at that point, the two most important people *in* my life are on the phone *talking* about my life. [laughs] But you give and you take: you can't be so demanding; you have to give an inch. Alicia, she's a very smart girl, and she's very tactful, and has very good arguments, being out and everything. [laughs] And also, I figured it would be more difficult for my sister to say all the things to her that she would say to me. So I let it happen. You have to let it happen—you can't stop people from doing things.

But then, as time went on, still she wouldn't talk about it. Sometimes I would come home with these great stories about what happened here, or what happened at CCP. I would be like, "Oh, this is so great." I would tell her, and she would just be like . . . [sighs] First of all, she watches TV *constantly*—she's, like, *addicted.* She would stare at the TV and go, "Mmm-hmm . . . Yeah." Biting her nails. And I'm a storyteller—I can go *on* and *on*. I can come home from the supermarket, and I'll have stories to tell, you know. Sometimes I would sit her down, I would turn off the TV, and I would start a conversation. And she'd get kind of hostile: she'd be like, *"I don't want to."* First of all, she doesn't think—she *doesn't* think. She just goes, *"I dunno"* to every question. "I dunno. . . . Don't bother me—I don't care. I don't want to think about it." You know? And I'd be like, *"How* can you say you don't know? *Everybody* has an opinion—especially concerning your *sister.* You don't have an opinion on *your sister?"*

She became better with it, but the last time this happened, which was a few weeks ago, I totally freaked out from her "I dunnos." I was ironing, and I wanted to bang on the ironing board because I was so frustrated! But you know, you can only hit an ironing board so much, because it is weak and fragile. [laughs] So I was standing there, going [mimes tearing out hair] because I *couldn't take it!* I can't believe I got so frustrated, because usually I don't.

She doesn't like it—but she wouldn't tell my father, she wouldn't tell family, she wouldn't tell friends, because it would be a reflection of *her.* You know what I mean? I really think that's what her motive is. She wouldn't tell *anybody,* because I'm her sister. And I know that I can tell her whatever, because of that. At one point we weren't close, because I was closeted. But now I feel closer, because I can say things that I couldn't before—but I can't talk freely. But, I mean, we're still close in that I'll do anything for her.

Did I come out to my dad? [She looks horrified, then laughs.] *No-o-o!* No *way.* I want to go to college, you know?! [laughs] My dad, he's pretty liberal compared to other Armenians—he's a very open man. I thought my sister was the same way. Honestly, I feel like it's such a natural thing that I'm afraid I might slip. [laughs] At this point it's so natural and so comfortable that it would be like saying, "Pass the salt." At one point I almost did tell him. I was very, very close; very close, but he changed the subject.

Remy Jardinel
Chicago, Illinois

S*he's amiable, with a low, gentle voice — words stream forth. As she talks, she turns her head from side to side — a lulling, rhythmic tic. She is eighteen.*

My mom grew up in the Philippines, and so did my dad. My mom does this thing where she gets the slang all wrong. [laughs] The big thing is you *mess with* somebody, right? My mom says, "Don't mess up with me! Don't mess up!" [laughs] I get a kick out of it. I say, "Mess *with*, Mom. You don't stick that preposition there." She's like, "But you *mess up!* You *mess up* your room, you *mess up* your plate, you *mess up!*"

I'm sarcastic with my mother at times, and insulting with my brother; and sometimes with my dad, I don't talk to him. I'm like, "What's wrong with you, Remy? These are your *parents*, they've given you so much, and you're bad to them." I'm not sarcastic all the time, only when they get on my nerves. My mom's learned how to put up with me —she shows a lot of restraint. And when she's talking about dumb things—there are just dumb things that your parents talk about—I let her talk on. It's normal family stuff, really.

My mom works at a manufacturing company. She completely hates it. She doesn't like working *at all*, but she has to, 'cause of me and my brother, basically, and the mortgage on the house. She's trying to make extra money on the side—she manages an apartment building. My dad works for a company, and there's like a conveyor belt and stuff passes by. My neighborhood is good. It's exactly middle-middle-class: no lower-middle-class, no upper . . . It's bungalow and brick houses, apartment buildings scattered here and there. And it's really diversified: Asians, Hispanics, caucasians; some blacks—not a lot.

My parents are divorced. My dad lives in the attic—he never got past that stage where he moves out . . . He has his little bedroom and a kitchen. It's totally separate from us, but he still comes downstairs, and mom still makes rice for him. I was about eleven when they got divorced, and my brother was nine. I wasn't surprised: they always fought, so it was OK that they were getting divorced. It didn't bother me, because my dad was still going to be around.

I went to a Catholic elementary school, and it was mostly Filipino kids. Filipinos are *really* Catholic, like ninety-nine percent Catholic. I go to church so as I don't get kicked out of the house. My parents are *very* religious: if I say I ate chicken on Friday, they're like, "Oh, you *weren't* supposed to—it's Lent." I'll be like, "Oh, sorry. Now I'm not going to heaven, right, Mom?" And she'll be like, "Remy, no . . . " I'm not too Catholic. Even though there's like all these Bibles, it's really hard for me to believe that a lot of this stuff went on—like miracles, Lazarus rising from the dead, Jesus coming . . . It's really hard for me to see him walking around the earth and turning three loaves of bread into baskets of fish, or whatever the story is. It just doesn't seem conceivable, or real. And the pope? He's *gotta* let go of that whole birth control thing. . .

Freshman year I went to a public magnet school, and that really opened me up a lot. It's better to have diversity—it's more awareness. I know better than to think a certain way about certain types of people. It was the first time I ever had a black teacher, and you figure out that things just aren't as different as you thought. I like it there. My brother is transferring out. He just didn't get along with *anybody*. I don't know if he wasn't giving them a chance, or if he talked to these people and found out they weren't people he wanted to be around. One big reason is he says there are too many black kids—he's like, "They're always so *loud* in the hallways. They're just so annoying, and I can't make them go away."

My mom has black tenants, and she's like, "They're so messy: they can't keep their kids clean, they can't keep their houses clean," blah-

blah blah-blah. I think my brother kinda gets it from her. She knows it's wrong to be racist, and she knows if she says something like that she'll get lambasted. I know *I* can't change her, so I just don't listen to her. A lot of the stuff that I thought about black people came from her, but I learned to pick what's right from wrong.

My brother mainly sticks to his own kind—all his friends are Asian. I'd like to think I have a more diverse group of friends, but my core group of friends are all white. It bothers me a little, 'cause you want to think that you can hang out with everybody, but you can't. Like, if we hang out with the Hispanic people then they fall into their Spanish slang, and you're like, "Huh? Huh?" You're kinda clueless, and, like, the big dork.

I have Asian friends, but it's a separate thing. My Asian friends are more straitlaced. Their fun is to go to a movie and then dinner, and the movies they pick would be different. It wouldn't be *Rocky Horror Picture Show*, at midnight, or *Go Fish*, because it'd be too radical, too deviant. My white friends, they're more social, more, "Let's burn up this town." What do we do? When somebody's parent isn't home we'll have a dinner party at their place. It'll be eight of us or so, and we'll play cards and Pictionary, get silly and have fun. Burning up the town is *Rocky Horror Picture Show* at midnight, and then go to the Golden Nugget and eat a lot. [laughs]

Is there cheating at my school? Yeah . . . [smiles] I've cheated all my life—all my life. I don't know that many people who haven't. I could say that grades don't mean that much, and cheating for a good grade isn't that big a deal—but we wouldn't cheat if grades didn't mean so much. Cheating is an adrenaline rush—getting away with something. Like shoplifting: most of my friends have shoplifted. They all have horror stories about when they almost got caught, or when they did get caught. I stopped shoplifting: it was like, "Oh, let's see if I can do it"—kind of like a dare. I figured out I could do it, and then I didn't need to anymore.

My parents never really gave me a sex and drug talk. The people I hang out with, we're aware—wear your condoms—but there are still so many people that don't know what's going on. But drugs are every-where. I like marijuana. I have a friend who's tripping on Friday. She's having three quote-unquote babysitters to watch her and make sure she stays under control. You want to maximize the fun you're gonna have, you don't want it to be dangerous, so you plan it: make sure you don't have to be home early, you're in a safe environment, stuff like that.

My parents know I've smoked marijuana. There was this dinner table conversation—it was *so* bad. My mother was like, "I want to ask you something, Remy. Have you ever smoked marijuana?" "*Yeah, I have,*" blah blah blah. She said, "I figured you probably would've. I know I raised you right, and that you have a good head on your shoulders. Just do it safely and take care of yourself." And then I came back at her with my own serious question: I asked her if she was a lesbian. I thought she was, and that that was the reason she divorced my dad. She said, "I did a bit of experimenting and fooling around when I was living in an all-girl dormitory, but that was the end of it." It was a bit disappointing, 'cause I still didn't know why my parents divorced. I say, "Oh, they just stopped loving each other," but still, in the back of my head . . .

My mom's got this guy at work who's kind of after her, but she won't go out with him. He writes these awful cards to her, like for Valentine's Day. [Sympathy washes across her face.] Well, they're not awful . . . They're tacky, sweet, lonely-man kind of cards. Some of her friends are lesbians, and she told me that when she was younger, a lot of her friends were gay men. So I was like, "Oh, what's going on?" See, my dad told me that was the reason. I was like, [challenging] "Yeah, are you *sure* about that one, Dad?" And he's like, "Well, look at all the facts." It was like, [humble] "Oh hey, you're right." [laughs] I think she's bi or lesbian or something, but I don't know . . . That's OK, it's not my business anyway. And either way I wouldn't care—it really wouldn't make too much of a difference.

I'm just glad she didn't flip out about the marijuana. It's better that way, in the sense that you should just go ahead and learn how to do it responsibly. If they intervene, you're gonna end up resenting them and being angry. Hopefully, you'll figure out yourself that marijuana isn't all that great; that in the end it'll just burn you out, and you'll do nothing for the rest of your life. It's like a coming of age to learn about that stuff. I don't want to learn about it in college when I'll be made fun of. It's getting younger, though. We have seventh and eighth graders going, "Yeah, we're cool, we're smoking up and stuff." It makes me feel really old. It's like, "Not yet, you guys—what's your rush? Don't do *this*—go watch *Aladdin* or something!" [laughs]

One kid in our school committed suicide last year—he was a junior. Counselors were pulling his friends out of classes, and you could see them crying in the hallways. It was this big hush thing. He shot himself in his parents' Lexus. I've had suicidal thoughts—like, "Yeah, they'll regret it, they'll be sorry." Sometimes you just want to see how much you affect the world you're in, so you want to take yourself out, to see how different things would be. But I'm not *that* curious—I don't think I'd really want to kill myself. But yeah, it definitely has run through my mind. I learned you kill yourself like this, [mimes slicing a line along the length of her forearm] up the arm, because that's the way your veins run; and that if you cut yourself like this [cuts a horizontal line across her wrist] you just, like, slit it—it's not as effective. Some girl from the suburbs taught me this. She's like, "And thirty sleeping pills and a shot of whiskey, too, will do you in." I was like, "*Oh* . . . " She wasn't suicidal; she said she had learned it from her friends . . . at least that's what she said.

I'm not too worried about the state of the world right now. A lot of kids are up on things—they *really* know what's going on in the world. We really don't want to mess things up for us and for our kids. Like, we know we have to recycle and stuff like that: "Buy *this* gas, it's better because of so-and-so." I think in the future it's just gonna be a sadder state kind of thing. It'll be really strange, all high-tech; all the low-income people won't be able to catch on to what's happening with all this high-tech computer stuff, so they're kind of gonna be left in the dust. It's gonna be really bad.

I don't agree with having housing projects, 'cause some people never leave, and all they see is this bad stuff going down: they have nothing to look up to, to make them say, "I want to do better." Like at school, in group work I'll give back as much as a group gives me. If I'm in a big slacker group, and I see that they're not gonna do anything, I'm not gonna do anything either. But if a couple of kids are like, "Yeah, we really should get together," I'll be like, "You're right, we should." You put out, if they're gonna do the same for you. If you're living in a project. you don't see that happen too often. If we get some mixed-income housing the high-income-class people won't forget about the lower-income-class people; it'll be a more cooperative, helping-type thing.

My friends and I, we talk about Social Security a lot. We don't like the fact that you guys are gonna eat up all our money—the baby boomer generation. It's really awful, it's not fair. Most of my friends work, so we complain about the Social Security that we're not gonna get. I don't feel betrayed, because I don't think the government walked into this saying, "Yeah, we'll spend all the money on this certain group of people." It's just how things happened.

I don't know if I want to get married, have kids. We'll see . . . I don't know if my parents divorcing really ruined it for me. I like little flings—I'm afraid of all that weird emotional stuff, attachment and all that junk. I'm too scared to surrender myself to another person; and the fact that that person is surrendering themselves to me isn't really that assuring. I guess I have a warped sense of relationship . . . I like kids though. I babysit, and I also work at a library as a page, shoveling books, and stamping date-due cards. It's not a fluff job—the books keep multiplying, you never stop. I like it a lot—it teaches the value of hard work.

One summer I worked the Taste of Chicago. [An annual summer food festival in Chicago's Grant Park.] I liked seeing all the people, all the masses; you see all kinds of people passing by, and you realize how average you are. It was affirming that, "OK, I just blend in—I'm not the odd nail that needs to be hammered down." A lot of times I've felt like an "other"—the Asian as in, unrecognized, kind of thing. Minority is either "black" or "Hispanic." I don't know why they don't recognize us. Maybe we don't pose such a threat; maybe people just take it in stride, accept us.

For a while a big thing was Asian newscasters, and I'd be like, "You can be a journalist. [feigns cheerleading] *Yeah, Remy, you'll be the next Connie Chung. Yeah, Remy! You can be just like Anna Quindlan. Yeah, yeah, Remy!"* It's like, "No . . . maybe *not*, Remy." I'm really lazy, and I'm a *big* procrastinator. I should get over those things—I probably won't. There's a low self-esteem, low self-confidence thing that I'd like to change, but that's not easy, and it'll probably stay with me the rest of my life . . . [laughs]

Another thing I have a hard time with is keeping secrets. *Big time!*

[laughs] There was some bad stuff that went down, like two weeks ago. It happened over a long time period, but I'll compact it. [shame-faced] This friend of mine, Paul, told me in confidence that he was gay. He couldn't say it, he had to, like, write it down. He was so hesitant: he'd write it down, crumple it up, scratch it out . . . Finally I had it on a piece of paper, and then he made me tear it up. I hadn't guessed, so it was like, "*Not another one!*" He was a casual friend—we just saw each other in the hallways and stuff. I don't know why he told me: I'm like, "Why are you telling *me*, Paul?" I didn't say it, but I was like, "Do you understand what you're doing to me?" [laughs] 'Cause now I'm completely worried and concerned about this poor guy.

I'm like, "Oh yeah, OK. Are you just gonna tell me, or are you gonna tell everybody else?" He was like, "*No.*" And I'm like, [gulps] "Great . . . " He told me that for the longest time he'd had a crush on his best friend, Larry. My friend Lisa is good friends with Larry, so I told her—with, like, good intentions—hoping she could figure out what's going on with Larry. Then Lisa told me all this stuff about how Larry had a dream about Paul coming onto him, and how Larry had been getting love letters for about two months . . . Later, Paul said he didn't write the letters. Oh, this sounds so sixth grade! But Lisa said to Larry, "They're probably from Paul." He was like, "*Who told you? who told you?*" And she's like, "Well . . . Remy did." [grimaces] And then Larry went and told Paul. "*You told Remy, and you don't expect Lisa not to know?*" and blah blah blah.

So I outed him without his permission. It was like, "Oh no—*I'm going to Hell, I'm going to Hell!*" I had to go to school the next day and see Paul—we're in the same gym class. It was, like, *so* bad. He looked at me, and I was like, "Don't look at me like that, Paul—I'm *so* sorry." He looked disappointed, hurt—he wasn't too angry. I think he knows me better than to think . . . He was like, "I can't help but not be angry at you."

I have a journal in my knapsack. [She fishes around in her bag and pulls out a spiral notebook.] I showed Paul the journal entry because I couldn't say anything—I couldn't look him in the eye . . . [She sighs and reads from her journal.] *What compelled me to tell Lisa, I do not even know. I actually meant it in good intentions: I wanted her to probe Larry to see if Paul had a chance. I'm such a fool, such a bad friend. This whole thing stigmatizes my soul forever. No more trust from anyone, let alone Paul. His trust in me was so rare and brave. I killed it. Dammit, I'm going to Hell—the deepest, lowest, most roasting-hot pit of Hell there is. Was it even your place to help Paul out without fully understanding him and his feelings? You ran blindly with your new piece of information, and look who it hurt. Oh, Remy, you're going to Hell: for betraying a friend, for abusing trust, and for just plain not having any self-restraint.*

Now he's able to joke about it and stuff. [She hides her face in her hands.] But it still weighs heavy with me—that was a *really* low thing for me to do . . . It's just an effort to tell a story, I think. Not really a story, but to let people know what's going on. But there was no reason for me to do it—I've just got a big mouth. I can't help it.

We Are Family

Jian Bari

Manhattan, New York

J*ian has nearly waist-length black hair, which she absent-mindedly winds and tucks up with a pencil. She has a nose ring—the subject of parental dispute for a brief period—and is gracious, self-possessed, and very much a young woman. She is seventeen. Asked about her family she answers, "I guess I'm an only child. It's a long family story." And it is. I offer a partial summary: Jian's Chinese mother married Joe Bari, an African-American/Italian man, and they were divorced when Jian was two. Jian's mother had a close friend, Susie, who is Japanese-American, and has a son named Taro. Susie and Taro's father split up, and Taro later was adopted by Susie's husband Alan. After Susie and Alan divorced, Susie began living with a man named Rick. When Jian was almost three, her mother started living with Alan. Susie and Rick and Taro were and are very much a part of their lives.*

I've called Alan dad since I was little—he's my father. And Taro considers him his father, so I consider Taro my brother. Taro's also crazy about Rick—he's part of the family too. Rick and Susie, they're not married; neither are my parents. They're planning on getting married, but they haven't for, like, fifteen years. [laughs]

I haven't seen my biological father since right after the divorce. I never saw his picture until a year ago. I think my mom has bad leftover stuff from their marriage, and she didn't want me to meet him. She was the one who cut off the contact—I haven't seen that side of the family since I was two. I never had any bitterness toward him, because I had a father.

I guess I was curious, but I never had the desire, the need to meet him. She'd be like, "He does call and ask about you, and he would like to meet you—but he's not gonna force himself into the situation because he doesn't want to mess up what you already have." I'd be like, "Cool, fine. I don't need to see him right now." But now I want to see him . . . I guess for a lot of reasons—if he were to die, I'd feel really bad. And I think it's important that I see him. I think my mother got scared and didn't want to associate with him, and she didn't think about how it would affect me. It hasn't affected me adversely, really, but it's something she should have thought about—she should've made sure the connection was there . . . [softly, gently] I think it was a mistake, but I'm not angry.

I just found out last year that I have a lot of siblings, and I want to meet them—I want to find out what they look like. I have an older half-brother who's all black, because my father married a black woman; and then my mother, a Chinese woman; and then a Puerto Rican woman recently, and she has two kids. [happily] So I have three brothers and sisters that I never knew about, that are all blood. I always wanted a little brother or sister, so I really want a connection with them. I want to meet *them* more, basically, than I want to meet him.

So, all these influences—Chinese, black, Japanese, Jewish. My dad's aunt taught me about Jewish religious things, and would celebrate Hanukkah with me. My Chinese grandmother is Presbyterian. My mom's Christian, and lately she's been like, "Oh, I feel bad I never sent you to Sunday school or church," and I'm like, "*Don't.*" 'Cause I don't want that: I don't want to be Presbyterian; I'm not sure I want to be Christian. I believe in God, but I think Christianity has been used in very oppressive ways.

One of my friends doesn't approve of organized religion; she goes to church to please her family, and I respect that completely. She's African Methodist and believes in God, but she doesn't believe in the Christian stories. My other friend is Catholic, she believes in it a hundred percent, but she's for using birth control, she's prochoice. She's Hispanic, and she goes to a different kind of Catholic church—they speak French, Spanish, and English. It's Catholic, but it's not the hier-archical thing that a lot of white Catholics experience.

When I was reading about Islam, I liked that the most. But the problem I have is the views towards women in the Middle East. Black Muslims can be a little . . . rowdy. [small laugh] But Islam—I think of Malcolm X, when he went to Mecca, and there were people from all over the world who were Muslim. But I also want to study Buddhism, and Hinduism, and Confucius.

When I fill out forms, I put black and Chinese—I check both. I think identity has so much to do with how you're raised, who you're raised by. So I identify strongly with Asian-Americans and Chinese. But I'm black, too, the color of my skin. When you see me on the street you can't deny I'm something—I have black in me. I think the second most important factor in identity is society, the way people perceive you when you walk down the street. I know a girl with blond hair and blue eyes, and she's like, "People look at me like I'm white, but I'm not a hundred percent white—my father's black." And the one-drop rule: you look a little black, you're black, automatically. So it's how people treat you, and then you internalize it. And, I mean, it's not a bad thing, but it's a real thing—that's just the way it is.

I identify myself as black, and Chinese, and American. I hate American, but in fact I *am* American, and nobody can deny that they're American if they were raised here. But America is *so* fucked up and ridiculous—the power structure, values . . . Our history is *so* sordid. I don't like things like the treatment of Native Americans in this country from the start to the present day, slavery, Japanese-American internment, involvement in the Korean War, Vietnamese War, Persian Gulf War . . . Our founding fathers, with the exception of George Washington, who was an alright guy—he freed all his slaves. I don't like Thomas Jefferson; I don't respect him, because of slavery. The power structures were white, elite men. I guess the good thing about the Constitution is that it can be amended and changed. And if there were more people of color in positions to do that, change could occur.

I know they're gonna do away with affirmative action, and it makes me *sick*. They want to get rid of Social Security, welfare, AFDC, everything. In New York City they're getting rid of financial aid pro-grams, work-study in colleges, and tuition's gonna go up like *three thousand dollars.* I think it's ridiculous! Who's gonna benefit? I hate Republicans! I *hate* Republicans! *I hate Republicans.* They want to get rid of *everything.*

There are too many white men in power . . . [sadly] And I don't think it's gonna change, because our society is structured on economics—there's *always* gonna be a glass ceiling—and why would you let all that power go, once you have it? I'm not encouraged . . . I don't know what I want to do with my life, but I have always thought about government. It's like . . . [She tsks and sighs.] I *have to* change it—political, social, I want to change *something.* I have to.

The power structure, economics, the debt—we're *always* gonna be capitalists . . . [sighs] I don't have another alternative—not communism, not socialism. I don't know—maybe socialism. . . I think a lot of things in our country are socialist—Social Security, welfare—and we just don't use that *label.* We get a lot of our roots not only from democracy, but from socialism, without realizing it. And that's fine; and to a certain extent it works—not as well as it *should*—but instead of looking for a way to make it work better, they look for a way to get rid of it.

In my high school there's one full-time teacher of color, and he's Asian-American; everybody else is white. We have an exclusive student of color organization, which causes problems every year: we can never put in the mission statement that it's exclusive, because that would be racist, blah blah blah, and "the school doesn't discriminate." But, by word of mouth, it's exclusive: only for students of color.

There's one Asian-American student, and me—one and a half! [laughs]The graduating class graduated two black boys. I mean kids got kicked out, academic probation, but the point is they couldn't exist in the structure, and there was no support system created by the school to support them. It's *just* about gaining social skills. You come from a public school, maybe, and you don't know how to react, interact with teachers and white students; you don't know how to keep up with the work—and it's not because you're not as *smart.* It's just a whole different place. I think that lack of support system shows that they weren't serious about the retention of students of color. So the students had to create their own support system, which is our organization.

I call myself a "girl" and a "woman," not a "teenager." Or "youth"

—I like that. *Teenager* has so many weird connotations, good *and* bad. Like "teenagers are rowdy, teenagers are immature." The problem I have is the automatic assumption that adults are always more mature than teenagers; that teenagers are in this constant state of hormones, whatever. They want to try new things, experience this, that, the other thing, but adults *don't* go through that. Yes, teenagers are still growing up, but adults are *still* doing that too. When you say "teenagers," there's the automatic assumption that adults are already grown up, and comfortable with themselves and who they are, which is not necessarily the case. I think you never stop growing up, and having crazy feelings. And sometimes, as an adult, you can't express them— and that's worse, 'cause you have no outlet—'cause you're supposed to have it together.

I'm a good kid; I don't do drugs and I hate alcohol. My friends are conscious about safe sex. We were in AIDS Awareness for a long time. We all practice safe sex. [laughs] I'm a virgin—what am I talking about?! And my friends are virgins too. But, I mean, the guys I know practice safe sex. But I do have friends who know, know, know that pulling out does not work—but they do it. They get caught up in the moment, don't use condoms . . . and it's incredibly scary.

I don't mind letting my parents know where I am, and I don't rebel. And it's not because they say *no,* I say *yes;* or they say *yes,* I say *no.* I never understood that—the more your parents say no, the more you want to do it? When they say no, I don't do it most of the time. I don't need to rebel, because if I really want to do something they usually let me do it. They'll really listen to me. [grinning] Even though I claim they don't. . .

I have three best friends. One is a Puerto Rican-American, Iris; Caprice is black, but her great-grandmother was white Panamanian; and I have a white friend, Jenny. I don't think I ever had a problem with being black and Chinese. I never wanted to be white—I never wanted to be white. At times I would've wanted to look more Asian, because when you look at me you can't really tell. I just started spelling Jane J-I-A-N. It was a declarative statement: like, "I'm Chinese, the part you can't see." It's a way to claim it.

I don't know how I feel about interracial marriages. If you're in love, fine, but I don't know about what it does to communities. [sighs]

Asian-Americans have one of the toughest times. They feel a lot of pressure to assimilate, but their family doesn't want them to assimilate fully: they want them to do well but retain the cultural thing. What they retain is this anonymity and quietness, and they can't speak up, they don't speak out, and they don't speak *against*. They get immersed in what's American. They assimilate so integrally into this society—they all want to succeed, they all want cars. They deny their culture, they deny where they come from, because it's different and it's not American. And most of them reach a certain economic level where all their friends are white, and that's all they know, and they act white.

Assimilation hurts the community. I was just speaking to somebody and they said it perfectly: in any marriage, whether it's monoracial or biracial, you're gonna sacrifice something of yourself to be with that other person, and I don't think it's worth the sacrifice when you're giving up your culture, or part of your culture.

I look at black women, and there are no black men out there— they're all in jail or killing each other. If I see black men with white women I wonder, "Are they really together for the right reasons?" I mean, I think it's not a coincidence that all these black men . . . Like, look at black basketball players: half of them have white wives, and the others, their wives are light-skinned, silky hair. Maybe they look at white women as the pinnacle of success, the trophy. And it's not a coincidence—it's too big a phenomena. I'm thinking that maybe it's economic: once they get that economic status, all they see is white women. Who they meet is, like, the trophy—and white is right, white is better. I think you sacrifice so much in interracial marriages—I don't like that.

I don't like white men. They scare me because I think they look at women of color—OK, Asian-American women—as exotic. And mixed women get a lot of shit like, "You're *exotic.*" And it's like, [angry] *I'm not a delicacy!* I'm not to be *eaten*, I'm not an *ornamentation for your home*—I'm not *exotic*. I'm just *me*. White men look at black women as sexual, like, earthy things, as objects, and it's disrespectful. I mean, I've met totally *down* white people, but that's not the point. On the whole, white older men are totally disrespectful, and there's a history with white men and black women. So I don't trust them.

I look at Jewish people differently. [laughs] I don't think of Jewish people as white. Jewish people and black people, they have a lot in common, whether they realize it or not. [laughs] The treatment by the larger society, the exclusion, the ghettos. They've achieved a certain level of success in this society, but historically they really are no more welcome here than the rest of us. Civil rights struggles—violence, lynching. . . And large scale, internationally, the Arabs in Palestine; and in Europe, World War II—Germany, France, Russia . . . *at* one point, they *all* hated Jews.

I guess I want to get married. [laughs] I want to marry a man of color: Asian-American, black, Hispanic. I don't have any Hispanic in me, so I'm thinking, you know, my kid could end up speaking Spanish with a Chinese grandmother. [laughs] What is family to me? [slowly, thoughtfully] Family is just people who you feel a filial bond with that transcends blood. Family is anybody who's associated, who you grew up with, who's always been around, and they know you. Family is the people you go to, or the people you can call anytime. Family is—family is the *people,* just the people. Your people.

Vincent Serrano

New Bedford, Massachusetts

I

t is the summer of 1994, and the local fishing industry has just crashed. There's of talk of a replacement industry—gambling casinos. Vincent is a husky young man, with dark eyes, dark hair, and a thick Boston accent. He speaks slowly, and evenly. He is seventeen.

New Bedford—there's nothing to do now. There's no jobs, it's dull. There's a lot of people on welfare, and people are not educated. When the casino comes, there'll be no excuses that we don't have no jobs— it should make a lot of jobs. My neighborhood is quiet. There's not too many teenagers around here, so that's why it's quiet. There's nuthin to do. If you want to do something you gotta walk . . . like, South End, North End. There's a lot of teenagers around there, outside, playing basketball. There's movies that teenagers go to; they can go to the mall.

I'm Puerto Rican. I live here with my aunt, Marguerite, and my uncle, Joseph. My mom is in Puerto Rico. She left me when I was young. I have never seen her face to face, or pictures. I just know her name: Inez something. My uncle is her brother.

My father . . . The last time I seen him was on Mother's Day—he came down out of the blue, and he left out of the blue. He came with his father, and stayed three days, or two, and then they left. I never saw him again. That was seven years ago. I know he's in New York, but I don't know where—I don't hear from him. He never sent me a postcard or a birthday card. That's sad. But, hey, that's life, I guess . . . I'm not mad. He's probably having a lot of problems. And my mother, I just know that she lives in Puerto Rico, but I never seen her in my life.

I heard different stories why she left, but most likely it's because she was young—she had me when she was fifteen or sixteen. So that kind of age, it's hard to raise a kid. Plus she had two, me and my sister—she's a year younger. My father kept leaving out of the house, and she was alone with us children. She was still at the teenager age, you know, outside, having fun. She made a mistake and she couldn't handle it, so from there she just left.

My grandmother took me for a while, but she was sick; and then my other uncle took me. I kept going back and forth, 'cause *she* wanted me, *he* wanted me . . . Finally she ended up dying, and I ended up staying with my other uncle, in Florida. He died, so I came over here. Marguerite has three daughters: twenty-five, twenty-three, and twenty-one—and they all have kids. [laughs]

My sister lives off the projects with her foster parents. She's doing good: she's living nice, she's happy. She was with me until what happened—the problem—and then she ended up leaving. It was because she stole some makeup from one of Marguerite's daughters, and she didn't admit that she did it; she started saying a lot of lies. I was living with my other aunt at that time, just for the summer. My sister called the DFS [Department of Family Services] to tell them to get her out of here. And then they started making a big problem out of it, and they put her in a foster home. She lives with my aunt's best friend, Ruby. I'm always going over there; she doesn't come here.

I used to steal, and I got in *trouble.* I was scared. I was real young, like twelve, thirteen; I was living in a foster home, with my foster mother, Terry. I went to a store in a mall with my friend, and I seen this hat, and I took it. It was an L.A. Lakers hat. It had the alarm underneath, on the inside of the hat. I put it in my pants and my pants was thick, and when I went by the door there was no alarm. We took off and slipped into the movies. My friend had stolen a knife from the same store, and he was telling me to get one too. So I went back, and I had my hat on. It had the ticket on, hanging—'cause at that time it was in style, having the ticket hanging, with the name of the brand or whatever. I went in and the alarm went off.

I thought I was going to *jail* that time. The store manager said, "If you participate with me, don't give me no hassles, I won't call the police." I said, "OK." I just gave him the address, where I lived, and how old I was—that's all, just that. And then Terry came and got me. [He shakes his head.] I was *scared* that day. I don't know why I did it—if I wanted to be cool or what. No reason, to tell you the truth—I just did it. Terry yelled at me, she didn't really discipline me. I was just real scared.

My sister was at that foster home with me. We were together all the time. She ran away 'cause they weren't treating her nice. There were a lot of older guys there, Terry's sons, and they were abusing my sister, like sexual harassment. I didn't know; she didn't tell me they were bothering her—she just took off on her own self, and then I found out that she was here. I was mad, because she didn't tell me—because I would have ran away with her too. She's my only sister that I know of. Girls, they're sensitive, they're not as tough as a guy: a guy can live off of the street, but a girl can't.

When I was smaller I used to abuse her myself—hitting. One time I went really overboard. I was ten, nine, but I was really big, the same as now. We were arguing for I don't know what reason, and there was a chain like this—[He motions toward chain strung across front yard.] I got mad and I pushed her, and she flipped over the chain, and then I started yelling at her and kicking her. My aunt came by in a blue car, and she seen me. I picked my sister up: "Tina, don't tell on me! *Shut up*—don't tell on me." But she was crying, and she told on me, and then Marguerite hit me with a belt. Since that day I started cooling down my temper. I started learning a little bit that hitting's not nice—especially a girl. I didn't want to hit her anymore, I felt sorry. I just like got out of the forest and looked at what I was doing. You know how when you're in the forest, you don't know what you're doing—other people know—but when you get out, then you can see everything? So that's what I did. And then since that day I've always treated her . . . a little nice. [laughs]

She's in a regular high school, and I'm at a vocational school. See, I'm not a smart kid: I have a lot of problems, like learning disability. They say that I'm slow, but I think I'm not. I'm in Special Needs right now. I got to work hard if I'm gonna go to college. I know how to read, but I don't know too good a pronunciation. There's some big words that I get stuck on. I can learn it, I *know* I can learn. [emotionally] I *know* I'm not slow! It bothers me that they say that, but it makes me *sad*, more. I gotta live with it though . . . [He slowly presses an index finger against the bridge of his nose, first one side, then the other, as though pressing back tears.]

When I was small I used to like to play around—I *never* concentrated. I was always hyper, I was always moving, didn't listen. And that's what messed me up, that was my problem. At that time, to tell you the truth, all I was thinking about was making love, kissing. That's all I used to go to school for, to bother the girls . . . I'm suffering now, 'cause I gotta learn more.

I was a little scrawny when I was small—I was like *this*. [He holds up his index finger as if it were a little person.] After school I always used to run home, cause I used to get beat up all the time. I guess they didn't like me. There was no reason, actually, 'cause I didn't do nuthin to them. Some kids don't like you so they want to do something to you. I used to run all the time—all the time. Now I'm not afraid, and when somebody bothers me and I can't stand it anymore, I don't run away. If they start throwing hands on me, I throw hands on back. If they want to hit me, I hit them back.

The hoods, they mostly dress up in pants a little big off their size, you know—*big*. They have it down to their butt cheeks. [laughs] But with a belt so it won't hang *all* the way down! They talk English, but their words are different than the regular English: like instead of saying "money" they say "loot," they say "dope," they say, "Whass up?" They give you "dap"—it's like giving five. I dress up like they do, but it's just that my thoughts are very different than them. Mine are about life, theirs are about getting high and stupid stuff—who can they get in bed, or how many girls they can get before they graduate.

They go to school, but the ones that are hanging around outside all day on the corner, or who dress up hoody, mostly they go to school just for two things: see how many girls are there and how fine they are, and to show off their equipment—their gear, clothes. They don't really care about studying; they just want to live large, live nice, make fast money. What's weird is, the kids that are into being hoods and all that are *smart*. They ain't smart in education, like in school—reading and all that; they're not smart, what they're doing—quitting school and hanging out. That's not being smart. But they *are* smart.

Some of them are nice people, but sometimes they like getting high, getting drunk, getting buzzed up. I don't mess around with that. I used to try, but I didn't like it. Plus, it's not that really smart for me to be smoking weed, 'cause that messes up your memory. I don't want to waste my brain. When I get older I probably will drink, but I won't abuse it. Some kids, they want to get drunk. They think that's being a man.

There are gangs in New Bedford. I almost went into one. I was fourteen—a lot of things happened in them ages. I used to hang around the basketball court on this one street. That's all they do is drugs and play basketball. They were making this new gang, and this kid asked me if I wanted to join, and I said OK. What I had to wear was a black jean, and a boot, and then a sweatshirt with a hood that's blue. I already had all that. The leader said, "If someone looks at you hard, you jump 'em." And I said, "OK . . . " He told me the things I had to do if I joined—it wasn't like I had to fight anybody, you know—like you got to fight somebody to get in, and then fight back out. He asked me if I'm afraid to shoot anybody. I said, "No, I'm not, but out of the blue, to just shoot them, that I will not do." He said, "No, I mean if somebody has a beef with you and wants to shoot—you won't be afraid?" I said, "Oh no, not that way." Then I had to carry a gun too; it was a nine millimeter, that's the gun I had to use they said. I told my cousin, and she said, "I don't want to hear it. No Vincent, I don't want to hear it."

I changed my mind; I didn't do it. Sometimes I get frustrated with my learning thing, and I get mad 'cause of that problem that I have—and I think *that's* my only way to get money. But I'm not thinking like that now. When I was fourteen, fifteen, I wanted to be a regular cop—then I wanted to be a bodyguard. After that I was thinking of going into the marines; and then I wanted to be a state trooper. I'm majoring in automotive mechanics, but that's not my thing—it's good as a hobby, just to know, but it's not my career thing. Now I want to be an actor. I was just in my first play in my whole life. I liked it, because I felt it's not me, I'm trying to be like somebody else, trying to be that person. And when you hear people clapping, it feels good, and you're keeping them entertained and making them happy. The only scary part was just to not mess up. I need to practice a whole lot, though. When I graduate I'm going to go to the community college and take courses. I think I have a chance of becoming an actor—I just gotta study harder.

I like the way I think, but there are some other things I'd like to change. My weight. [grins] I'd like to be nice and thin. So change my weight, read a little more better—a *lot* better. Since I want to be an actor, it's got to be perfect. And change my voice, cause I don't like it, it sounds shitty: like Sylvester Stallone, like a retarded person. I'd like to sound like a lawyer, an educated person—a nice voice.

My uncle's the one that I'm really close to. He gives me discipline, and tells me about school, education: "Don't drop out, don't do foolish stuff." He's kind of making sure I don't fall, and if I do he just gives me a little nice boost. If I mess up he tells me the consequences, and how I'm going to be paying for it in the future. Like if I drop out of school, I'm not going to be having a good job, I'm always going to be in a factory; I'm gonna be making minimum wage, and I'm not gonna live nice. These days, being a garbage man you got to have a diploma!

Him and my aunt, they're really nice people. I'm doing good with them, I just gotta do *better*. One time I just like got mad, and I told them a lot of things that I didn't like about this house. I said, "I think I would probably live better if . . . " 'Cause I'm thinking about my reading, I'm putting all that in my mind—and I said to myself, "I probably would have done better if I was living with my family. Maybe I would have known how to read better." My uncle said something like, "God sees a future, and he looks at the future, and if he sees that you're not going to do well over there, he will take you out of there and put you in another way of living."

Like, for example, if I'm still living with my parents I probably would have been selling drugs or whatever—I probably would have been dead by now. I probably would have dropped out of school. You never know . . . So I thought of what my uncle said: God probably took me out of there and put me here. And that helped. I couldn't argue with that, because it was true what he said: my father was doing drugs. I probably would have been lost by now.

One time I went to my sister's house. They were talking about my mother. Ruby's husband asked me this question: "What would you do if your mother came and visited?" First I said, "We'll talk." He said, "Would you talk about what happened, why she left you?" I said, "Yeah, I would. But I wouldn't do that right away—she could tell me that later on." There could probably be a reason—she didn't have no other choice but doing what she did.

I couldn't get really mad at her. I could forgive her because if I put myself in that position, I probably would have done the same thing. See, I put myself in their shoes, their way, how they feel: if I was in this position, what would I do? So first I'd ask what she did, and then I'd probably tell her it was a mistake what she did, she shouldn't have done this, but hey—it's already passed, and I'm just glad that she's here. I would hug her, I would kiss her, I'd be happy. My sister started saying, "No, I would be *mad* at her, I'd be *yelling* at her!" [shrugs] I can't do it. That's her. [fondly] That's her way of expressing that she loves her.

I'm planning to have kids, a family. I want that big time. It's not nice to live alone. I want to raise my kids the right way: give them a lot of love and show them that they're not alone. If they have a problem, they can talk to me. And I will discipline—I will hit 'em for a really, really good reason. Not a stupid reason. I'd help him with his homework, I'd go everywhere, see how he's doing in school, make sure he's not falling apart. I'd be really with him all the time.

I think I can do whatever I want to do, and right now it's acting. I'd like to know basic of everything, like computer, because in these days you *gotta* know computer. After I graduate from college and I become an actor—when I have my own house, when I'm settled—then I'd like to go to another college and take some law, learn something about the government. I'd like to know about psychology, to help people. You don't come here just to live, to work, and have kids and that's all. You gotta do more than that—you gotta do *something* before you die. That's what I think.

Megan Riley

Foxboro, Massachusetts

W*e talk at a picnic table in a large yard, not far from a scenic and very populated duck pond. Megan appears athletic, with a warm open manner. It is the end of her first summer after high school, and she is more than ready to go to college. She is seventeen.*

I would definitely have to rate my teenage years as pretty boring. This is the boringest town. It's *so* boring. I've only done your basic teenage things—I haven't rebelled or anything—so . . . [shyly] there's not really anything to tell.

My mom died when I was four. I remember: one day here, one day there, or something reminds me of her. But I don't know if it's just 'cause I've heard a bunch of stories, or if I really *remember.* She died in her sleep. It was early on the morning after Thanksgiving. She just didn't wake up. She had some heart condition—and I have it. It's nothing serious, except that if you get bacteria, an infection, you're susceptible to it easier, and it can kill you. My brother Jim was eight, and Danny was nine at the time, so they remember more than I do. My sister Kathy was too young, three months. I remember having nightmares about my mom—I'd wake up screaming. I remember my dad coming in. I remember some Christmas when my sister was in a crib and me and my brothers snuck down, and my mother wasn't there. Just one or two things I remember.

I ask to hear a story about her every now and then, because my dad tells stories about everything. *Anything*—he's lived it and got three stories to tell you. [She laughs, shaking her head fondly.] The same stories. I'm like, "Dad, we *know!*" Every now and then he'll be like, "Oh, I remember once me and your mom . . . " It's kind of weird, 'cause I don't really know her. Sometimes my grandmother's like, "You remind me a lot of your mother"; or she'll me a story. I hate getting my picture taken, and there's all these pictures of my mom where she's bawling because they were taking her picture. It's so weird, but it's kind of neat.

I don't remember Marge and my father's wedding at all, but I remember in second grade when I found out they were getting married. My parents were friends with Marge and her first husband and their three kids, so we knew them. She used to take care of us. It was kind of weird when they all moved in. I got booted out of my room! [laughs] The rooms got switched around 'cause they had to, I don't know, re-figure. I just remember that once I had a big room, and I got moved into the biggest room—except I had to *share* it with Beth and Kathy . . . [laughs]

My stepsister Beth is seventeen too, but we're in different grades. We get along, but if we didn't live together—our families were separate—I don't think we'd hang out together. I have friends in her grade and she has some in mine, and they're *totally* different. It's kind of stupid, but in my school there's people who do sports, people who are in the band kind of thing—and I'm people who do sports, she's people who are in the band. We're *really* different. Like if we go out, you can almost guarantee we will *not* be doing the same thing. [laughs]

Today I had to drop Beth off at color guard. I've done sports all four years, and it just seems weird 'cause I was thinking, "Right now I should be at captain's practice for cross country." I did cross country all four years, I did basketball my first two years, and did winter track the second two. I was captain of all three. I feel a little nostalgic, already . . . [laughs] and I haven't even been out long. I liked high school; it was fun.

My junior and senior year I would go to school, go to practice, and then I'd usually have to go to work as a waitress. [She cringes.] It's horrible. I liked it in the beginning, because it was more money than I'd make anywhere else—but I *hate* rude people. I hate it when people are snobs. I'd never been treated that way myself. It just makes me so mad: they treat you like you're *dirt.* And I'm like, "Someday I'm gonna be smarter than you, and I'm gonna make more money, and I'm gonna come back and *stomp all over you!*" [laughs]

I don't know what I'm going to major in at college. I'm the person that always wanted to be four different things. One day I'd be like, "I'm going to be a hairdresser," and then, "I want to be a doctor." I can't make decisions—I'm kind of flaky that way. Sometimes I get in moods where I just don't feel like doing *anything.* I don't feel like going out, because I don't feel like getting up, getting dressed, making plans; but I don't feel like sitting home either. I just get antsy, and like, "I'm in a weird mood," and I whine about it. [laughs] I had the biggest problem picking a college. I'm like, *forget* the major—I'm having enough problems picking a *school.*

I definitely want a career; I don't know in what yet. Probably business, just 'cause math is easy for me. I kind of want a family, but I can't picture myself as being a housewife. I don't think there's anything wrong with that, but it's totally not me. Plus, I'm not going to college to be a *housewife.* My family makes fun of me: "Oh, who's gonna do all the cleaning? Are you gonna marry a husband who's going to stay home with the kids?" I'm like, "I don't really care who stays home with the kids at this point, but *I'm* not going to school four years and then stay home 'cause my husband wants to work. I don't think so . . .

I hope I'll be married, but at this point I don't know. If my dating life is going anywhere *near* like it's going now, it's not gonna happen. I'm just not into the committment thing, I guess. My longest thing was three months, and I was like, "*Whoa!* I can't do this anymore." I have a lot more guy friends that are pals than people I date. Guys that I went to school with, I'm like, "I can't date them—I've known them forever." One of my friends, we get along so good—we can talk about *anything.* People ask me about him: they'll be like, "He's *so* cute." I'm like, [look of surprise] "He's Dave." He says, "Thanks a lot." And I say, "I'm sorry, you're just really not a guy to me." [laughs] My town, it's like everybody knows *everything,* but they don't really—they make things up. So in school things were going around like, "They must be dating 'cause they're hanging out." And we're, "Well, actually we're just friends." I can't wait to get away from where everybody knows everybody else's business.

I have two, three best friends. I'm with them almost all the time. We can just do nothing, hang out, and talk forever. Every now and then people end up having parties, which I'm not really allowed to go to, but . . . [She giggles, looking over her shoulder at the house.] That's another thing that's really different between me and Beth. One day I was talking to her about a party and she said, "You know, I've never been to a party." And I was like, *"Really?!"* I'd never thought about it. Kathy is more like me—outgoing. Danny was really outgoing and really smart, and athletic, and a lot of people liked him. And Jim was really good at track, and had friends. I don't know how outgoing I really am. Compared to Beth, I see that I am.

One thing that was a downfall being the same age was that they'd compare us: "Why can she do this? Why does she do this?" They do that now about our friends, but not as much about anything else. Our parents seem to think that my friends are these *hellions* or something. If my friends do normal teenage things, they're like, "Oh my God! *Beth's* friends don't do that." They seem to think that every single one of my friends drink. I'm not going to lie and be like, "No, none of my friends drink," because that's ridiculous—half of our high school drinks. I *am* friends with people who drink, but not *all* my friends drink. They pass judgment on people; and half the friends that they think are the little Miss Don't-do-anything-wrong, are smart, and they're in this club and that club . . . but you've never been out with them on a Friday night! [laughs]

I don't drink all the time, but I have every now and then. One time I told Beth, "You know what? The stupidest thing is that the main reason why I even drank was because all week long they've been going off about how my friends do nothing but drink, and I was *so* sick of it." I was like, *"Fine,* if that's what they think, I might as well just do it." I used to never do anything wrong, *ever,* and they never trusted me—and I didn't understand. I don't know how crazy they think I am. I'm like, *"Really,* you overestimate me. [laughs] I don't have *that* much fun."

One of my other friends found marijuana in her mother's house, and she *flipped.* She was like, "I wouldn't even do that—how could she? This is my *mother.*" So, from then on, it wasn't like it was her mother: they're like friends, not mother-daughter. But I mean, when you're sixteen years old you need someone. Her mother once packed up and left the country with a boyfriend, and she was shipped off to relatives: her mother was like, "Well, why can't you deal with this?" She's like, "I'm in junior high school! You're supposed to share my *prom* with me!" She never had a mother who acted like a parent.

I can't say I'd want *that*—because I saw what she went through— but it's a little *too* strict here. Half the time I don't think they know me at all: they know the outside that everyone else knows. They can tell their friends, "She's in the National Honor Society, and she's captain of this sport, and she got into these colleges"—but they don't know the inside me.

I confide in Beth some. Sometimes we'll lay it on the line. We've shared a room forever, and now it's just me and her, so we'll come home at night and start telling stuff. "What'd you do?" And then we'll both be horrified, like *"No way!"* And then we won't say anything for a while. And then every now and then—and I know she does it too— we'll tell each other half, get the reaction. I'm always curious about what the older ones did when they were my age. I think it's just because what I do is so different from Beth. I'm like, "Am I really off on this one?" I just want to make sure.

Our parents are *really* strict. They're *so* paranoid about stuff. Every now and then they'll be normal, and you'll be like, *"Whoa."* They're usually like, [panicked] "Where are you going? What time are you going to be home?" Instead they'll be like, "You're going out tonight? OK, bye"—so you double-take. I get so puzzled. Then I get used to it, and then all of a sudden they're like, [interrogating] "Where are you going? What time will you be home?" [laughs] And I'm like, "What happened here?!"

Sex . . . The basic communication is, [laughs] "Don't have any or we'll kill ya"—in so many words. Here's another thing that was just like, "You've got to be *kidding* me." We were not allowed to date until we were sixteen. But, see, with me, by the time I was sixteen I was a *junior.* I think the basis for the sixteen-year-old rule is 'cause when Marge was younger she got pregnant in high school, and it's always, "We don't want that to happen."

It wasn't even just dating one on one—it was like you can't go out with people if there's guys there, you can't go to a coed party, you can't do *anything* with guys—even just your guy *friends*. It's probably going to be harder for Kathy, 'cause she's a tomboy. When I was Kathy's age I was like her. I was into sports, so I hung out with guys. So it was weird: "Why can't you come to my pool party?" "Well, 'cause you're a *guy.*" I could be friends with them all school year long, and then summer came and I couldn't talk to them again until September. We go to school with them every day: it's ridiculous to think that we're not friends with them, or that we don't like them. I guess there should be a certain age where you can date—I think sixteen was a little extreme. But I think there's a difference between going on a date and hanging out.

A couple of weeks ago, when I wanted to go out of town with some friends, we had this *big* fight. I got a lot of things out in the open. I was like, "If this was Jim . . . " And my father said, "*Fine, maybe it is unfair, but girls can get hurt.*" And I'm like, "Oh, *please!*" They were like, "*Well, what are we supposed to do about it?*" I said, "I don't know. It's late for a lot of stuff you could have done, but you have to ease up."

For them it was, "You can't go away with your friends," but for me it was, "You have to *let go* and let me live my own life." My father was like, "When you go to college, I have to let you go." I'm like, "What do you mean you *have to?* It's a given: I'm going to school." He said, "See, I don't want to." I'm like, "I'm going to be eighteen years old, you have to get a grip on reality." I never thought how he was thinking: "I *have* to let her go, I don't have a choice." But that's exactly how he felt.

Daniel Nagorian

Manhattan, New York

We meet at the Hetrick Martin
Institute, where Daniel attends
*the Harvey Milk School, an alternative high school for gay, lesbian,
bisexual, and transgender youth. He is large-boned, with a hint of
baby fat still, and very pale and blond. Though his lineage is Puerto
Rican, Hungarian, and Greek, you might think he was Polish. He
is seventeen.*

I come from a family of—well, there's gonna be nine children now.
There's my parents and my aunt, so that's twelve of us in one house.
I'm the oldest. My sister's sixteen, then we got another one that's
gonna be fourteen. I have a brother that's eleven, twin brothers that
are ten; I have another one that's eight, one that's eleven months, and
the other one's five. My mother's a foster parent. She adopted five of
us, and over the summer she took three more. I've been with her for
six years, since I was eleven. I call her mom.

I don't know how old I was when my real parents separated . . .
[sighs] Maybe four or five, something like that. I keep in contact with
my biological father, 'cause he doesn't live far from me—in New
Jersey. My mom moved to Florida, but I don't know if she's still living
there. I haven't heard from her in, like, three or four years . . . [sadly]
But eventually, one day, I'm gonna look for her. She told me I had a
sister, but I never met her, and I don't know where she is. I'm trying to
look for her, but I just don't have enough information. It's really
rough, 'cause I know nothing, not even when she was born. My mother

just told me, "You have a sister. I gave her up for adoption when she was two years old, and I forgot where she's at."

My mother flew off to Florida with my stepfather, but then he passed away—he got hit by a car. I don't know if she's living by herself, or if she's staying with his family in Florida. I don't know if they're still in Florida—they might have moved back to New Jersey, or to Puerto Rico. I'm not sure where she is right now. . . When she left, my biological dad didn't want me; he, like, signed papers and all that. I was eleven—that's when I was placed in foster care. I've spoken to my biological father. I've said, "Have you seen my mother? Have you spoken to her? Do you know if she's in Jersey?" He goes, "No, I haven't seen her."

I want to see her. She always wrote me letters: "I'm coming back to get you some day. I just don't have the money right now. I'm trying to stand on my two feet." We were very poor and all that. She used to write me letters and give me her address and phone number. There was this one night I was very angry, so I tore up all the letters and threw them out. My mom used to draw on them—she was a good artist . . . [sadly] I had, like, thirty letters, and I threw them all out. So now I don't have any letters—I have *nothing*.

My mom went through a lot of garbage—she had a rough childhood. She saw her mother die in front of her, and she said that her father molested her. She ran away from home when she was fourteen. Bad things happened to her when she was young; she was abused, and then she abused me. [sighs] She hit me with belts, shoes, broom handles—she literally abused me. She just had so much anger, I guess. She did pot and all that, sometimes. My stepfather was a real heavy drinker too, and he abused me as well. He used to smack me around, and he did all these bad things to me. They *always* fought, always beat each other up. I was always in the middle of that; I was always trying to stick up for my mother—I hit my stepfather back.

I don't know anything about my father's childhood—it's not like he comes from a dysfunctional family or nuthin. He was an alcoholic, but not as bad as my stepfather. He's living with his sister's family. They're very loving and everything—they always ask after me. They always tell me, "When are you coming over? We want to see you again." I wish I was with my biological father sometimes. I don't ever remember him, like, hitting me or anything. At one time he was working in a factory, but then he lost his fingers in a machine. Now he's working in a hospital. He's very responsible. My stepfather, all he ever did was drink—and *drink*, and *drink* . . . That's *all* he did every day. He did work here and there, like he would load things from the truck or something. That was it—he never had a decent job. Now that he's dead, I'm wondering if my mother's got another guy, or she's on her own.

My mother—my other mother, my foster mother—she helps me sometimes. Like, we would call through the whole state of Florida, see if there's any people by the name. And we tried New Jersey—there are some people by that name, but just not the right people. Then we did Pennsylvania. And then I tried to contact my biological mother's brother in Vermont. I'm trying to go on looking, but I just don't have any information . . . [sighs]

When I was in fifth grade I had a few friends; it wasn't that bad. I always wanted Spandex for Christmas and all that—I always asked my mother for Spandex pants, and she finally gave them to me. I said, "Well, I guess that's what I like to wear to school. This is me: I like to wear tight pants sometimes." And *no one* liked that. My foster mom told me, "Well, don't wear them to school." And I says, "Well, I want to—I don't *care* what other people say." Everyone looked at me, like, "*What?!*" They were *real* tight, and they were like fishnet—with holes in them. This was when I was about twelve. The other kids looked at me and they backed off. From there on I says, "Well, I must be feminine. This is what I like to wear most."

When I got to sixth grade, oh, it was *bad*. They were talking about me: "Oh, you're a faggot. You're gay." They really tortured me. They threw things at me—rocks, pens. Some of the straight boys would like blows kisses at me and all that stuff when I was walking down the street or in school. "Oh, you're *sexy!* You're good-looking." Ugh . . . They were really teasing me a *lot*. Sometimes I was afraid of being followed home, or being hit on the bus. Sometimes they would smack me in the head.

My foster mom tried to help me, but there were just too many of them; there's nothing that you really can do. You can't call everybody's mother—and not that their mother will care about what their kids do half of the times. The teachers stuck up for me sometimes—

they know that I went through rough times. In seventh grade I asked to go to a different school—I went to a Catholic school. That was bad too, but not *as* bad.

The first day at that school, we were interviewing each other, and one question was "Who's your best friend?" The kid I was interviewing said, "Grant Muller." I said, *"What?* You *know* him?" He says, "Yeah—he's my best friend." I says, "Oh my God . . . " 'Cause he was from my other school, and I had a fight with him one time, in sixth grade—he gave me a black eye. So that day, he went home and told Grant, "I know this kid, Dan—you know him at all?" And Grant told him, "Oh, yeah, he's gay. You better stay away from him." Next day the kid came to school and patted me on the shoulder, and he goes, "I understand you're gay." I went, [despairing] *"Oh my God."* I wasn't expecting nothing like that to happen.

When I graduated eighth grade, my aunt told me about Harvey Milk High. I said, "Wow! I never heard there was anything like this before. What do you mean there's a gay and lesbian high school in New York?!" [smiling] *Of course* New York would have stuff like this —that's the way the city is. But, you know, there's nothing like that around where I come from.

The Harvey Milk School is small—there's forty students, at the most. It's all kids who were being picked on in other schools. They come here, being that this is a safer environment, and they can do their work at a different pace—they don't have to rush. There's a drop-in center—an after-school department, for students from all over the area to come and hang out, make friends, have fun . . . There's an after-school photography class for the students, and we do writing and artwork. There's a training resource department, where they train you to do a job. I have trainers teaching me how to become a peer ed—to go out and teach other high school students about gay and lesbian issues and to practice safe sex. And if you need someone to talk to, there are counselors there for you—you can talk to them about anything. I haven't gone to them: I can always talk to my mother.

My foster father is Armenian. I wouldn't say that he hates me, it's just that he's having a rough time accepting me. My mother told him, she said, "What if I told you your son was gay?" And he goes, *"Don't tell me that*—I don't want to hear it." [sighs] He was, like, *shocked:*

"Oh, *stop it!* Don't say that! What do you mean he's *gay?*" I don't like wearing women's clothing *all* the time—only when I'm in the mood . . . But he doesn't feel comfortable if I'm wearing makeup, or if I'm wearing women's clothing. Sometimes he says, "I'm trying to accept that my son's gay. I don't need to *see* him wear makeup. I'm trying to take it step by step." Sometimes I'm angry about it—but for a guy that's not gay, you know, he's doing the best that he can.

My mother tells me I can wear makeup or women's clothing when he's not around. There were times that I used to tease him: I'd put makeup on and he'd go, "*You're disrespecting me, aren't you.*" One time my mother yelled at him. "He's doing this because look at what you're doing to him: you're making him feel uncomfortable. You're telling him that he can't wear his makeup—that's why he's going to disrespect you."

My biological father doesn't know . . . [He sighs, and looks worried.] I don't know how he would react to it. I look at it this way: I don't think I could go to his house if I ever have a boyfriend. He asks me, "Who *is* this person?" What do I say? I don't want to lie to him and say, "Oh, he's my friend"—I don't want to *lie* about it . . . I'm sure there'll be one day where I just have to tell him—it's not like he's gonna smack me or anything . . . I don't know how he's going to react, 'cause I don't know the type of guy he is, you know? I mean, he is a loving person, and he always cries about me, he always asks about me, and he always misses me. I'm his only son that he's got. He might be angry, a little bit, but I wouldn't say he'll beat me up or anything.

I don't know if my biological mother thinks I'm gay, but she didn't care if I wore her clothes—she was always comfortable with that. She always said to my stepfather, "Oh, leave him alone. He's not bothering you—let him be! If he's happy that way, then let him do what he wants. As long as he doesn't go out like that then it's OK." But my stepfather, he always said, "*You're a faggot*—I don't like you," and "I hate you—you're such a *queer*, you're such a sissy. You should wear a pocketbook on your shoulder . . . " Stuff like that.

The younger kids, they all know. My foster mother explained to them, "Your brother's gay, he likes guys. You like women, but your brother likes males." Sometimes my brothers, they'll go to school, they'll tell their teachers: "My brother's gay, he likes boys." [He throws up his hands in exasperation.] *Oh, God*—sometimes it embarrasses me. Oh, *please,* don't let the whole world know. My sister, she goes to the high school that I was gonna go to. I told my sister, "Tell all the students about me—tell them that I'm your brother now." 'cause everybody knows me in high school. Sure, at one time or another they say things about me, and so what? But they still ask for me: "Oh, well, Dan should come back to high school." Everybody misses me . . . Yeah—they miss me because they used to like beating me up, so that's what they miss. *Mmm-hmm.*

We just had a meeting last week at another high school. They're peer educators too, on multicultural issues. We talked to them about gay and lesbian issues. There were some students that were very curious: "How do gay men and women have sex?" And that's OK, because that's how some heterosexuals get—they're curious. I'm saying to myself, "Wow, these are like *kindergarten* students. I'm sure they know." There were students who came up to me, "Do you ever masturbate? How do you masturbate? How does it feel?" There were some students that said, "Oh yeah, I masturbate too." I don't know if they were saying that to tease me, 'cause you don't have to be gay to masturbate. I'm sure every male in this world did it once.

My mom always tells me, "Don't *ever* have sex without a condom. *Always* use a condom, *always* practice safe sex—*and I mean it!*" And she goes, "I don't really want you to do drugs." And I don't. My mother always says, "Dan is such a wonderful kid—he's a very good student, he gets good grades in school, never does drugs, never drinks, never smokes." I don't do none of that. She says, "Your brothers always look up to you, and they *should* look up to you."

I love everything about my mother: she's very accepting, she's very warmhearted. And she's with me all through me being gay. She told the whole family about me, she tells everybody—she's not ashamed. I'm adopted now—two years ago, December of '92. [He smiles and wipes his brow.] *Phew.*

Elvy Aguilar

San Francisco, California

I *meet Elvy at her parents' house. Her year-old son toddles around the living room until she distracts him with a video of* The Lion King. *Her face lights up when she gazes in his direction. She is seventeen.*

My dad grew up in the Philippines and came here when he finished college, and my mom came when she was eleven. I have two older brothers—twenty-six and twenty-three—and then my little brother is twelve. My dad works for the post office. My mom was an executive secretary, but she became disabled from arthritis. She has pain, but she doesn't really show it that much.

My mom says that I'm always spoiled by my dad, because he gave me more things than my brothers got. Like I always got a room by myself—I got the television, the cable, and the phone. But my brothers have more in common with each other, so *I'm* left out. I always feel like I'm the black sheep of the family. My brothers are so much smarter. My oldest brother became a police officer; he was in the military. He took care of all of us, and my mom is proud of him. And then my other brother, he's really smart and wise; when he has problems he knows how to settle them. So my mom, she's proud of him. And then my little brother, he's getting good grades in school, he's in honors . . . [sighs] And then there comes me, who's not that great in school, and always wants to go out, and always wants to be on the phone . . . She has problems with me.

When I say black sheep, when I feel like the odd one, it's because I always see what I'm doing wrong, but I never really try to *change* it. I think it's 'cause I get so carried away with what I'm doing, I don't want to stop. Like when I started going out with my friends, and I wouldn't come home—my mom would get *so* mad at me. Yet I'd do it again the next time, because I always felt, "I need my friends, Mom" —I didn't want to be left out. And then I'm the one that had the baby; the first of her children to make a real big mistake—bring a shock to the family.

We lived here when I was born, and then we moved outside the city, and we came back when I was nine. It's quite mixed; there's a lot of Irish and Chinese, and Filipino . . . There's tensions. When I was in seventh and eighth grade at my grammar school, there was mostly Irish kids that went there. They used to call all the dark people names; and I used to have problems because I wouldn't let them pick on me. They used to call me *nigger*, and say they were gonna kill me, this and that. At first it hurt, but then it made me mad. My mom always says that when people talk back to me, try to stay away from the problem. But if anybody ever strikes me, no matter what, I should fight back.

When we moved back here I was *so* depressed; I think it was the fact that I left all my friends. I started to eat a lot, so I became really chubby. And I was always shy and quiet, because I felt that nobody would like me. My grades were low, and I was too shy to ask for help— but it seemed like they wouldn't want to help me, like they felt, "*Oh, she's not doing well in school anyway* . . . " They seemed to favor the kids with the better grades, and kind of forget about the kids with the low grades.

It was better in high school. I go to an all-girls Catholic school. At first I wasn't used to not having boys in class. It just seemed more funner with boys, and you learn to communicate with them. But then I got used to it, and I realized that it's kind of better when it's all girls —it's more comfortable. Sometimes girls can't really be themselves around boys. The girls try to impress the guys, and the guys always talk about girls . . . If you go to an all-girls school, you don't have to worry about what guys are gonna say.

There's a lot of different nationalities: Filipinos, Mexicans, Chinese, blacks, and there's white people. I hang around with lots of different groups, but the ones that I basically stay with are mostly all Filipino. I guess it's because there's kind of peer pressure: everyone's in groups of their own kind. When I have friends of different nationalities, my friends say, "Why are you hanging around with *them?*" They talk about other people, you know, people that's not Filipino. My baby's father is Mexican, and they always used to say, "You're Mexican, you're not Filipino." They tease, but it doesn't really bother me. At first it did: I used to feel like, "Maybe I shouldn't be with him." It's kind of peer pressure, you know? But then I said, "Well, if they're true friends, they'll still be my friend no matter what."

My baby's father used to live around the corner. I started going out with him in eighth grade—he's two years older. Two years ago he moved down to the Mission area, and he got involved with gangs . . . When I started going with him, that's when me and my mom first started having problems, because I would *always* be thinking of him—like when girls first get into relationships. My mom always told me to be careful, because I will be the one stuck with the responsibility for the rest of my life: the guy can stay if he wants to, go if he wants to; but the girl doesn't have a choice. I guess I didn't listen. And she did start to like him, because she noticed how nice he was to me in the beginning.

But when he moved, we started separating; he started getting so involved with his friends and hanging out in the street. I always used to say, "Oh, he'll change, he'll change." And every once in a while he kinda seems like he's changing: he gets a job and he helps out. Then he starts going back and forth, and his friends are still hanging around. I've kind of given up . . . [sadly] Right now my mother kind of gave up hope on him also. She kept telling me, "wait, maybe he'll change"—we were both hoping, but he kinda kept making us get disappointed. It just seems he's lazy. But then I feel like, "Oh gosh, I should understand —he comes from a family that doesn't encourage him." His family, they have war inside the house. And his mom does drugs.

When I found out I was pregnant, he didn't believe me. We were using protection, every once in a while. That was when he had joined the gang, and he didn't really want me to be with him anymore. So I was kind of scared—like, "Well, I'm alone . . . " I told some of my friends, and they were telling me if I needed money, they'd give me money—if I didn't want to have the baby, you know? They were like, "Maybe you *shouldn't* have it." They said I was too young, and I had too much going on: problems with my boyfriend, and nobody in my family to turn to, and I might get kicked out . . . I felt like, "OK, I'm going to have an abortion." But then there was a little bit in me that didn't want to, and I didn't want to regret it.

I was *scared* . . . [The story comes out in a torrent.] OK, because before, when I was a freshman, I got pregnant. My grandmother had just passed away, and my mom and dad flew to the Philippines. I found out while they were gone, and I didn't know what to do—I had nobody to turn to. *His* mom found out and she was putting things in my head, saying, *"They're going to kick you out—I know how you Filipinos are. You're dad's gonna kill my son!"* She was, like, *brain-washing* me. One day she gave me money and told me to go. She did-n't give me a chance to think about what I wanted to do—she was pushing me—and I didn't know what to do. I had nobody else to turn to. I was fourteen.

After I'd had my abortion, I went through a *lot* of problems. I'd wake up in a cold sweat. I'd have dreams that I'd hear the baby crying —*a baby crying!* . . . In school I'd have daydreams of seeing a stroller or a baby come by. I couldn't concentrate—I'd always be daydreaming about having a baby, hearing it, seeing it . . . [Her voice cracking] And then one day—I kept getting anxiety attacks. I noticed the voices were getting louder and louder and louder, and my friends kept talking and talking. I got so mad I threw my books down, and I started yelling, *"Just leave me alone."* I started crying . . . We had a teacher that was really close to us, that we could really talk to. I told her— she told my counselor, and she had a psychiatrist come in. My parents didn't know.

After I got over that, and then when I got pregnant again, I told the same teacher, and she told my counselor. I told my counselor that I was having pain, and she said that I'd have to tell my mom, otherwise *she* would tell my mom. So my mom came to the school and I told her, with the counselor there. First she broke out and cried, and I started crying too. And then she goes, "I was praying so much to come here to hear something like you got kicked out, or your grades are failing— that'd be something better to hear than you getting *pregnant*." I started thinking about all the times that me and my mom got into fights, and how all I keep doing is causing problems.

I said, "*What do you want me to do about it?*" She said, "No, it's up to you—I can't make this decision for you, because this is a decision that you'll make about the rest of your life. I don't want to be responsible if I decide wrong for you." She goes, "Because I don't want you to hate me . . . " I said, "Well, could you just *help* me? Could you just tell me what *you* would do if you were in my position?" And she said that she would have the baby, because no matter how old she was, she feels that a baby shouldn't suffer for her mistake. In the car I said, "Maybe I should keep it." But I still wasn't sure, and she could tell. When we went to the doctor's office, he went to make a schedule for regular appointments. She also made a schedule with the doctor to make an abortion, in case I changed my mind. She didn't tell me that until later on.

We came home . . . [sighs] and my mom called my dad and my oldest brother over. I started crying, and I clutched my brother. I was like, "Please don't get mad at me." And he was, "*What happened? What happened?*" And I just cried. My dad started to panic, "*What's wrong? What's wrong?*" Like he wanted to know *now*. My mom was like, "Well, tell him, Elvy"—I said, "I'm pregnant." My dad kind of sat down, and started to take a deep breath, and then he looked at the floor. Then he talked to my mom in Tagalog—I don't understand it. He does speak English, but it's hard for him to understand it, and we always have my mom involved whenever we talk to each other. She turned to me: "*Tell him who the father is.*" And I said, "It's my boyfriend—it's Carlos." He didn't talk to me—he wouldn't turn to me, he wouldn't *look* at me. I was expecting him to at least yell at me, to say *something*. I started crying more, because he wouldn't even look at me.

He told my mom that since I'm Filipino—I've already made a disgrace of the family—I had to marry so I don't make a bigger disgrace. I said to my mom, "We're having problems—I can't marry him." My mom talked to him about it: she goes, "Elvy would have to support her baby and him. And right now who's supporting her is *us*." My mom called his mom up, and she goes, "Could you and your son come over, because I'd like to talk to you guys about something." And his mom said, "Well, is she pregnant or not?" My mom goes, "Well, yes, she is."

And then his mom goes, "Well, *you* pay for this abortion, 'cause I paid for the last one." That's how my mom found out about that.

At first Carlos goes, "It's up to you"—and then his friends would call me up and say, "Carlos doesn't want a baby. He said he's not ready." He talked to my mom, he goes, "Well, what? Do you want me to marry her? I'll marry her, then." My mom was like, "I don't want to force you guys into marriage." She goes, "It has to come from you, it has to come from your heart." Every once in a while it seems like it's coming from his heart, but then . . . I don't know. [She manages a pained shrug.]

I was depressed in the beginning; I was crying a lot. And then me and Carlos, we would get into fights—not only verbal fights, physical fights. He hit me, and when the police came, I didn't say nothing. So after I had the baby, and I tried to file for full custody, they were like, "Well, you don't have any proof that he abused you."

When the baby was born, I kept calling him from the hospital—I couldn't count on him being there. And when he *did* come, he came with all his friends . . . It was kinda embarrassing. They'd leave, he'd stay for a while, and then he'd leave—go out with his friends. I was a week late, and I had pre-eclampsia, so they induced my labor; and then I had a high fever. Finally I had a cesarean. My mom had been there for me, so I asked her to be in the room. He waited outside, and then when the baby came, he stayed with him for a while. When the baby went to sleep, he left.

I had to stay in the hospital for two weeks. Every time I'd call his house, they would say, "You can't talk to him," and hang up. They made me feel *really bad*. It was so hard for me to get him over to the hospital—I'd have to beg. Afterwards, his mom—they had a fight— and she kicked him out. He started living with his dad, around here. He was coming over every day—we were happy. Everything started getting better, like how it used to be. That's when I started having hope for him. He got a job, and started being a little more responsible. When it comes to money, it's hard to get it, because he's kind of self- ish—like his family. Then his father passed away, and he started living with his mom again.

I told him to come over to watch over the baby today, and it's either that he doesn't come, or comes real late. [disgusted laugh] You can't count on him. I'm used to it, so . . . [She rolls her eyes.] Since I see it like that, I started seeing another boy. I haven't told Carlos, because I know that he's gonna try to make me mad by fighting over the baby. We did that before, when his mom told him to get custody of the baby. I always say, "You can't take care of the baby." I try to make him realize how hard it is.

The doorbell rings: Carlos. He's a scrawny young man, who barely acknowledges an introduction. He trails after his son, or holds him, but rarely speaks to him. Eventually, Elvy asks Carlos to go to the back of the house. He does, but regularly meanders back in, seemingly at a loss as to what to do with his child.

When I was pregnant, me and my mom got really close, and that was the only time I did really good in school. I think it's probably because I didn't go out! [laughs] Before I had my son I used to get into fights with people, you know, on the street. When I got pregnant I stayed out of trouble more. My mom goes, "I think it was a sign from God that you got pregnant—because you never really cared about yourself before." I told my mom, "I'm going to finish my schooling. Even though I have a baby, I'm going to try to accomplish the things that you want me to accomplish." And there are things *I* want to do.

When I'm at school, I act like a teenager, and people say, "You don't seem like a mom." But then when I go out into the street by myself, and I see kids my age, it's not the same for me. I used to feel secure about the streets, like I know them. I didn't used to be scared —because I knew everybody, and I knew all the bad things that they did to other people. But since I have a baby and I haven't been going out, it makes me scared, because now *I'm* the other people.

As I grow up, society keeps getting *worse*. I know how people are. Even though our school is strict, people even do drugs in the bathroom and stuff like that—at a Catholic girls school! *Nobody's* scared of adults, nobody's scared of *anybody* anymore. It makes me worry about my son's education, because even younger kids are doing bad things now, bringing weapons to school . . . I worry about that.

I came from a very loving home, but yet, the people that I came to know—it's a lot of peer pressure: everybody wants to be like everybody else, *nobody* wants to be left out. Or like Carlos had problems with his mom, and so I guess he was looking for love from somebody, and the only place to run to was the street. Kids get more rebellious, because when you're out on the street you feel insecure—you always have to keep looking, watching over your back. And you don't want to feel like that, so you hang around with other people—even though they're bad—cause you feel safer. I always see it in those three different ways: the society, family, and people who are scared—people who are insecure about where they are. They want other people to help them out, so they join—whatever, a group that's out in the street.

My mom takes care of the baby as long as I go to school. But if I go with my friends, the baby comes with me. Now that I'm back in my old school, I don't want to miss out on anything. Before, when I would go with my friends they used to drink or smoke, but now when we go they don't do that—it's different now. When I go to school and sit at the table, and they talk about things that they did yesterday, or the plans they're making . . . I kind of feel left out—like, "Why don't you guys ask *me?*" And they tell me, "Because you have a baby." In a way I don't mind, because I feel proud about my son, you know—the way he is. I don't regret having my son; I just regret having him at such an early age. You have to really think about the decision before making it —and then, expect *big* changes in your life. I could *never* have imagined how much things would change: no more going out and coming home whenever I want, no more being foolish and stubborn . . . [laughs] Losing freedom.

I get tired every once in a while. Last week I was so worn out I felt my head was down to my shoulder. I was up on the computer on Monday, typing a thirty-page essay, and with my son crying, I always have to stop—and it gets *so* frustrating. I notice that when I get into arguments he always pulls on me, and wants me to carry him, and he cries and cries. I feel like, *"Be quiet!"* and I start yelling, and I feel like I want to *strangle* him. One time I got really scared because I thought, "Gosh, why was I thinking of *that?* What kind of mom am I to even *think* like that?!" I know he's just a baby, but I'm a child *also*—I still have a child's anger. I never really thought about it until I talked to my counselor . . . but sometimes when I'm upset, the reason he cries is because he can feel my tension.

When I was pregnant, people always used to point at me. I used to cry because I noticed that people were looking at me in a disappointed way. My mom would tell me not to go to church or my old school. She goes, "If they look at you pregnant, they say, 'Ooh, look at *her*—she's pregnant, and she's *so* young.' But then, you come around, you have a baby, they'll be like, 'Oh, how *cute!* You're baby's so cute!'"—I used to think people were looking at me, thinking, "Oh, there's another girl on welfare, and I'm *paying* for that girl." I feel like welfare is good, but I think it should only go so far—'cause I've heard some girls get pregnant just so they can get on welfare. And I've seen some girls get on welfare, and they don't really use it on the baby—they use it to buy other things. I think welfare should help you get an education, to help you get a good job in order to get *off* of welfare.

I want to go to college; I wanted to be an accountant—the only thing I'm good in is math and algebra. [She grins and shrugs.] I don't even look at the book—when I see the problems, I can just *do* them! When I was pregnant, I had to leave my Catholic school and go to a school for pregnant girls and girls with babies. Since I went to that school, I've seen their problems: I started thinking about psychology a little bit. I want to get involved with other teenagers, and teenagers that get pregnant at a young age. I'd like to be there if they ask me for help.

Moms and Dads:
Anything Can Happen

Diamond Moore

Baltimore, Maryland

Diamond is a tall, African-American, beautiful girl. *Her long hair is divided into several braids gathered up ponytail-style. The interview takes place at a friend of mine's apartment, where we pause often for cups of tea and bowls of soup—Diamond has a cold. The temperature is meanly chilly, in the thirties, and she coughs and wheezes. I notice she's not wearing socks. She says, "I washed them all, and they weren't dry when I left—I didn't want to wear no wet socks." She is fourteen.*

I lived in Perkins Project my whole life. My mother has two other boys. One live with me, he's seventeen; and one live around the corner with his girlfriend, he's twenty. They're real protective of me, they watch everything I do. If I like a boy or something, it's like they think it's wrong for me to like somebody. I guess it's 'cause I'm their little sister, they don't want to see me hurt or nothing. But they gotta realize, I'm getting older now. They'll like peek around corners, ask my friends who I be talking to. In a way it's good to know they care, but sometimes it get on your nerves.

My eldest brother, he got a *real* bad temper. But me and my other brother, we're real close. He gives me advice about boys, like, "They'll cheat on you, they duds—they don't do much." I told him it's all in who you pick: If you go out looking for the wrong person, you're gonna find it. But if you find the right person, they're not gonna treat you like that. I told him, "They're only gonna treat you how you *let* them treat you."

I think they're, like, hypocrites because—well, my oldest brother, like I said, he has a real, real, real bad temper. He used to hit on his girlfriend and stuff. But he learned to deal with his anger, and he try to hold back—they try to work their problems out. My other brother, he just jokes with his girlfriend too much. He's an easygoing person; and sometimes he just don't know how much he's playing. That don't bother me that much, though, 'cause I guess that's his way of showing that he loves me instead of saying it. That's *his* way of saying it. My brothers can be fun, but at other times you wish you was an only kid.

My mother got a mental illness, and it's called manic depressive schizophrenia. She stayed in the hospital from time to time, and she got a social worker to help her work out her problems—advise her about things, and make sure that me and my brothers was getting what we needed to get. The first social workers, they was *mean*. My brother, he don't go to school, and they were dogging him about that, like, "You don't go to school, you ain't going to be nuthin." You shouldn't tell *nobody* that, no matter what.

I guess my mother had this illness all her life, 'cause she said when she was younger she had a real, real, real bad temper. She used to see a counselor, but it probably wasn't really taken seriously. As she got older it got worse and worse, and she went into a depression. The first time she went to a hospital I was about nine; and then she just, like, went from time to time. I stayed in a group home before—four times. I guess by her illness, it caused us to have family problems, and sometimes we needed time away from each other—we needed a break. Well, mainly I needed a break, away from my mother. Because, you know, it was hard for me to deal with that she had an illness. And sometimes I need to break away.

My mother, she's medicated now. A lot of times she went to the hospital cause they was trying to get her medicine organized. I think now they finally got the medicine under control, where she don't act so mean and depressed. Since I was younger, I grown to realize when she's getting sick; one thing I notice, her eyes get real bold, *big*, like she's happy. Her eyes pop out—and when it'll be like that for a while, then I call my social worker and tell her, or I tell my aunt. That's how I realize it's time for her to go in—'cause she'll be like real depressed, stay in her room all day, just lay there . . . She like to bring everybody down to her level, like everybody else would be depressed like her.

It's a hard thing to grow to live with, 'cause that's your mother—it's hard to actually realize that your mama have an illness. But after a while, I guess as I got more mature, I've just grown to deal with it. When I was littler I went to live with my aunt. That didn't really do much better, 'cause I was more depressed. I wanted to stay at my aunts because I didn't want to be around my mama, 'cause it was hard for me. But on the other hand, that's my *mama*—I was *nine years old*— and I was really attached to my mama. I cried every day. It was, like, hard. I had no brothers living there: one of them was living with my father, and one of them was living with my uncle. I had my cousin living there, but it's not the same as people you grew up with all your life.

I feel like I didn't have my whole childhood, and I grew up faster than I was supposed to. I mean, I always had somebody there for me —I didn't *raise* myself—but I basically grew up by myself . . . Partly I *did* raise myself. I don't feel that I really got to be a child, 'cause I always had to be there for my mother. I would make sure she took her medicine and stuff. And, you know, people might not think so, but that's hard for a child to keep up with, 'cause sometimes my mother didn't want to take her medicine. I'd try and help her, try to talk her into taking it. I had to make sure, I had to make sure everything was OK in the house, and I had to cook for myself. I'm not mad at my mother for it, but I just regretted that it happened.

But I don't necessarily wish that she didn't have illness, because it taught me things about life. It helped me look at people and the world in different ways: don't be judgmental about people, things like that. But I just wish my mama was more outgoing, 'cause she stays in the house a lot. Even if it's taking a walk, going to a library, going to a show, the movies—I just wish my mama would be more active.

My father? When I was born I guess they stopped going together. Me and my father don't really get along 'cause . . . he don't never come to see me. He'll turn it around on me, like, "Well, why you didn't come up there and see *me?*" He got a car—he could come to see *me*. I feel, as a parent you're supposed to be mature. He should have been the mature one, and came and saw me, and he shouldn't have tried to, like, pin it all on me. Last time I saw my father it was Father's

Day, and I didn't really say anything to him. Lately I been thinking about him a lot. I want to be close to him, but I'm not gonna sit there and let nobody use me either. Not, like, *use* me—but I feel, if he really wanted to see me, he knows where I live at. He moved, and he never called around my house to tell me where, so I don't know where he live at . . . I'm not going to go see nobody just because I want to see them, if they don't really want to see me.

I got *real* bad nerves. In fact, when I see fights I don't cry—but you know how you feel when you found out somebody died that was close to you? That's how I feel inside. My heart will beat *real* fast. One day when I was going down to school—this boy, he like *really* beat this girl up. He stomped her and made her tooth fall out. My hands were *shaking.* [She presses her palm to her chest again and again.] My *whole inside* felt, you know, like you feel you got a dark light inside or something. And that's how I feel, when I see fights like that. And my hands were *shaking*—I have asthma, and when I saw that fight I didn't have my atomizer—I was breathing like . . . [She pants frenetically.] My friend had to sit there and calm me down, 'cause I was like . . . [She shudders violently.] She had to hold my hands, 'cause my hands were shaking . . .

I've lost people—I lost three uncles. One of them died in a car wreck, one of them died from a roller skating accident, and the other one, he died from AIDS. I think about them from time to time. Sometimes you sit there thinking and get real, real sad. I been feeling like my mother's gonna die for some reason—and I'll just sit here actually *crying* over this. It's like a phobia. I'll sit there, I'll think about it, and I'll start crying. At one time I was thinking about it every day.

I've been doing this all my life. It started when my mama first got sick. One day I had a dream that the doctors, they *killed* her—like, they was drugging her up and stuff. See, she used to get shocks. My mama, she loved her brother, and she couldn't remember how to *get up to his house*—stuff like that. And that was *real* scary. It felt like I was slowly losing her. And ever since, I'll go into a panic, 'cause I'll be thinking, "What if my mother dies?" I'll be thinking how it would feel and what would happen. Everybody thinks about that from time to time, but it was like I got depressed over it. Like, "*What if my mother died?*" And I just couldn't get it out of my head.

I don't see myself handling it, 'cause we've been through *so much*. My mama, she's my best friend. I feel I can tell her anything—but it's just some things I'll be shy about . . . [giggles] Boys. I tell her who I like and stuff. It's just sometimes you get shy about it. But if I ever had to tell her something, I know I could.

Sometimes now I feel like I'm a teenager, but sometimes I still feel I have to be an adult. But I know how to deal with it. I deal with it by talking, just talking. I used to keep things bottled up; I would keep it in so much that I would just cry and cry and cry. Now I let it out. I talk to my aunt—she's like my best friend too. Or I'll talk to anybody I feel can understand me, that's gonna be mature about it. It helps. I think that's why I want to be a psychiatrist when I grow up. I'd like to help people and stuff, and that's what psychiatrists do. But I'm the active type, so I want to go in the Coast Guard first. I want to travel, plus, that would be a good way to help me pay for my education. I'll go in the Coast Guard, and then maybe become a police—I find it amazing how the police do; I like the things they do.

I want to be a psychiatrist when I'm ready to settle down, 'cause I don't want to be forty years old or whatever and chasing a burglar! A psychiatrist, that's a more mature job—like another level. See, I'm *real*, real hyper: it's weird, it's like I'm in a different body than mine —like I just jump out my seat. That's why I said I couldn't see myself as a psychiatrist when I'm young, 'cause people that come see me, I'll be like, "*Let's walk and talk!*" [laughs]

You know how when you're in elementary school there's always a teacher every year that asks you, "If you had three wishes what would they be?" My wish would be to go to college and be successful. That's *all* I want in life. People think I'm crazy, 'cause a lot of people say if they had three wishes it'd be for money or boys or something. But I'm saying, that's *all* I want in life. Being successful is like . . . [A long pause, then she resumes with conviction.] Being successful is *putting your heart* into whatever your task is. *Just be good*—just put your heart into it, just to put your heart into it . . . If I'm going to be a police, I'm going to put my heart into it—not just go there and do work! Sometimes people don't necessarily need to be locked up— they might just need to be *talked to* or something. And if you help *one person*, that's being successful! [She presses her fist into her hand again and again.] It's just the point of me helping somebody. If it's just like one person, I'd be happy—*one person.*

I think it's good to have a plan. I ask some of my friends, "What you gonna be when you grow up?" And they're like . . . [shrugs] They don't know. I worry about what people are gonna do with their life. It's not really a worry, but I think about it. I think about, like, mainly this one girl. She said she wants to be a housewife. And it's a lot behind it, why I think she said that. It's partly cause of her mother—her mother kind of neglect her—and she just don't care about *anything.* School? If she goes, she go, if she don't, she don't—she don't care. She's my best friend. I think about her sort of like my little sister, 'cause I'm always advising her about things. On the outside she portrays to be a big bad person, but on the inside she's just like a little soft teddy bear. I try and help her. She's real depressed, and I worry about her killing herself or, you know, getting into trouble. Somebody might get smart with her, and she'll just be like ready to fight, *vicious.* She worries about being mature right now, and I tell her, "Don't worry about being mature. You got to be *yourself,* and if that's being immature, that's being immature—if that's being yourself, be *you.*"

It's good for kids to know what they're gonna do. Especially in the neighborhood I live in, 'cause it's good for you to be *somebody,* you know, and don't just sit around the house. Mainly, people are like on welfare or SSI (Social Security income), like my mother is. Or people might have jobs, like a janitor. It ain't people living around there that's like a doctor or something like that. I think the best thing people is around my way is maybe like people who work in nursing homes. That's why I try to encourage my friends, like, "What you wanna *be?*"

I was in a special program for people at risk of dropping out of school. I liked it—it's just, I didn't get along with the lady—she was sort of like a counselor. I don't mean to sound mean, but I don't *like* that lady—she's phony, and I can't stand phony people. She'd tell us that she was going to do something, and then didn't do it. The government, I think, gave her five hundred dollars. I guess they thought at-risk kids didn't know about culture and art. She was supposed to take us to see stuff like that, but she didn't. What she did was bought us pizza every Friday. She wasted the money. I didn't respect the lady, and if I don't respect you, I don't trust you; and if I don't trust you, I'm not gonna like you. And that's how I felt about her.

She liked to embarrass people. One day we was outside playing, and this boy, he had a condom in his coat pocket. It was hanging over the rail, and the condom fell out. I was standing right next to her, and she's like, "*It's Diamond's condom!*" And one day she had asked us what boy we liked. I told her about this boy; and she was like, "What's his name?" She was asking all these questions. After a while I see she was trying to make it funny, so when she ask, "What school he go to?" I said, [sullen] "I dunno," like that: "*I dunno*, I dunno, I dunno." She said, "You're not supposed to go with nobody that you don't *know about.*" She was trying to put it to my mother like she knew me—but if she knew me, she would have knew I would not actually take that much interest in a boy if I didn't know how they was. She wanted to be my friend so much, but I *hate* that lady with a passion. She know it too—I told her. She said she never had nobody hate her.

This one girl, her father used to hit her, and she had a bruise on her face. The girl was telling everybody that she had fell down the steps and hit her face, but she told me and my best friend the truth—that her father had abused her. So the lady was like, "Come on, tell me the truth." And it was in front of a big group. She was like, "Come on, tell me, didn't your father hit you?" And that just made me really, *really* hate her. [She becomes *very* upset.] That made me lose *all* my trust and respect in her. I mean, 'cause why would you?! I don't care if she's a teacher, and I don't care if she's *who*—she's supposed to be an *adult*, she's not supposed to do that! Kids want to *confide* in adults. She's not supposed to go and try and embarrass her. [disgusted] She *knew* what she was doing.

She shortchanged us about school, too. She was supposed to organize and collect teachers together. We had social studies, math, English. They beat up the science teacher, threw crayons on her, and chairs and stuff. So we had no science teacher—she went to another part of the school. But the lady was supposed to hire a permanent substitute teacher—never hired her. We had graphic arts. I stopped going to that because I didn't trust that teacher. He used to look at me too wrong. He would say, "You look nice today, Diamond," but it was the way he would say it, you know? He just made me feel uncomfortable. And he was, like, down in the basement, and his door, when you shut it—it locks and so, you know?—I was like, *no.* I wasn't taking any chances.

People shouldn't get on kids about sex, or they shouldn't say it's wrong, because it's not wrong for everybody. It's best to wait, but it's individual—everybody got different maturity levels for different things. And it's not wrong. You should teach a kid what love, making love, should mean to them. You should teach them to make love, not sex. Anybody can have sex—you can take a hooker and have sex with them. But love is between two people who love each other. And you shouldn't down a person about it, you shouldn't make them feel uncomfortable—you should just make them feel, "Don't do it for the *wrong* reasons. It's not *always* wrong for young kids to have babies. I'm not saying go out and have a baby—but if it happens it happens, and you shouldn't *down* your kid about it. You should teach your kid to take care of *their* kid. If a parent teach their kid all the right things, they don't have to worry about them doing the wrong.

If you teach a kid about sex at a young age, about the risk you take —if you prepare your kid for it—then you just gotta leave it in the hands of the kids. I'll never put myself in a situation for me to get AIDS, because I'm gonna use protection. But you should talk to your kid so she won't, like, feel shy about it. She should feel, or he should feel, comfortable talking to you—like you're having a conversation about pizza or something, instead of trying to make it a bad word. Sex or making love, whatever you want to say, is *not* a bad word.

I'd like to get married. But people are like, "If you're married that's a big step, somebody you got to be with forever." That's not necessarily true—you could always get divorced. There ain't nuthin wrong with divorce: everything is not meant to be. But yeah, I'd like to get married, yeah, I would. My parents weren't married—they were just like a girlfriend and boyfriend. If I get married I want to make sure he's the right way—that if me and him decide to get divorced, he's not going to shortchange my kids: he's gonna be there for my kids. And maybe we *do* go together. My child's got to be his first priority, you know, no matter what. The child's got to be his first priority over everybody. Because that's your child, you know, and kids, they *need* love. They, like, need love a lot.

Tyler Williams

East Lansing, Michigan

T yler *is a student at Michigan State. He is eighteen.*

We're Dutch and German on my mom's side, and on my dad's side it's German and Polish. My great-grandpa came to America, and his last name was Wilhelm. I'm really not sure on the story, but he had a bakery, and it got stoned—the windows were all crashed—so he changed his name to Williams.

I grew up in Caseville, Michigan; it's a *really* small town. I think the average population is eight hundred, but in the summertime it gets to like three thousand, almost four thousand people. It's a tourist town: you get all the city people up from Detroit and Ann Arbor, and Bay City and Saginaw. In the wintertime, in the fall and spring, there's really not much to do.

I've got three younger brothers. We're all three to four years apart: the next youngest is fifteen; I'm three years from him, and then it's four years from there. The youngest is ten years younger than I am: he's nine—he's a little punk! [laughs]

All through elementary, junior high, we were like the *perfect* family. We had a nice house, nice cars; we've always worn nice clothes, and had more than enough food on the table. We're probably between upper-middle and middle . . . My dad worked a lot—he's a commercial fisherman—so in the spring and the fall, when their busy times are, he wouldn't be able to eat with us, but we had dinner together every night. All my friends *loved* my mom and my dad—I *always* had friends over. I didn't have any problems, never got grounded; I was really a good kid. I mean, I did stupid stuff, just around the house and stuff, but I wasn't a troublemaker. My mom didn't work then, but she went to school for nursing; she just recently got a job. So we were a real close family, went to church every Sunday together—Methodist.

I was fifteen when they got divorced, and it was really traumatic. I kind of put that time out of my life. I guess they say traumatic experiences, you forget some of them. That's what I did . . . When it came, it was a *real* shock. I don't remember much—I just remember it hurt. When it finally happened, my dad moved upstairs with me—'cause like, I dunno, they didn't sleep together anymore. That's when we became really close. [softly] And I'm glad for it, but I'm sad for it also.

It's a happy-sad, because I took the side of my dad during the divorce, and I kind of shut my mom off. It was tough on her. I didn't realize what I was doing until not very long ago. I wasn't very nice at that time; I was really mean. I'd go in stages: I'd be mean to my mom, and then I'd be mean to my dad. I couldn't be nice to both of them at the same time . . . but *now* I can. She reminds me of when I was really mean to her . . . [little laugh] She's like, "Oh, I'm so glad you're not like you were."

My dad and I were really open to each other during that time because he had no one to talk to, and I was a good ear. My dad kept on saying, "I'm sorry for getting you into this." But, I didn't feel that I was getting into anything I couldn't handle. I didn't talk to my mom much; I tried not to turn her off, but subconsciously I did. I remember her trying to take me to a counselor and all that crap: she was like, "Oh, it'll be *good* for you." I didn't want that. Me, her, and all my brothers went to a counselor, and I got *really* mad, because I didn't want to talk to a stranger. I probably *did* need to talk to somebody; I don't know if I wasn't ready, or if I was, like, being too macho . . .

Eventually we moved out, just me and my dad. It hurt my mom a lot that I moved out. I didn't want to just live with one of them—I wanted to live with both of them, but it wasn't possible . . . [softly, very sadly] If I could change anything about my parents it would be that they loved each other again.

I still think of myself as a teenager, but if a situation occurred where I would have to fend for myself, live by myself, I could . . . I basically did that when my dad and I lived together, 'cause he worked a *lot*. I would make dinner for myself, I would do everything. I did my dad's and my laundry. I'd make somebody a *good* wife! [laughs] I know how to cook and shop—I *like* to shop.

My dad had talked to me before about work, and other things. I was his first son; I went to work with him when I was ten or eleven. At first it started out to be, go down and fool around at the fish company, but then I started liking doing it—it was fun. He didn't pressure me at all. If not with him, I would be working with the other employees, and *that* was tough—a *lot* of criticism from other employees.

The employees there, they weren't really educated people. I don't want to say "scum," but they *were* scum. They couldn't get *any* other job . . . Commercial fishing, it doesn't take a lot of brains to get into it. And so these guys gave me a lot of crap because I'm the boss's kid: "*He gets to do this and this and this.*" But they didn't realize what I had to put up with. I didn't have to put up with just a boss, I had to put up with my *dad*. And my dad had the problem with not always being able to separate me being an employee and me being his son. I remember walking out a few times crying 'cause I couldn't handle it. I'm kind of emotional, so it would get to me every once in a while.

A year or so ago, I went out on the boat, like five thirty in the morning—it's about a fifty-foot boat. I worked really hard—I was always a good worker—and got the fish in. Big load, a really big load of white-fish—probably twelve, thirteen tons of whitefish. We got back on dock about two, three o'clock. Everybody else went home, 'cause they put their day in already. And I wanted to go home: I asked him, "Dad, I worked a good day and I'm exhausted. Can I take the van home?" He was like, "No—there's more work to do. Keep on working."

Everybody else left—they're employees, they did their work, they're done. And they're not good inside. I was the all-purpose man: I could wait on customers in the store; I could clean fish; I could go out on the boat . . . I could do just about anything that needed to be done. I said, "Well, I'm *gonna* go." He's like, "No, you're not. Don't take my van." I said, "I'm gonna call up a friend and get a ride." We were both very upset, and I think I was crying and yelling. It wasn't a very good scene. I got *really* stubborn—which I do a lot—and walked

outside, and pouted. I stood out there, and a guy going to Caseville
gave me a ride. My dad told me I was fired . . .

It was a really busy time, and I understood where he was coming
from, because there was a *lot* of work—and everybody else left, so I
should have stayed. But I was *really* tired, and I didn't think it was
worth staying, because I'd be, like, in a zone where I wasn't really
thinking. I don't remember if we talked about it or time just resolved
it. I think it happened like, he said, "Are you working this weekend?"
and I said, "Yeah."

I like the work, I really do. I like being outdoors and going out on
the boats. But the last three summers I've worked somewhere else,
because I didn't want the impression, "Well, he's always worked for
his dad—he took the easy way out." Working there made me feel sort
of grown up. I felt good because I'm working the same job that these
adults are working; I'm doing as good as if not a better job than they
are. But I felt bad because I was in place of someone else that could've
been hired, that's got a wife and kids, and really needs the money. I
feel kind of guilty, but I don't know—I think, "Well, it's better me
getting money for college than them scamming welfare and working."

In Bayport, where the fish company is, there's this guy that claimed
he hurt his back, and he didn't hurt his back. And now he's collecting
welfare, food stamps, ADC, or whatever. It's *such* a scam. And then
two black guys come into our fish company: Armani suits, gold
around their wrist, around their neck, nice shoes—I mean, they're
top of the line. They're driving a brand-new Cadillac, gold-plated
Cadillac. They buy X amount of pounds of fish—they pay with *food
stamps!* That's not right. And it's *not* just black people. The guy that
"hurt his back" was white. It's both races; *everybody* that does it is a
scammer. It's not right.

My mom had food stamps for a while, after my parents got
divorced. I was totally disgusted with that. I was, *"Don't go to the
shopping mall with me and buy food with that."* It was *embarrassing*
—it was really degrading to me. She's like, "Go get me some milk,"
and hands me these food stamps! I said, "Get those out of my hand!
I *never* will use those in my whole entire life." I just get *totally* disgusted—that's not for me. I understand there's people out there
physically handicapped, they can't work—*they* deserve them. But

the majority of people are just lazy; they ought to get off their butts and get a job. I'm conservative, Republican—very much so—and my parents are. It's more or less because they are that I am. I do *some* stuff—like, I got my ear pierced, and that's very nonconservative. I got a lot of hassle from my uncle and stuff, and down at work.

The brother underneath me, Danny, doesn't work at all. He's, unfortunately, *really* lazy. But the brother under him, Lou, he enjoys going down to the fish company. We're really close, and he's getting the same kicks out of working for dad as I did. I'm not really close to Danny. I'm starting to get to like him—I used to not like him at all. The only reason I can figure out for it is when I was like ten, eleven, Lou almost drowned.

We used to live in a house on a river. My grandparents were up, and we were all watching TV or something, and we lost Lou—he was two or three years old. [His voice fills with anxiety.] I ran around the entire island, superfast, and I came back in—and I'm like, *"Go look for Lou! Go look for Lou!"* All I remember is Danny sitting in front of that TV, watching some stupid cartoon, when he could have been outside looking for his brother.

I remember going and looking where we used to fish, and seeing my brother, face up in the water. I screamed at the top of my lungs, and my mom got there, jumped in, and grabbed him out. He's perfectly fine now, but he was like an inch underneath the water—his *mouth* was underneath water. I can picture it right now. Face up, with the red overalls with little dinosaurs on them . . . I thought about it, and the reason why he went down there is 'cause we always fished down there —my dad, and my brother Danny, and I. And we wouldn't let him come because he was too little—and it was *really* tough to get down there. He went there because he couldn't.

I wish I was closer to Danny, because I could help him a lot. He's kind of like I was at the age he is . . . not a lot of friends. When I was a couple of years younger than he is now, I had two very best friends. We did *everything* together: we were the studs of the playground, as little as that might mean. They moved away, and I had zero friends. I was in sixth grade, seventh grade, and I felt so naked without them. I just wanted to do *anything* to belong and be accepted. It was a real relief when I made a new friend.

My mom helped me through that. She saw me in great pain—I was very much to myself, just to myself. I wasn't, like, a vegetable—I still was involved in the same activities—but I just didn't have the same, I don't know, *spunk* as I did before. Something was missing. She talked to me and said, "There are plenty of friends out there; you'll find a good friend"—and I eventually did. The basic thing my dad told me was, "You're gonna make friends through high school, and you'll probably have one or two that you're gonna keep up with. But they're high school friends—they're just building blocks." I look back now, and I'm glad that I did have a best friend; and I think everybody should have one. But if you don't, you'll find them in college.

Danny is in the same situation where I was—no friends. Everybody picks on him. And that's the way I was too: everybody picked on me. For me, it was because I was small and, back then, I was smart; for Danny, because he's *really* smart, and he likes different stuff than those kids like.

In high school there were basically two cliques. The people that were smart, athletic, popular; the people that were not smart, not athletic, and not popular. We didn't totally shut 'em out; we talked to 'em, we were decent to 'em. I graduated with twenty-three kids—you can't *not* talk to people; everybody is friends with everybody, eventually. The guy that became my best friend was a kid in my elementary school, and we used to get in fights every day—we were like *mortal* enemies. It got to the point where his dad and my dad, they almost got into it. His dad was saying, "What are you gonna do with your son?" *My* dad was like, "What are you gonna do with *your* son?" It was *crazy*.

This kid really got on my nerves, and now we're best friends. I mean, I'd do anything for this guy—I would die for this guy. It sounds kind of dumb . . . I mean, not *dumb*—I don't know how to say it. I don't want it to sound homosexual. But seriously, I would do anything for this guy; and I would have to think twice about doing anything for the girls that I've gone out with. I just recently broke up with a girlfriend, and I wouldn't do *anything* for *her*.

There's a lot of homophobia in my town. I guess I have a little— I've only met a few people that are gay. Two of them I didn't realize were; I don't think any less of them now. Another person I met was a friend's cousin, and he brought up his boyfriend, lover—whatever you want to call him. It made me a little uncomfortable, but, I mean, I *shook his hand*. It was very awkward for me, but now I look back at it and laugh almost, because it was nothing! I'm just so naive about the whole subject that I draw myself to conclusions about these people. The more people you meet, the more different people that you meet, the more you start to change your attitudes toward everything.

My friends drank during junior high and the first part of high school, and I didn't want to, because I knew I'd like the taste of it, so I didn't. What's really sad, and the reason that I don't remember a lot about my parent's divorce, is because that summer I drank. A lot— too much actually. Almost every night. Beer . . . I was a total robot; I showed no emotion. It was sad, and not a very productive summer. Looking back, I have mixed emotions, again. I'm disappointed with myself: I should have thought about it, and not done that stuff. But, truthfully, I think it was good, because it helped me not think about what was going on; it put it out of my mind. I needed an escape. It was a very bad escape, it's a poor excuse, and I don't want to say it worked, but it *did* work.

I had a really good friend try to commit suicide. I talked to him a lot, and I promised not to tell anybody. He wasn't saying it straight out, but he was *really* depressed. He tried overdosing on aspirin or something—some over-the-counter drug—and I just couldn't handle it. I had to help him; I didn't want to see him die—so I talked to the counselor confidentially, to have him get some help. He went to some psychiatric hospital, and he got it all worked out. I try to do a lot for people that are in need, I guess you could say. Maybe I should be a psychiatrist or something. I've always had this sense of knowing when people were in need of someone to talk to.

There are so many different people here at Michigan State—there's like forty thousand students! I love it. Right now I'm undecided—I'm just getting the basics out of the way. Three, four years ago, I was thinking I'd love to be a fish biologist, so I could help my dad's business. But now there's no jobs, and it's not really good pay. So I'm more or less thinking about being a teacher, which still . . . [laughs] There's no jobs, it's low pay.

I really want to be a teacher because I had a teacher, and he was inspirational almost—just his whole level of thinking. He was *very* strict, and he demanded respect, but he was a nice guy. He made you work hard, and I respect that a lot. I'll remember him for a long time, and if I ever am a teacher, I'll model my teaching after him.

I want to live better than my parents. They have a good life, but I want more. I want more toys, more vacations. It would be nice to get married, but I'd have to be really, really in love—I mean *really*, I mean *crazy*. [laughs] Truthfully, I want to have a son, but I don't want to get married. It's not a continue-the-name thing—that's a big deal to a lot of people. But it's not about that, it's just . . . I don't know—I want to be *proud* of somebody.

Diana Koehler

Chicago, Illinois

W*e meet at Diana's home, the top floor of a two-story building on the northwest side of the city. She sits at the end of a very long couch, which makes her seem small and somehow fragile. Her hair is long, wavy and blond; her eyes an Easter-egg blue. Her mother, Anika, is home. Although they both agree she knows pretty much everything going on with Diana—"It scares me sometimes, she tells me so much"—she offers us privacy and goes to another room. Diana is thirteen.*

If I had a chance to go back and do it all again, and my dad not get sick, I wouldn't let him do any drugs in the house, because I would know what was coming. It wasn't my fault, but I always think maybe I could have helped him live longer than he did.

My dad died when I was in fourth grade. Cancer in the esophagus. He didn't know about it until I was in second grade, and didn't tell me until the beginning of third. Then I knew he was going to die. He always said he'd be there for my graduation, but he won't be. But I know he will be in heart.

Him dying doesn't bother me as much as it did, but if I wouldn't have joined the Big Sister program with Maggie, I don't think I would have come out like I did. My old school got me hooked up with it because they thought that maybe I could use someone to talk to. If somebody said something about my dad, I'd run down to the principle's office crying—I ate lunch down there a lot, too. We did a lot of stuff, me and Maggie, and the other kids. The other kids were in the program 'cause of divorce and death mostly.

I wanted to keep going, but they wouldn't let us, 'cause we'd been together longer than any group was supposed to be—we were together for three years. I liked having someone I could talk to that I wouldn't, like, necessarily have to tell everything to, in every detail. I told Maggie mostly everything—before sometimes I'd even tell my mom. And if it was serious enough, she'd make me tell my mom. Like one time last year I went to this club called Boppers [for teenagers and young adults]. I told my mom I was going to a friend's. It was kind of a mistake, and Maggie told me to tell my mom. I was with my boyfriend, and I tried drugs there, but I didn't feel right—I felt kind of stupid.

I was going out with this guy, and I started getting stoned and stuff. My boyfriend got in the gang around here after he started hanging around with them, but then he got out. He introduced me to a kid who introduced me to another kid who ended up being my next boyfriend. I just kept getting deeper into this gang. It felt like they were kind of family for a while, 'cause I was always with them; I was, like, barely home. It made me feel, like, "Wow! I got friends I can talk to." That boyfriend got a job, but that was after we broke up. We stayed friends, and now we're going out again. He's fifteen.

My neighborhood, this whole area is white. I'm German and Swedish; most of the people around here are Polish, and Italian. They're prejudiced too: we have one black family down the block and *nobody* will talk to them. Nobody. They stay in their house, they're scared to come out. I've seem them, I've said hi, but the gang around here—if they see them, they'll totally beat their butts in.

The kids in the gang are mostly Italian, and they don't get along with the Polish people or the Irish people. They started a fight with the Irish people over the summer: they bet five hundred dollars they'd beat them, and they did. They beat them up pretty bad—they got them *good*. There was cops and ambulances . . . I was there, fighting for the Italians. It was in the alley down the block. I wish I wouldn't have done it, because it was *really* stupid, and the girl that I was fighting got hurt. The kids in the gang around here are *really* into drugs. They were either stoned on coke or tripping on acid, so they were real crazy—I was like the only straight one there. But before we went out to fight, maybe I had a cigarette or something, and like four sugar cubes, and I went crazy. I was hitting this girl up in the ribs with my fists. I came out with bruises on my knuckles, but she had a broken rib. I could have done worse—but, I mean, when I saw her laying on the ground, crying, I just said forget it, and I walked away.

I wasn't sad, because she deserved it. This is the thing that everybody goes by around here: you don't fight unless someone says something about you, they lie to your face, or they start with you. I go by different: if someone lies to my face, that's OK—I'll get them another time. But if I go up to them asking them if they said it, and I *know* they're lying—because I heard it, or because my best friend told me or something—yeah, I'm gonna *really* kick their butt. [giggles] If they hit me first, I'm not gonna stand there like a moron—I'm gonna fight *back*. And if I don't win, oh well . . . I'm not scared of guns; I even know where to *get* a gun. *Everybody* I know knows where to get guns. One of my friends, her father is a police officer, and all she'd have to do is go into his room and take the gun. I can get whatever kind I want. If I wanted a bazooka, it'd be kind of hard—but I think I could get one.

Most of my friends are in school. My best friend, she's fifteen, she goes to a public school. She only goes to classes that she knows she'll understand: she'll go to algebra; she'll go to English; she'll go to driver's ed, 'cause she wants a car. She won't go to, like, history or biology. Her class was the largest at her school, and they used to explode pens. They light the tip of the pen, and when it starts to bubble they go, "*Here, catch!*" and throw it at the person, and it explodes in their hand. One girl got burned pretty bad, I remember . . . They burnt down their library . . . They used to kick the faucets and break them, and flood the school. Those kids were all from, like, *bad* families, where their parents yelled, beat each other up and stuff, or they cursed around their kids—so the kids were cursing and doing all kinds of stuff. And at the time a lot of the kids were in gangs.

I go to a Catholic school and it's not so bad. At my old school, I was like, Miss Attitude. This school's a little more strict, and now I'm an angel, a perfect angel. I *never* talk back, I don't make any jokes, I'm really silent, I do *all* my work. I don't like missing Tuesdays, because we have a psychiatrist. The girls see her all in a group, and then the boys. She's only for the eighth grade; we can talk about anything with her. She has questions on how we feel about certain things—the main topic now is sex. One sixth grade class she told us about actually *pressed charges* against all their boys for snapping their bras and saying stuff. We could charge our boys with sexual harassment—they snap our bras and everything. We wouldn't do it; we make a joke out of it. If the boys did that, one of the girls would turn around and hit him in the nuts, or take him and slam him up against the lockers or something. Everybody thinks they're all preppyish, but our girls are pretty violent.

At school we have dweebs, nerds—dweebs are the lowest you can go. They lack *anything*, they're ugly—they try to make fun of you, and they can't even do it! The nerds are like the OK group. Then there's popular, and then there's the clique. The clique is based on my five best friends at school.

As soon as I started hanging around with the gang around here, that's when I stopped hanging around with the clique outside of school. They don't ask me to—they don't invite me to any of the things, 'cause they know I'm always with my boyfriend or with my best friend. They don't really like her because she doesn't like them, and she'll fight any one of them. They talk about her a lot, they call her names—sometimes they'll call her a whore, and yeah, sometimes she can be. I mean, she's known with the gangbangers around here *really* good. Really good. She knows them all inside and out. But she went in for her AIDS test—they all thought she had AIDS—and she doesn't have it.

The gangbangers have another friend, but she kind of went on to a different gang, and doesn't hang around with us—we don't talk with her, *won't* talk to her—and that's what we call a *real* whore. She had a lot of things, like genital warts, and crabs, and all that. We're hoping she dies of AIDS, because she sleeps with *way* too many people. She's done a lot of things that have really ticked me off. She slept with my boyfriend when I was going out with him, and then she tells me, "Oh, I didn't do it." My best friend was there too—she wasn't going to let it happen. My boyfriend was trying to push that girl off of him, but she wouldn't get off—she was like totally high on weed. She gave him a joint and he smoked it, and he was high too, and it just happened. I didn't let my boyfriend off the hook—I dumped him.[little laugh] That was a different boyfriend, because I had boyfriends between this one.

My boyfriend's mother and father are divorced. He used to live with his mother but it wasn't working out—she'd, like, beat him and he'd hit her back, and he ran away a lot. Then her boyfriend raped his sister. That's when he decided that's *it*, and he and his sister moved in with their dad. [lowers voice] My ma doesn't believe that my boyfriend and me are gonna last till graduation. I told him, "I want to get married to you—I want to have your kids, and everything"; and he said the same thing. But we ain't planning to do nuthin—I'm not planning to sleep with him for a while again, because we've already done it. I haven't slept with many guys, but I *have* slept with a few. I slept with one at school, and now I've got kind of a reputation as a whore: he told them, "Well, she's loose." I'm like, "Well, I don't *care* what you people think." I'm kind of thinking I'm gonna wait till I get married to have sex again.

I pulled my mom in my room when my grandparents were here, and I told her I'd had sex, 'cause I knew she wouldn't yell. She was kind of upset, but she took it pretty good—I was *really* surprised. I wasn't planning to tell her until I was, like, sixteen; but it was something I was thinking about, and I didn't want her to find out on her own . . . 'Cause I could be talking about it on the phone with my best friend, and if my ma accidentally picked up the phone and we're talking about it, I wouldn't want to feel all stupid, and, like, lie to her about it. I was thirteen the first time, it was just this year.

Kids' parents, all of them, always say, "Don't have sex, *period.*" But my mom's a little different, she'll understand. She knows I've tried drugs—I've done it in the house and she's smelt it. My dad used to do drugs, so she knows how it smells. I've never done anything but pot, and I refuse to. My dad had done coke, and that messed his life up. It's not like I could smell it or anything, because I was normally in my room when it happened, or wasn't home—or he was out in the garage. He was normally drunk at the time, too, so I wouldn't know the difference. But he quit doing coke on my eighth birthday as my birthday present—I asked him to, at my birthday party.

I was twelve when I started smoking pot. The first time I tried it was when I was going out with my boyfriend for the first time. That was before Boppers; Boppers was when I decided, "I don't want to do it anymore." That night I lied to my mom because I wanted to go, and I *knew* I was going to get high. But everything scared me—it was like I saw things that *weren't there!* I still do it . . . maybe once every few months. But the lifestyle of you *wake,* you *bake,* you *wake,* you *bake,* that *really* freaks me out—that'll mess up my life forever. I won't be going to school, I'll pawn stuff to get drugs, and I don't want to do that. My best friend did that for crack rocks. She tripped, she's done coke, she's smoked heroin. She quit everything, except for doing pot.

With the gang, we'd hang out right down the block. That was the main place—that was where everybody did their drugs. They used to hang out at this place called the Mansion, but it got closed down and raided. And then they started hanging out with me, and *this* automatically became the Mansion—they'd come over in groups of ten right after school. They were high and they'd get mad 'cause I wouldn't open the doors—'cause I was *scared!* They broke stuff; my door was broken into, my windows have been broken. When the neighbors really started complaining and stuff, my mom was like, "That's *it*— you're not hanging out with them!" I didn't want to hang around with them anymore. . .

Most of the people I hung around with over the summer are either locked up, escaped, or dead. This kid I used to hang around with, Vic, he's in jail for two more years for hitting some guy. Vic had other felonies, drugs and stuff . . . Another person we hung around, Short Man, he's in there for ten years for smuggling. He ran to Costa Rica— he had warrants on him—they caught him, brought him back. Now they're sharing a cell in Cook County Jail. They're older—like twenty-five. One of them even went to my school—and that *really* scares me. I didn't know that anybody from my school could get as messed up as he was.

I know another kid that graduated from that school, and he spends every day from eleven till two twenty-five smoking pot: he's literally baked *all* the time—and that scares me, 'cause I could be as messed up as him, if I wanted to be. If I could go back and change, like, hanging around with a gang, I know I would. I think that was just a little phase. I made a wrong turn—but I turned my little car around, and I went home.

I figure I might as well go to school, because every day you go is closer to graduation. And it puts more into my mind, so I can get a good education and go to college. I want to go to Notre Dame, that's my dream. I went there with Maggie for her parent's reunion, and I *really* liked the campus. I want to be a fashion designer. Mostly I like writing, fashion designing, and I want to be a lawyer. I love arguing— I *love* arguing with my mom. We get in the best fights, *the best!* I'll swear at her, and then she'll swear at me. And then I'll slam doors and break things, and throw things across the room. When I'm mad I go *crazy!*

Sometimes I mind that she's at work. Sometimes I want my mom to be here so nobody will come over after school. Sometimes I don't though, cause I like being home alone. It gives me a chance to do my homework with nobody to bother me. And then I could do whatever I want, blast the music as loud as I want, smoke my cigarettes if I want. I'm quitting when I get my braces. I want to have perfect teeth in case I ever want to model. I just want to have perfect teeth, that's all I've ever wanted.

This is what I learned when I was ten: if I put my mind to it, I can achieve anything that I want to. I gained responsibility when I was ten with my dad being sick. But I gained more responsibility than I was really supposed to have. Sometimes I feel like I'm the adult. Like once in a while my mom'll go out drinking, and she'll come home twenty minutes after curfew, and I'll tell her, *"Get in this house now!"* I lecture her a lot.

I'm scared that something will happen to her. Like when she goes to work every morning, I'm worried. What if the train falls over? What if she has a heart attack and dies? But it's like, why am I worrying about her? She can take care of herself. I think it's because I felt like I had to take care of her instead of her taking care of me. I mean, I had a *lot* of responsibility when my dad was sick at home. She was working— and when I came home from school, I had to change his feeding bag, 'cause we had like a little hospital in the house.

Before he went in the hospital I thought one day I was gonna come home and he'd be lying dead. I had to watch things. Once he left the oxygen tank on while he was smoking, and I had to run over there and turn it off. I thought the house was gonna blow up and everybody was gonna die—*I'm gonna be dead,* isn't that *just great!* I thought what if we don't die? What if we just sleep? What if there is no Heaven? What if there is no Hell? I mean, that's what I always thought about. What if you just die and you're dead? You're just *there.*

Honestly, I think there is a Heaven and a Hell. I believe in ghosts and spiritual stuff. I'm *really* into witches and black magic. I believe there's life after death; I believe in reincarnation. I had a dream the night before my dad died. My dad was sitting on the bed, talking to me. He was telling me, "OK honey, I'm dying tomorrow." I was like, *"No you're not! No you're not,"* and I was crying. And I remember he put on the radio, and there was this one song on. I don't remember what song it was, but I heard that song when I got home from school the next day. That's when my mom walked in the door and told me he was dead.

I worry about getting cancer; maybe one day overdosing on a drug or something; having too many kids and going crazy; having a spirit visit me from another world. I don't know what I would do if one did. I'd probably sit here and talk to it—I know I wouldn't run out of the house. I think it'll never happen to me, but I kind of wish something would, just to see what I'd do.

If I saw my dad's spirit, I'd scream, I'd cry, and I'd talk. I'd say . . . [sadly] that I wish he wouldn't have done his drugs, because maybe he could have lived longer and been there for my eighth-grade graduation, like he promised. And that I love him. I have his ashes— sometimes I'll talk to them . . . At first when we got the ashes, I wanted them in my room, so I'd feel like I'm protected. I always thought, like, if there was a fire, what I would take? We had to do a report on that in school, and I said, "My dad's ashes, and my mom." That's all I'd really need.

Some day I want to live in a white house with a little white picket fence. I know I'll have, like, two or three kids. I don't know if I'll have a husband. Well—I know I'll have a husband—but I mean, I don't know if he's going to die on me or divorce me or whatever. No matter what, I want my kids, and I want a dog. I *gotta* have a dog!

Leo Allen

Chicago, Illinois

L eo is thin and handsome, with a surprisingly deep voice. He *is friendly, but there's a reserve, a certain sense of distance. We sit at the dining table in a large country-style kitchen. His biological parents, Judy and Martin—both militant political activists—are in jail. He was adopted by another couple, Rob and Vivian, many years ago; they're also activists. When I arrive, he's just finished watching twenty minutes of* Schindler's List—*a movie he's already seen, but likes to watch again, in small bits. He is fourteen.*

My parents were underground when I was born—until they were put in jail, they were underground. They were arrested when I was fourteen months, and for a few months I lived with friends of theirs, and my grandparents. Rob and Vivian were underground when their kids were born, but turned themselves in when the oldest was three. So they'd gone different ways, and disagreed about what was the proper way to continue, but Judy and Martin agreed that they would be the best parents they could find for me while they were in jail. And Rob and Vivian were gonna have a third child anyway: I was the cute, chubby thing that came along . . . [softly] I suppose my parents wish they'd done what Rob and Vivian did, but what are you gonna do?

I call Vivian "Mom," and Rob "Rob," "poppy," "dad," whatever . . . I call my parents in jail "Judy" and "Martin." I have two brothers: Ezra's eighteen and Ben's fifteen. I'd say we get along better than most other brothers do; we're very close, and I trust them probably more than I trust anybody else—there's nothing I wouldn't feel safe telling them.

We didn't always get along. When I was nine, eight, seven, me and Ezra *hated* each other. We fought, and it was horrible. He was a certain way, and I looked up to him and tried to be with him a lot, and it sort of bothered him—he was trying to have his own life. Like, an example of the difference between our relationship four years ago and now is that Ezra would *kill* us if we went near his room— but now we're the *only* people he lets go into his room when he's not there.

We moved here from New York eight years ago. None of us wanted to—we didn't want to leave behind what we already had: our house in the country, our friends, our city life. And we didn't see it as something that we could easily replace—our friendships, or me with visiting Judy—I didn't think I'd be able to visit her anymore. Now I just fly—it's not a big deal.

My neighborhood is mixed. I think I've always been more scared when I see blacks on the street than I am when I see whites. I've been raised with a lot of blacks all around me—homosexuals, everything —and I have this more diverse background, and I *still* feel that way. Our society is racist to a certain extent, and that sort of rubs off: you're raised not just by your parents, but by society, and by your friends, and by the news, and everything contributes a little bit.

I go to a private school. Most kids whose parents are in jail aren't going to a private school, or don't have pretty wealthy grandparents, or even parents. In all of my classes I pay attention exactly as much as I need to to get a good grade. A lot of kids sort of get mad at me for getting good grades. I know that I sound sort of very conceited, but I'm not gonna worry about that, 'cause everybody already thinks I am anyways. But like if I get a ninety-four, and I say, "Dammit, I *knew* that! I should've gotten that," they're like, "*Fuck you,* I got an eighty-five! You're not happy with your score?"

That school's so easy it makes me feel like maybe I should do something to get challenged; but it also makes me feel like if I can go through high school not doing any work and getting straight As, I'll take it—and then I'll challenge myself in college. It's not like I don't learn anything; I find certain things interesting, but I'd rather not have excessive amounts of work. Like, there's an advanced math class for my grade, but the only way I can get into it at this point is by taking summer school, and the advanced class has twice as much homework. I think high school is gonna be harder, so I don't know about going to that class . . . School might be challenging next year anyway—and if it's not, I think I might be OK with that. [He smiles a big smile.] I think I'd have a lot of trouble next year if I didn't breeze through it— it'd be pretty weird. But I could start working . . . See, that's the thing: I always have the option of *actually* doing work.

At this point, grades are more important to me than learning, because if I get good grades now I can get into whatever college I want to, and that sort of counts more than actually learning something at this point. It shouldn't—it shouldn't to me, and it shouldn't in general—it should count how much you learn. But the way our society works is that if you get good grades, you go to a good college, you go to a good graduate school, and everything sort of falls into place. I mean, that's the idea—I don't know how much that's true, I'll know in ten years . . . A lot of people think I'm gonna be a lawyer, because I like to argue and debate, and I'm sort of interested in that. But then again, I like money, so maybe I'll be an accountant.

When I was little, I loved counting out my pennies—I'm sort of weird about that. But it's one of those things where you never know what's gonna happen. Now, my grandparents on my mother's side died in the past five years, and they left a trust fund: it's for college, it's for education. But you never know: what if something happens, and that money needs to be used for something else?

I hope I don't get married. I can't see living with somebody in the way my parents or other parents do, for more than . . . at all. I *can* see living with a lover—I could even be married—but I'd end up getting divorced, I think. I've never been in love, so I really wouldn't know what it's like, but I can't see being attracted to the same person forever—especially if you're living with them, sharing a bathroom, sharing a shower, sleeping, you know . . . [He throws up his hands.] It makes me *sick*, it really does! I just don't see how living that way you can still be attracted enough to each other to have sex. I mean, putting it quite simply, there's just *no way!* But if I had kids, I'd want to have a steady relationship with their mother—so that's why I don't think I'd have kids. But that's what I say now—in ten years I may feel completely the opposite. I say to myself, "This is the way I feel now. . . "

My parents, they're great—I mean, for all their flaws, they're *great.* They're raising us a very different way, a much more relaxed way than their parents raised them. But in general, even people who were loose in the sixties and seventies now are more conservative and high-strung and uptight as parents. *Especially* parents of girls: they're more protective, worrying about their daughters being raped and used and abused, and getting pregnant, being taken advantage of. Boys aren't in that same sort of position.

If everybody brought up their children well, they wouldn't have to worry about it. Basically, you shouldn't put yourself in a position where you can get raped or anything like that. I'm not blaming women for being raped, I'm just saying—even me—I'm not gonna walk down the street by myself late at night. A lot of rape that goes on is date rape, and it just seems to me, you shouldn't put yourself in a vulnerable position, you shouldn't get drunk, high, whatever, with somebody you don't completely trust. If it were a perfect world, and men didn't have all the flaws they do, then women wouldn't have to worry about that in the first place. Obviously, they shouldn't have to worry about that, but they *do.*

You're not gonna stop kids from having sex and doing drugs just by saying no. There was this girl in my grade last year, she gave this guy a hand job, right—not even that big a deal . . . So this girl wrote a letter about it to a friend of hers on the computer, and said *way* more than she should have. I don't even think she saved it, but she printed a couple copies, and she threw one in the recycling bin. Her mother happened to see it—her mother's an absolute *freak.* I was at a birthday party of hers in fourth grade, and I was showing a girl where the bathroom was—the mother came and said, "Children, we don't go to the bathroom together in this house . . . " Ridiculous. So you don't want to leave something like that around your mother. If that's the way she is in fourth grade that's the way she is in eighth grade, only *much* worse . . . So her mother found the letter, was very upset, and literally said, *"We're moving to the suburbs!"* Now that's just *ignorant.* The suburbs is just as bad, if not *worse:* there's less to do, more free time, and more availability, more privacy—big open houses everywhere, parents commuting to the city . . . To say the suburbs is *better*—now that's somewhat of an extreme, but a lot of parents are like that. To expect her kid to stay away from sex, without talking to her about it at all—that's *ridiculous!* If she's gonna have sex in high school, which she is, then *talk to her* about it.

I don't always agree with everything my parents do, but in general they do ten times as well as any other parent. Them trusting me makes me act eight times as responsibly as I would otherwise. Them trusting me to call them makes me *want* to call them. That's the one thing they're uptight about, and it's not a lot to ask. What's great about my parents is there's no reason for us to lie, and therefore they know what we're doing, and we can call them if we're in a situation we don't like, and they're gonna be understanding about it. If certain parents were to get a call from their kid at two in the morning saying, "I'm at a party and I'm scared," their parents would get mad at them, and say, "What's wrong with you?! You get home *right now*—you're grounded for *six months.*" I've never been grounded in my *life*. Sometimes my mom is, "Go to your room, you're grounded," but that's just the heat of the moment.

I haven't had any religious schooling whatsoever—I'm quite happy about it—but our family made sort of a big deal about our thirteenth birthdays. I don't really like birthdays, people buying me presents . . . Everybody likes to get presents, but if I don't like something, I feel really bad. I'm not gonna say, "I don't like it": they spent the money on you, and you know you're never gonna wear the shirt or use the game. God, it just makes you want to kill yourself . . . So even though I love getting presents, just as much as it's great, it's *horrible.*

My parents raised me in a way where I can be religious if I want; but since they didn't force it on me, I chose not to. I'm atheist or agnostic; there's no evidence of God. If there is a God, then I'm going to Hell, frankly—I'm fucked, and it's too bad that my parents didn't force religion on me; it's a big mistake. But it just doesn't seem very realistic. I'd like to think there's some kind of an afterlife . . . [laughs] 'Cause if there is no afterlife, this is all meaningless—and it sucks that everything stops, there's just nothing, blank . . .

I've thought about it a decent amount, but there's not much point in thinking about it, or being scared by it—that's the way it is. I know fear is not logical or reasonable, but I've managed to sort of suppress pain, and to some extent fear, by saying, "It's gonna pass, or it's not reasonable, or what's the worst that can happen?" Now, it doesn't always work—especially with fear—but with pain it's good. If I stub my toe or cut myself, it's gonna pass . . . You just think about the time when it's not gonna hurt. Fear is harder—but thinking that way helps my conscious mind. I mean, I say to myself it helps, but it doesn't really—in my heart, I'm still scared. But it helps you cope.

The good thing about having four parents is I have another two people to turn to. Now, it sounds kind of weird, but I have a different relationship with Judy and Martin than I have with the parents I live with. It's a different kind of trust than I have with my other parents, because there's nobody for them to tell. Now, while they do talk to my parents, if they were to do something which lost my trust in them, I'd never have to talk to them again, and they *know* that. So, for all the difficulties it causes, there's a lot of benefits, and not only that, but I'd say most of the difficulties are for them as opposed to for me. [He nods toward his surroundings.] I think I might even be living better than I would otherwise, had they not gotten put in jail.

It doesn't bother me to talk about it at all—I even enjoy talking about it sometimes. I like to be able to educate people who are ignorant about the subject. There's virtually nothing anybody could ask me that I haven't been asked sixteen times already. Probably everybody in my grade at this point knows my parents are in jail, but even good friends of mine ask me from time to time, "I forget, what'd they do?" I say they were charged with some form of second-degree murder, that they were involved in a robbery with a huge number of people.

They were robbing an armored car, and my parents were in the getaway cars, the switch cars—they didn't play an active role in the actual robbery. During the robbery one of the cops pulled a gun, or a radio, I don't know . . . I think one police officer got shot, and two armed guards got shot. I read lots of stuff on microfilm about it, so that's how I know some of it, and I talk to them about it. They were caught that day. My mom managed to get a plea bargain and was sentenced to twenty to life—she's already served fourteen. My dad got seventy-five to life, and he's served fourteen too. I was only one-year-old when they got arrested. The original plan was for just one of them to go, and for the other one to stay with me, just in case, but they both wanted to do it, so they put me with a babysitter. It wasn't for money —they weren't going to keep the money. It was to help, I think, underprivileged black people, to help get better housing, and schooling, and food, and education—everything. They weren't going to keep any of the money.

Once somebody asked me—and they were trying to be mean— how I knew my parents weren't lying to me. It's not really all that far-fetched a question, considering that a lot of the parents in jail tell their kids that they're in a university and there's police just for protection 'cause there's a lot of robberies in the area. A lot of kids whose parents are in jail don't know what's going on. I just told the person I'd read it on microfilm, and I knew, and he should shut up right away or else get punched. I never, never considered they weren't telling the truth. I've been told by eight thousand people the exact same story, without a flaw, and I've read about it in the *New York Times*. That's what happened. And they didn't lie to me anyway—I mean, I just know.

From the time I was two, when I tried to visit them, the prison would do their very best to make sure we had a horrible time getting in and wouldn't come back. Now some of the guards are nicer, but a lot of the times they'd just be very difficult with us. They have a lot of rules, a *huge* amount of rules. I remember that at one of the prisons they stayed at during the trial, there was a big, inch-thick divider between us, and I couldn't touch them, I couldn't play with them . . . I had to talk to them on a phone. It was horrible. We got them taken down—we sued. There was a time when I was mad at them, and wouldn't talk to them—when I was two, three. People would take me to visit and I'd just stare away. A lot of things have been weird like that; I could literally fill up eight hundred tapes like this.

Judy's never moved since she was sentenced. She's very lucky, she's been in a very good prison, all things considered. Martin's been moved around a lot—he's sort of run the circuit of the worst prisons in New York State. The worst experience with them moving him was when I was in the middle of a visit. I was like five, and I saw him one day, and after the visit was over we went to a hotel. We go up the next day, and they tell us they moved him at two in the morning. And the only reason they did that was to spite us, to be pricks.

I don't see Martin nearly as much as I see Judy. When I visit him I do trailer visits, which are a kind of weekend visit. We sleep there, and cook our own food, and it's much, much better than a regular day visit. With Judy I'm not allowed to do that, because she's maximum security and the trailers are minimum security. So, with Martin I have more intense visits, but I've seen him as little as once a year. With Judy, it's a huge visiting room, we can walk around together, we can go outside, have snowball fights.

There's all this stuff on the news where they're gonna stop giving prisoners weights and stop giving them TVs. We were raised up till the time I was about twelve without a TV, and so because of that I read and am more active in sports and things like that. TV lowers your metabolism—basically it takes no brain power. But most every family in America has a TV—that's the way they're raised: a TV is as necessary as food. So it'd sort of be like saying, "You're addicted to cigarettes, you come in here, you can't have them."

Now with the weights—you could say these people going to jail after they've done some crime, they get buffed up, they get out, and then go kill some more people 'cause they're all big and strong. But if the prison system worked, if it taught them, and educated them, they'd be able to get jobs. But it *doesn't*. They're locked up: any minute a guard can put them up against the wall and make them spread their legs and pat them down, and hassle them, give them a ticket, beat them, kill them. Anything can happen.

It sucks for them that they're in jail. They did it to themselves, but still I wish they weren't in jail. But—and it might even sound horribly mean of me—I'm happy the way I am. My life's pretty good, all things considered. I'm happy with my life now, and I'm glad I have brothers; I'm glad I was raised the way I was, I'm happy with the person I am now. No doubt I'm privileged, and lucky in many ways.

Lucy Anderson

Chicago, Illinois

L*ucy lives in Minneapolis, but is in Chicago visiting her sister, Becky, who works at a local bookstore. Lucy's face is pretty and round. She has blond hair, and dark-lashed eyes that turn into horizontal slashes when she smiles. She laughs from deep inside, a rich chuckle. She is sixteen.*

I have four other siblings. They're all older, there's like a *big* generation gap. I have one brother, he's thirty, and then I have three sisters, twenty-five, twenty-seven, and twenty-nine. They all had a dad, who was my mom's husband, but he died. After that my mom met *my* dad, but they didn't get married—I have my mother's widowed last name. He was in the navy, and my mom just, like, met him. [giggles] I've never met him—except I did come close a couple of times. . .

See, my mom works with my dad's brother, Eric. My dad's name is Hans. They're Swedish or Norse or something . . . [laughs] So my mom was talking to Eric one day on the phone, like a year ago, and they were bragging about their kids—he has a stepdaughter. My mom says, "Well, Lucy's in the choir of her school," and he goes, "Well, so is my daughter!" They were talking about what schools, and we both went to the same school! It was so neat, because it was my friend. So we're connected in some odd sort of way. She was gonna bring some pictures of my dad, 'cause I've never seen him, but she kept forgetting. She graduated last year, and I never got to see them.

I'd like to meet him. I called his family, just out of the phone book, and got a hold of his mom—my grandma. We talked for a while. She was surprised: I don't think she *knew* about me. [little laugh] So it was kind of . . . It was really weird, actually. I told my mom after I did this. She doesn't disapprove of me trying to find him or nothing; she suggested, though, that I should be careful, 'cause she doesn't want me to get disappointed if he decides he doesn't want to have anything to do with me. I know that his family is really nice from talking to his mom. I asked her something like could she tell him to call me—and nothing ever happened . . . He didn't call. What do you expect?

When I was little, my mom worked a lot, especially with all those kids. She was a 911 operator on the graveyard shift. The older ones would take turns watching me. Of course *nobody* wanted to, because they were teenagers and wanted to do stuff themselves. After a certain time they'd lock me in my mom's room so I would go to sleep. I'd always sneak out the window and run to this nursing home down the block—'cause they'd always give me treats. And then the nursing home would call the cops, and they'd send me back home. [laughs]

This was, like, *routine* for me. A couple of times they called child protection on my mom. And see, it's funny, because my mom is a police dispatcher, you know, so . . . [laughs] One time she was on a ride-along—with a cop, driving around—and she was sitting on the passenger side. This call came over the speaker: "*We have a runaway child at this nursing home.*" And my mom was like, "I think I know who *that* is!" [laughs]

We live in a double bungalow—each one has their own little number, but they're attached. It's public housing. When I was growing up. our neighborhood was lower-middle-class, but it was still a decent neighborhood; a lot of people knew each other and all that . . . Each little section of northeast Minneapolis is either kind of low-class or a little more richer. There wasn't really any bad neighborhoods until recently. Parts of the area are bad now: it's dirtier, and there's more slackers—people who stand on the corner and get drunk, people who just walk around, don't do anything, sometimes cause trouble. The crime rate is higher—car theft, stuff like that. You don't really feel at home much any more. Before, you could sleep outside and not have to worry about it. Now you'd worry.

It used to be all white, pretty much; now it's more diverse. North-eastern's a big Polish community, and there's a lot of Mexican people, and some black people. I don't know what *I* am! [laughs and shrugs] My mom was talking about her great-great-grandfather who comes from Norway, I think. Maybe we're Norwegian. It's no big deal. I'm an American—that's basically how I think. I feel the same way about all kinds of people: I want to get to know them first before I can really judge them. Actually, I'm kind of glad that I don't really consider nationalities, because I can't tell the difference—I'm not very good with that kind of thing . . . [laughs] But I suppose that could be to my advantage too, because then I won't judge people.

And I have all kinds of interests: I'm involved in band, choir, swimming, gymnastics, softball—and I like art. My work is right next to my school—so I'll go to school and then I'll go to practice, and then there's an hour before work, so I'll take a shower—and maybe stop at a coffee place—and then go to work. I'm a telemarketer, and I bug people. We get a list of people who have subscribed to certain magazines before, and call them up. It's robbery, in my opinion, that's really what it is. You tell them, "You get five magazines for free," and you ask them to pay a shipping-handling fee, and that shipping fee is $2.99 a week. You're trying to con them, and I feel kinda bad about that. But I have to make sales.

For a little while, between thirteen and fourteen, I was kind of rebelling, running around with a bad crowd. I think most people do that. It's a big thing: you're turning thirteen, you're gonna be a teenager, you gotta be older, act older, whatever . . . It made it seem like you were older when you did rebelling-type things—sneaking out past curfew and causing trouble . . . A lot of people hang around with older friends, or older sisters, whatever, and they know all the privileges they get. And it plays a big role, who you hang around with.

A lot of my friends smoked pot and stuff, but I didn't do that. And a lot of them would drink. Actually, a *lot* of my friends were having sex, too. You'd be surprised at the age people are having sex. In fifth grade I knew people who were—it was a big thing to not be a virgin. At that age it's like, "Alright, I'm about to be a teenager, I've gotta be ahead of everyone else." But then as you get around my age you don't really care too much about all that: you realize that it's not a big deal —it's very little compared to school, and thinking of yourself. A lot of

my friends are still virgins. And a lot of the people I know, they've
tried pot—but they don't smoke it all the time—or they've tried
drinking. All teenagers try a little of everything.

Back then, my sisters were all moved out, and my brother still lived
with us, in the basement. A lot of times I'd go down there and dig
through his stuff. He'd recognize that, of course, and he'd get really
mad and upset: "*Are you digging in my stuff?*" I'd always say, [inno-
cently] "How come the first time anything happens you blame me for
it right away?" [laughs] I'd convince myself I didn't do it, and I
thought I could convince *him* too. I'd always say, "You can't prove it,"
or, "It could've been mom—how can you just blame *me?*" [laughs]

Maybe I'd do bad things because people would just assume it was
me anyway. It's hard to explain why. A lot of times I would just do
things to do it. No reason—just do bad things. I would steal his socks
all the time! [laughs] I wouldn't steal money, but if I came across
something that was really neat I'd usually take it. Like he had this neat
switchblade knife, and I took it. [laughs] He had a cigar from some
friends who had a baby, and I took that *too.* I didn't smoke it or nothing—I just took it. I kinda knew it was wrong, but I just loved digging
through people's stuff. It was weird, but I'm over that now.

Maybe it was because I always felt like people were invading my privacy. Maybe it had something to do with I wanted to find a way to get
back at them . . . I didn't have my own room when I was little—I usually slept with my mom, or else in the living room. And I didn't really
have a lot of stuff. I figured everyone knew everything about me,
there's nothing I can hide, no place I can hide things—I felt no privacy at all. And so maybe that was a way to even the score. I never really
thought about that. Now I have a lot more privacy, but I have a secret
box in my room that's locked up. It doesn't have to be things that I
shouldn't have or don't need, just stuff that nobody needs to look at
—notes from friends or whatever.

My sister Becky was my favorite person to dig through. She had
tons of neat stuff: lots of jewelry, tons of bracelets, colorful things. Of
course, she was the first to move, too—she moved when she was sixteen. Becky's gay. My mom, she sort of guessed—she had a feeling.
And then finally Becky built up everything—and told my mom when
she was twenty-one. I was twelve or thirteen. My mom was kind of

hinting: she was saying, "You've got to know something about Becky," and I'm like, "She's not pregnant is she?" My mom started laughing and said, "*No,* it's far from that." I said, "Well, is she sick?" "No." And I was like, "What is it?" And my mom said, "Well, she's gay." I was like, "She's gay?! *Really?*" I was kind of surprised, like, "Well, that's weird." I wasn't like, "I don't want to talk to her." She's still my sister and everything.

I tell people. Well, I don't, like, just blurt it out: [laughs] "Guess what! My sister's gay!" One day at school we were on our bus, going to a gymnastics meet, and they were talking about gay people, and dah-dah-dah. Not so much saying, "I'm gonna beat up this gay person," not so much like that. But they'll call people fags and dykes and whatever. And I said, [proudly] "My sister's gay"—and *everyone* shut up! [laughs]

Because I'm on gymnastics, and you have to wear leotards, and like with swimming and stuff, I could lose a couple pounds. I'm not bulgy or nothing, but I got a lot of muscle. So I get self-conscious sometimes; but it's not a huge deal. It was an obsession for a while—I was bulimic. I threw up like two times a day for a month or two, but after a while I got sick of doing it. I figured if people aren't going to accept me then . . . [shrugs] I was fourteen, fifteen, and I wasn't that much overweight either—but I *was* bigger than a lot of the girls I hung out with. I have a big structure, and they were really petite, so I thought that I was outcast in that manner. I suppose that was around my rebellious time, too.

It's weird being a teenager: you can't do things with the adults, because they do things that you have to be over eighteen to do; or they do things that you wouldn't understand; or things they think you wouldn't be interested in. When you deal with adults you're not really respected as much as an adult would be. But then you don't want to play with the little kids. You're only really accepted by other teenagers, you know? So you gotta kinda have your own little world— and that's why it's weird being a teenager.

When you're sixteen, you get freedom, or special privileges— you can get a job, and maybe that could be your escape. Or when you get your license, it's like, "*Yes!*" Me and my friends, we just find *any* reason to go driving. We won't have any particular place to go usually;

we'll just drive, and talk, listen to the radio, waste a lot of gas . . . [laughs] But it's fun. We're escaping from being in the middle, I guess—from not really having anything else to do. It's kinda like our thing, our privilege. What's accepted, or expected: what we *should* do. I just got my license. My mom doesn't have a car, actually—she doesn't drive. But it's neat having it. It gives me a goal too: I can save up for a car.

My aunt and my cousins come over and have dinner, and we sit around, and talk about politics and TV, all kinds of stuff. My cousin's a couple of years younger, and when we start talking, we get interrupted *all* the time. We start to say something, and one of our parents or my brother will just all of a sudden start talking. Me and my cousin look at each other like, "God! *What's* going on here?" They act like we aren't even part of the discussion—like we wouldn't know or anything! Once, when my cousin started talking, she said something stupid, that didn't make any sense—on purpose—and no one said anything or even *looked* at her. So it's like they really *weren't* listening to us! [laughs] It's weird, but we're kinda used to it . . . It's hard to explain how you feel— isolated or something, like you're invisible. A lot of adults feel that teenagers are aliens. [laughs] Adults are, a lot of them, out of touch. They think that they know because they were a teenager, but they don't realize how much things have changed.

Do I worry about the future? Yeah—*if* there's gonna be one! Actually, it hasn't gotten much worse now that I think about it— poverty levels and that stuff, when you think about the Depression. And in the sixties there was lots of protests and war. Way back in the Wild West people had guns and were shooting, so I guess it's not really different. I mean, it's not like better or worse, it's just a different way of being bad. I think every society has sort of had it bad—except the fifties seemed kind of boring. It's sort of like a hill starting from the turn of the century—kind of uphill. It started really bad, and then around the fifties was like the peak.

But nowadays there's so many random things, so many ways to get hurt. It could be an accident, you could just be doing nothing; on my way home to Minneapolis I could get into a train accident. You think about what you're gonna do the next couple of days, but still—you never know what's gonna happen. *Anything* could happen. There's so

many ways you could get killed or hurt. I could get a terminal illness
—there's a ton of things that could happen to me. Probably, I should-
n't watch the news so much . . . I watch the news almost every night
before I go to sleep.

I don't really care about going to college; I want to go to a special
training type of a school, 'cause I want to be a police officer. It's kind
of in my family: my mom was a dispatcher, I have a couple of uncles
who are police officers, and I know lots of cops . . . [laughs] I feel
strongly about gun control. There's no reason people should have
guns. If nobody had any guns in the first place, you wouldn't need a
gun for protection. All that guns do is hurt people, that's *it*. And I
understand that if I was gonna be a police officer I'd have to have this
gun strapped to me all the time—but I just feel strongly about guns,
even for hunting purposes. I don't think they should have *ever* made
guns—there's no good purpose for them.

I haven't actually told my mom I want to be a cop, but she wouldn't
mind, I know she wouldn't—she's very supportive. She can't really
help me out financially, because right now she doesn't have a job. See,
she became agoraphobic, and now she's housebound. She doesn't go
to many of my gymnastics meets and things like that. I gotta pretty
much do everything on my own. I used to get *so mad* sometimes, I'd
be like, "*Mom!*" 'Cause I'd feel *really* stupid or embarrassed. Like we
have parents night at school and my mom never comes! Everyone
else's mom comes . . . She used to be very involved in stuff like that,
but now she's kind of lost. I have mixed emotions: sometimes I'll feel
really angry, sometimes I'll feel very supportive. I just want to say, "*Do
something for yourself.*"

My job, that's the only paycheck that comes in. She's on welfare,
now . . . It's hard. It bothers me to to be on welfare, 'cause I'm against
that. See, when it comes to politics I'm kind of Republican. I believe
that way, even though we're on welfare now. I think they spend so
much money on it. I can understand for somebody who's agoraphobic
for example, or somebody who has a lot of kids and can't really do
anything. But somebody who can get a job, who's able to work, I think
they shouldn't have welfare—or they should limit the benefits. It's
complicated, but I just think people on welfare get way too many benefits. We get dental, medical; I go to the doctor a lot because I get strep

throat all the time. I can't imagine how much money those bills would come to, and the *medicines* . . . Like a regular person—they probably wouldn't get it because they couldn't afford it; but if you're on welfare you get tons of benefits. It's the benefits, and also the rent—'cause with our public housing or whatever you call it, it costs less than when she had a job. But I'm not really into the Republicans either—I don't know what party I belong to.

I wish I'd had a father figure, but with my mom's condition the way it is, I'd be afraid that he'd be disappointed in her. We'd probably be financially secure, a lot better off—but if he wasn't supportive, then she'd be more stressed out. And there's always the chance that he'd leave her . . . She hasn't been to the doctor for a *long* time, for even a checkup. I think she's scared she could have something wrong—every once in a while she has pains. That really worries me. She's overweight too. She's not very healthy.

I kinda want to get married, I guess. Maybe . . . [laughs] I don't know . . . I have a boyfriend now—we've been together for more than two years. My mom was kind of nervous at first, but then she got to know him, and she likes him—they talk a lot. When I'm out with Josh she lets me stay out pretty much as late as I want, 'cause she trusts him —he's a *great* person. Josh's parents don't really know about my mom's condition, and we were watching *What's Eating Gilbert Grape?* [a film about an obese woman and her children]. His parents were like, "God—that lady's *so* fat," and "Can't she just do anything?" [sadly] I was upset—I almost started crying. I don't know—she's not *that* over-weight . . . She weighs three hundred pounds or something.

She gets kind of nervous talking about it, too, 'cause she feels like she's been a failure. I try not to make her feel that she hasn't accomplished anything, or that she's no good. I try to make her feel better so that maybe she'll be encouraged to get up. She goes out some-times—she'll take a walk or check the mail. She tries. I mean, she'd *like* to, but I think she's just scared mostly. She gets panic attacks, gets nervous . . . Maybe she thinks that people are looking at her weight or something.

I just want her to get out and be healthy, that's it. 'Cause there's a goal, we have a goal: for her to go to my high school graduation.

Michael Mboya

Manhattan, New York

H*is apartment is the top floor of a five-story walk-up on the Upper West Side, on Amsterdam Avenue. His father is African, his mother Caucasian. He is beautiful: very thin, very dark, with huge eyes, and a meltdown smile. He has a relatively new, hyperactive puppy, who barks and yips through much of our conversation. He is fourteen.*

I'm Kenyan, but I was born here. I think of myself as black, usually as black. White a little, but mostly black. I don't know why . . . [sighs and thinks] I don't really know. My mother's family always made me feel comfortable. Sometimes when my mom comes to pick me up some place, or when I'm at her family's at a get-together, I'm the only black person there, so I feel a little bit uncomfortable. But then, I think to myself, "Why am I thinking about that?" and put it out of my mind. It doesn't mean anything—I love my mom, I love my family, so I shouldn't be worrying about it.

First I lived down the block, when I was a real little baby. Then I moved with my mom far uptown. Then we moved here, 'cause my mom homesteaded this house. Homesteading is when you and a group of people become part of an organization for, like, community-owned buildings. They got together and decided they wanted to homestead this building, and so each person picked an apartment, and started working on it. It was messed up, before: there was rats; the stairs were messed up; there was no door on the front, so everything was just open

—people could come in and do crack if they wanted to, and stuff like that. The *whole* building—she helped with *all* the apartments. She made the interiors, and then she did *this*. [He sweeps his arm proudly around, encompassing the room.]

I was over at my godmother's house a lot of the time while my mom was working on this. My dad was out of the picture. They divorced when I was four or five. He had children before me, and I would hang out with them sometimes, but now I hardly ever see them; they're older —they graduated from college already. My mom still loves him because that was her husband at one point. She knows he does stupid things.

It was a bad divorce. All I remember is he was driving me home, and he was drunk, of course, and I didn't really know it. We got home, and my mom started arguing, and they were yelling. Me and my mom left. He was taking us in the car to our friend's house so we could stay there, and he was like, "I'm gonna get my gun out of the back of the car, and I'm gonna shoot you guys." I was like, "*Oh my God!*" I started crying. Me and my mom got out of the car right in the *middle* of the highway and we hailed down another car. We didn't care —we were like, "Take us to the police station."

After that everything went downhill for him. Now it's going up a little bit, 'cause he's looking for an apartment. He *loves* to cook. He always tells me about how when I was a baby I used to jump in the kitchen and ask what was for dinner—I don't remember that . . . But now he's at least trying to get an apartment. He was playing soccer, he was playing all kind of sports; then he started drinking. I think a lot of it was 'cause when my mom divorced him, he got very lonely . . . [sympathetically] A lot of the reason probably why my dad started drinking was because he had a hard time when he was a teenager. He was in the Mau-Mau—the independence movement in Kenya. He got caught—he had shots in his back and everything— and they tortured him. They dragged him by a jeep over gravel. They *tortured* him. And so that's probably a lot of his hardship . . . Yeah.

I see him sometimes. For a while he was sleeping in movie theaters . . . [sadly] Sleeping in movie theaters! He'd call up from outside and go, "I'm sleeping in the theater over here—you wanna come see a movie?" I was like, "No *way*; I'm not coming over there." Now he lives in an office. He used to be a chauffeur, but the guy he worked for had AIDS and died. The guy gave everything to his friend and told him to take care of my dad, because he's been such a great friend and loyal to the company. So that's where he stays. He answers the phone and stuff like that. He's not in good condition; he has Parkinson's in his joints and his legs—it's like arthritis—so he goes to the hospital a lot. But I don't see him a lot 'cause . . . I dunno . . . [pained expression] I get along with him—it's just, he drinks, and he says he doesn't. Sometimes he'll call up here and act like he's drunk. He thinks he's slick, but he's not.

I don't lecture my father, but I'm gonna when it comes the right time: [deep voice] "Time for your lecture, Dad—go to your room. Sit down." [his voice building] I'm gonna say, "You've been dumb all these years—it's time for you to straighten yourself out. I know it's a little bit late, but you gotta do it sometime, 'cause I don't feel like going to see you when you're lying to me about not drinking. I don't feel like hearing all those lies. You wouldn't like it if I lied to you, so don't you lie to me."

One time my mom told him to take care of me: he took me to the park or something, and he had his little girlfriend with him. She looked slutty—she had all these nasty pimples and stuff on her. I didn't look at her arms 'cause I didn't feel like seeing if there was any needle marks . . . [sighs] He brought me back here, and put me to bed—he was like, "Give me a kiss good-night," and I gave him a kiss good-night; and then he was like, "Give her a kiss good-night." I was like, "Nah—are you *crazy?* I don't know if she's on drugs or something." Then she came, "Give me a kiss"; he was like, *"Give her a kiss."* I was like, *"Nope!"* I said, "Get out of here," and I shut the door.

He loves the dog, and he takes care of the dog sometimes for us. I thought having a dog was going to be easier, but I was wrong . . . You have to spend a *lot* of time with a puppy; a *lot* of time! We have him on the weekends, and my godmother has him during the weekdays, since we're busy—my mom working, and me going to school. But two weeks ago my godmother had a stroke, so she went to the hospital. She was in ICU [the intensive care unit], and they didn't know if she was going to make it. Now she's better, which is good, but she's not fully better—she still can't move the right side of her body. We've had the dog ever since—every day—and then he got sick with a deadly virus that dogs get. Luckily he got better, but the bill was high.

We just had a hard week last week. A friend of mine was going to come to New York, and he didn't, so I was upset about that. He's my best friend in the *whole* world. Our mothers were friends before we were born: we knew each other in their bellies! I wanted a friend 'cause I was crying cause of the dog—'cause I was scared he was gonna die . . . Crying 'cause of my godmother—'cause I was scared *she* was gonna die.

I know if I take care of myself, which I will, and if I don't drink or smoke or do anything like that, which I won't, I'll be healthier than my father or godmother. Sometimes I wonder, why couldn't my dad get it together? I know it would've been much better. I would've had somebody to, like, maybe coach a team for me. My mom had a boyfriend at one point, and he coached my basketball team, but he was like Dr. Jekyll and Mr. Hyde: sometimes he was a sweetheart, but when he got mad he was a jealous, stupid asshole.

[He points to a shelf filled with sports trophies.] Those are for basketball, baseball, soccer. I like basketball the best. I say that I want to go to the NBA, like every boy does. I don't know if I would have a chance, but just to have a hope of it—it's good to have hopes. My mother wants me to do something else. I said, "Fine, I'll be a basketball player in the NBA, and then I'll write a book about it." [grinning] She says *that's* OK. She says, "You might not get in." She encourages me, but even I know I'm not gonna get in. But I don't *know* I'm not gonna.

My mom's a full-time teacher, she's the head of the department. I feel sorry for her lately, 'cause she has a lot of stress on her back: she's getting her Ph.D., she has classes to go to, and she doesn't have time to do her homework. She goes to bed at *three in the morning* sometimes. She wakes up, just on instinct, at like five-thirty. I keep on telling her, "Get your sleep, get your sleep. You really need your sleep, or else you're gonna get sick." Stress can give you ulcers, it just can give you so many things. I say, [firmly] *"Go to bed."* She listens sometimes. I know some people expect teenagers to be rebellious and fight with their parents, but I'm not gonna be like that, because I need my mom. I'm not gonna treat her with disrespect, because that's dumb.

I've never been to Kenya, but I might go this summer. I'm not sure

I'm going yet. Once I'm *sure,* I'll be excited; I don't want to get my hopes up and then find out that I can't go. Both of my grandparents on my dad's side died. My other godmother uptown—they live in our old apartment—they're from Kenya, so I know about it. I just have to start taking the language, so when I go there they won't think that I just disregarded my Kenyan side. I spend time with my godmother's family, and they're very close to us. We're like family—we *are* family! I have a lot of second families.

There's no perfect family—that's what I believe. [forcefully] *No* perfect family. Everybody has a past, or something's gonna come up, or they're hiding something . . . A lot of perfect families have kids that are being sexually abused, and it's just ignored—'cause they're afraid of telling you 'cause it'll make them irregular. There's nobody perfect in the world—nobody. [cheerfully] Not even the pope!

My mom's side of the family is Christian—they're from Scotland. I celebrate all the holidays 'cause I go there with my mom, but I don't have a religion. My mom said I could be in any religion I wanted. Sometimes I think Jewish, Christian, maybe Catholic—*never* Muslim. The Muslims, they're tense, their religion is tense. They can't do certain things that I would usually do—no birthday parties, no times where you get presents. And I don't know if I could fast, 'cause I'm already pretty skinny as it is! I don't think anybody's right about how the world was created. The only way you can find out is going back in time. It's a mystery.

I'm in ninth grade—a freshman in high school. I go to a performing arts school. I have two good teachers. My other teachers are just like, [robot voice] *"Copy down the stuff, you'll have a test on this next week. If you get a sixty then you fail the whole term, and you just aren't good enough."* My vocal teacher's too uptight: she's too focused on you having a perfect voice, perfect pitch, and all that. She's not making it fun—let's put it that way. It's boring.

In high school there's a lot of pressure—tests and stuff. If you don't do well, at least passing, they consider you kind of delinquent, and teachers don't treat you with as much respect. I want to get my homework done 'cause I don't want to be, like, a failure. I want to make my mom proud and my family proud . . . It's not *that* bad; it gets worse as you get *older.* My elementary school years were the best years of school in my life. I didn't realize it then, but I realized it once I got into eighth grade, and now in ninth. I wanted to turn back the clock and go back.

I went to a great elementary school. There was homework, but it wasn't like if you didn't bring it in, you'd fail. There was no failures, numbers—there was no *anything*. It was just basically your behavior: cooperation, and sharing, stuff like that. I learned a lot of things, and those were fun years. I want to go back to having fun in school. We don't go on any trips—like to museums, and the aquarium—it's not really interactive. If I'm a teacher I'll take my kids on trips. [with bravado] I don't care *where* I am—if it's in high school, if it's all those other places, I'll get the courses done in the museums if I have to! It's important for kids to enjoy it while they're learning: if they don't, that makes them not want to go to school. If they have fun, it makes them want to learn more.

The first time that I realized that I was a teenager was when I kissed a girl. [smiles] Not a little peck. That was way back in sixth grade. [laughs] We played spin the bottle, and truth or dare, stuff like that. Now it's none of that. Go to a party, drink, smoke—and it's not just cigarettes they smoke either . . . I don't do any of that. When you come into school, that's all you smell, smoke. It's *so* stupid. I feel like hitting them in the head with a baseball bat. If someone offers me a drink, I say, "Leave me alone." They do, 'cause they know they're acting stupid.

It's peer pressure a lot: *"I'm cool smoking."* I'd like to say to them: "Have your own mind! Don't follow somebody who's doing the wrong things. Follow what your parents say, and if they're telling you to do the wrong things, stick with yourself, have confidence in *yourself*." If I had a sense of peer pressure I would be smoking right now, and drinking, and, like, having sex *right now*. I could if I wanted to, but I don't: I want to take my time, and it's a little bit early. But, you know, everybody starts at their own time. I don't have any problem with somebody having sex at an early age, except when it's like *real* young. You have to be in double digits, at least.

I don't think I want to live in the city when I'm older. This is a ghetto—an Hispanic ghetto . . . [shakes head] Drug dealers—I *never* hang outside. I don't need that in my life, I don't need it. Three weeks ago somebody got shot *right outside my building!* God forbid if I was out there. When I'm walking, sometimes I look behind me, just to make sure. But I've been here so long I'm used to it by now.

I don't know if I want my children growing up in this kind of environment, but I want to have kids. I'm going to be a good father, I know that. What's going to make me good? Not drinking, trying to make a good environment, spending time with my kids, not embarrassing them, being cool . . . When you think about bringing a life into the world, it's wonderful—having a baby. Yeah, I'd have a baby if I could, if I could bring somebody into the world.

The Need to Work

Walter Brooks

Chicago, Illinois

At the Anixter Center Factory Branch School, which is affiliated with the Cook County Juvenile Temporary Detention Center, we sit in a small classroom packed with books and posters, pictures, warmth. Outside in the large factory room, other young adults, mostly male, work at assembled piecework—much of it involving the construction of cardboard boxes. Walter is black, not especially tall, but solid, a presence. His expression is most serious; when he smiles it's almost startling. His voice is low, he stares straight ahead. "My street name is Poet. It's tattooed on my leg. They started calling me Poet cause I was quiet, but quick to do something." He is on home monitoring, the result, I'm told by others, of a residential burglary charge, which he is reluctant to discuss. He is seventeen.*

I grew up on the South Side. Two, three years ago I moved up to the North Side. It's just me, my older brother—he's about twenty-six—and my mom. My mom works. My parents weren't married, and me and my mom, we had lost contact for a while, and then I told her I wanted to come home with her. I see my father every once in a while. He works at a rehabilitation center—maintenance and stuff like that. I lived with him, his wife, and my stepbrothers until I moved in with my mom. Me and my stepmother, we didn't really get along. She had two boys—they was younger than me. We would go out, she'd be with a couple of friends, and they'd be like, "Oh, are these your kids?"

She'd be like, "Yeah, these are my two boys." And they're like, "*Who
is that?*" [coldly] "Oh, that's my husband's son." I'd tell my father
and he'd talk to her about it, but then she'd still do it.

My old neighborhood, I can't say it was good, I can't say it was bad.
One time during the summer, you couldn't even stand in front of the
building, because they'd be out there shooting so much. You gotta
creep to school so won't nobody try to jump you. I didn't start carry-
ing a weapon to school until my best friend got shot in front of me.
We was close—we was like brothers. I knew him from when we were
little. He was in front of the school. I was coming out the door and I
heard gunshots, so I run back in. He didn't come in after me. After it
stopped I ran out, and I seen him there dead on the ground. That's
when everything changed; I started thinking about how I had to protect myself. I didn't know if they were going to come after me next or
what. I carried a gun eighth grade, all through high school. You know,
it wasn't what gang you belong in then—we were just looking out for
ourselves. It could be your friend who live right next door to you, you
knew since you were four years old, and he'll *still* try to jump you—
maybe something you said or something you did.

I grew up one way: try not to fight unless you have to. And maybe
he grew up with somebody saying, "The only way you can survive is if
you fight." By the time I started fighting—once I got in high school
—it might be more than one person, it might be three or four. So then
I'd have two or three of my friends, and we'd just be fighting in front
of the school.

There wasn't that many gangs back then, maybe just a couple. Now,
every corner you look, you see gangs. You gotta look out for yourself.
That's the main reason people join gangs anyway: they know you hang
with this crowd, you live on that street, they're gonna jump you as soon
as you come home. So you go ahead and join a gang. That's how it is.

Most of my family were heads of gangs, leaders. All my family was
up into it. My father was a Black Panther. It's not like something you
run away from, 'cause you turn around you see your cousin over here,
you see your cousin over there . . . I'd hang out, they'd be, "Why don't
you just click in with us?"—join up. It didn't seem right at first: I was
like, "No, I don't want to do this." And then after a couple of years,
and after my friend got shot, I was thinking, "Yeah, that could happen

to me, so I need somebody to help me." That's when I finally said OK, and I *finally* joined.

Some people are like, "Well, I'm in a gang, so I don't need to go to school," but I was still going to school. All my teachers would tell my mom, "He's smart, but we've just gotta get him to come to school and do the work." You got friends who are like, "We ain't going to school. It's just one day—what's *one day* going to do? We're just gonna go hang out." So they'd convince me, and I'd be, "OK, one day, that's it." Then maybe one day next week I wouldn't go. And soon it just started being whole weeks and whole months I wouldn't go to school. After that they kicked me out. That's when I started selling drugs. I was fifteen, sixteen.

When you're not in school you ain't got nuthin to do but hang around all day. One of my friends was like, "Why don't you just come and be selling drugs?" I started and it was like, "Man, this is easy"—it felt good. I didn't know many people who could make five hundred dollars a day. So I'd come in the house, I had jewelry on, and clothing, shoes—my mama'd be like, "Where did you get *that?*" I'd be like, "My friend went shopping, I went with him, and he bought me something." She'd wash my clothes and find hundred-dollar bills in my pockets. She'd say, "*Where'd* you get this from?" I'd say, "I went to the store for somebody," or "I took out a lady's garbage." She believed it.

My brother, he's a band manager, he finds talent—he's bringing money in the house. He was like, "I know what you're doing—you better stop before you go to jail." I was like, "*Man,* you don't know what you're talking about! I'm out here making money, I'm putting a little money up, and I *still* have money in my pocket." I was like, "I don't know no other way besides selling drugs where I can get five hundred dollars a day." He was like, "You better start making an honest living."

Back then, I was working for someone, but I finally started buying my own stuff. I had people working for me, and I'd always have money coming back: I'd just give them their little packages of cocaine, their little sacks—the work. After a while the police started coming around looking for me. The first time I got arrested they let me off—they sentenced me to six weeks of drug school. Every Saturday you go, you talk —about what happened, what made you start selling. People want jobs, not everyone out there want to sell drugs, they just see it as a quick way of making money, and people want money. *Everybody* loves money.

After drug school I stopped, but then I started back up again. I kept getting arrested—I mean, OK, the way I'm dressed now, [He gestures to his jeans, sweatshirt, sneakers.] if I walk down the street, I'm gonna get stopped. I'm a teenager, I'm dressed in nice gym shoes, they're gonna stop me. I can see 'em coming. They're gonna drive past you, they're gonna look at you; they're gonna go around, they're gonna come up behind you, they're gonna grab you: *"Get on the car."* They're gonna check you. If you ain't got nuthin on you, they let you go. You walk up two more blocks, another cop gonna stop you. When you're driving, they gonna pull you over—they're gonna think the car's stolen, you bought it with drug money, or you're driving without a license. When they see me, they're like, "He ain't nuthin but a thug, he's no good—we're gonna lock him! We *know* he got some kind of drug on him." And the police officers, they'll plant drugs on you.

I got caught up by the police. He was like, "How much money do you have?" If you know how much is in your pocket, he knows you weren't doing nuthin. I had two hundred and fifty dollars in my pocket, and I said a hundred and fifty. He's like, "Where'd the other hundred come from?" and I'm like, "I dunno." He took it. I was like, *"Damn . . . "* I got locked up in County—in Audy Home—for like two months.

After that I stopped selling and started hanging around with my girlfriend. With the money I saved up, I'd take her to the show, get something to eat, do stuff—go roller skating or something. When you're selling drugs, you're on the corner—you ain't got *time* to be no teenager, you ain't got time to have *fun.* You remember the time when you were a kid and you think, "Oh, I can't wait till I turn fourteen, fifteen"—like *yeah*, I'm a teenager. You look to what's ahead of you now, and you're like, *"Man,* I wish I was about six, seven again." When you was a little kid you don't gotta worry about, "I can't wear this color, I can't walk down this street, I can't wear my hair this way, I can't do this . . . " Sometimes I'll be in the room, I have the music going, and I'm thinking, "Man, I wish I could go back, and come back forth and change everything that happened up until this time."

My juvenile probation officer, she was cool with me. "Well, I ain't gonna violate your probation, but you gotta do one thing: I'm gonna get you into this school." I hadn't been to school in over a year. It's not like a regular school: you go to school half the day and you work half the day. The thing about the work—you don't get paid by the hour, you get paid by how much you do. Was I excited? Yeah. I was like, "It'll get me off the streets." You get some peoples who are like, "Man, you *still* going to school? What's *wrong* with you?!" I was like, "I ain't fittin' to go back to jail and end up going to prison for a couple of years. I can't see myself like that." But I'm still in the gang. That's the thing people fail to realize: once you're in, it's hard to get out. You get out of the gang, it's like, "OK, you left us, but I know you're gonna tell the people about us"—so they're gonna come after you. I'm still in, but I don't hang around much anymore.

Most of the time we don't be out there gangbanging, we're just hanging out. It's like, OK, you walk down the street and you see a group of white kids at the bus stop, and they're talking, they're rough-housing, and people, they'll keep walking forward. When they see us, they will cross the street, walk down the street, cross back, just to get past you. Sometimes I want to say something, but they'll just say I *did* something, try to get me locked up—'cause some of them's like, "That's all they need to do is be locked up. They ain't nuthin but no thugs, no ways." I respect my mother, my father, people older than me, people that taught me stuff; but it's hard to have respect for somebody that's scared of you.

Some people think all gangs do is fight and sell drugs. Where I'm at now, during the summer we got Saturday cleanup: everybody gotta get up, sweep the streets, pick up the papers and stuff. You got some parents who're like, "It's nice what you're doing for the community—at least *somebody's* trying to clean it up." You got little kids, six, seven, going, "You're cool—I want to hang out with you." We tell them, "Y'all can't be hanging out with us because it's too dangerous around here." They're like, "We ain't gotta worry about that." It's like, "Yes, y'all *do*—if something happen to y'all, your parents, they gonna blame it on *us*." They come home from school, we send them to the store for us, give them five dollars, tell them, "Get me a bag of chips, keep the change." We see little kids walking with their hats turned, we tell them, "*No*—y'all gotta straighten up your hats. Don't do that around us." We see them out late at night, we're like, "Y'all get in the house." They look up to us. Some of the parents are like, "Yeah, they're trying to help out the community." Then you still got other people, "Well, they're still out there selling their drugs, shooting people."

I still carry a gun sometimes. But like, say, my girlfriend'll bring our little girl over for the weekend—when I wasn't on house arrest, I'd take her home—then I wouldn't have *no* gun on me. It ain't right you got your daughter in your hand, you got a gun in your pocket. I ain't never shot *nobody* in my life. I got shot, but that still ain't no reason for me to be shootin' nobody. It was last summer. We was all up in the park at night, partying. Somebody walked through the park: he's like, "*What you lookin' at?*" We didn't say *nuthin*—he pulled out a gun and we started *running*. He shot once, but it went through my coat. Right before I jumped the gate, that's when he hit me in my leg. I flipped over the gate—I didn't know I was hit until when I got to the house and I see all this blood, and I just *freak*. I'm hollering, "*I'm gonna die!*" I put my finger in my leg, [behind his thigh] and I'm like, "Ma, I got shot!" She's like "*What'd you do?!*" "I didn't do nuthin."

Everybody was talking about, "Yeah, when you get out, we're gonna find him." I was like, "Y'all is, but I ain't." Revenge is not really something I think about. OK, somebody did something to me; I'm gonna be mad about it—I might think about how I'm gonna get him back . . . but if I do something, they're gonna come back after me. Then I'm gonna go back after them, then they're gonna come back after me—and it's gonna be an endless fight. Which is why you have to stop it there. Just quit it.

Mostly everybody was selling drugs, like, this is the only thing we can *do*. 'Cause there are some people who ain't got *no* money. When I was selling drugs, one of my friends was that way. I was like, "Tell you what. I'm gonna give you this pack so you can get on your feet and make some money to take care of yourself." He goes, "How much do I owe you?" I was like, "You ain't gotta give me nuthin back. You my boy; you gotta get on your feet, man—just go ahead." After that, he came to give me my money back, I was like, "You ain't gotta give me my money." Now, I ain't saying *everybody's* like that—you got some people that's corrupt and like, "You give me my money or I'm gonna do this to you." I ain't like that. I said, "I helped you out, now you go help somebody else out, and then the next person will help somebody else." That's the way it's supposed to be, really. I ain't in it just to have no money. Yeah, money's fun, but money gonna make everybody greedy.

I don't go around showing my money off. I ain't got no car, I don't wear no jewelry. The only thing I got's a beeper. If my lady needs something for the baby, she'll beep me, and I'll bring it to the house. I've been with this girl for three years. After we knew each other about a year, both of us got tested to make sure we ain't had nuthin. After we knew we didn't have nuthin, we were both clean, we stopped using condoms for a while, till my daughter got born. When she told me she was pregnant, I was, like, *amazed.* Then after a while, when she was born, I was happy, 'cause I had a *daughter!* I didn't want her to have an abortion, and she wanted to have the baby. She told her mother, and I told my mother; them two got together, us two got together, and we started talking about it. I was thinking, "Man, if I have this kid, I'm not gonna go *back* out there and sell more drugs." I'm thinking I can go get a job, or I can go to school and work. I turn eighteen soon, and we're gonna get an apartment. We might get married—we've talked about it; we're just not ready yet.

I had a summer job when I was fifteen, going door to door for a consumer group. It was telling people about pesticides they were spraying on fruits and vegetables and stuff. I was looking in the newspaper one day. It said, *Help wanted, canvassers.* I'm thinking "*What* is a canvasser?" So I went down, filled out the application and started training. You only get a certain percent of what you make. But that drug money just kept pouring in: during the day I'm thinking about, "Man, if at night it's coming in like this, *what* would it do during the *day?*" So I stopped going in, and started selling drugs. At first I was making five hundred dollars a day, and then I was making fifteen hundred dollars a day, so I was like, "*Damn!*"

But you think about it—you're out there selling drugs, you gotta watch your back to see if the police coming after you; you gotta watch your back to see if the dope fiend gonna come after you say, "This dope wasn't good, you trying to poison me"; you even gotta watch out for some of your own friends. When I started coming here, that stuff started making sense: *an honest day's pay for an honest day's work.* You don't gotta worry about the police saying, "Where'd you get this money from?" You don't gotta worry about running. You ain't gotta worry about getting caught. I ain't gotta come home and mama's like, "Where you get that money from, boy?" She come home, she's like, "How was work today? How was school?" "It was OK." I'll be so tired I just lay on the couch and fall asleep. I wake up, "OK, what I'm wearing to work tomorrow?" Go and iron my stuff.

My mom's Buddhist. My father's Christian. I believe in God and all that—it's just, *why* you gonna sit in church and have a preacher tell you, "You do *this*, you're goin' to Hell, you do *that*, you're goin' to Hell"? And he probably doing the same thing. Why you got to give money to the church just to listen to the Word? And most of the time I think them preachers be cheating that money *anyway*—that's why I won't go. But I got a Bible in my room: when something's bothering me, I read it—think maybe it'll calm me down. [sounding anxious] Sometimes I get *real* depressed. Say, I can't go outside, 'cause the boys from the opposite gang are in front of my house. I'll be sitting and thinking what if I just go out here and somebody come up and blow my head off? I'm paranoid. It's not that I'm afraid, I'm *paranoid* —thinking I go out there something's gonna happen to me.

You read the newspaper, watch the news, hear about little kids getting shot for nothing . . . Little kids getting ran over by people who just keep goin'. Kids getting thrown out of five-story windows, stuff like that. It's like, everybody *just be at peace,* everybody just *get along.* All the gangs, just *be at peace:* leave all your differences aside. 'Cause I'm from this street and this street got Folks over here, and I'm from this street and this street got Vice Lords over here, it ain't no reason to *fight.* I got a friend, he in one gang, but his brother in another —what's the reason he gonna fight his *own brother* for?

I can't say I don't miss the drug money, 'cause how many people can say they make fifteen hundred dollars a day? Still, you gotta watch your back everywhere you go. Here, though, you work, you get a check stub; they stop you, you show them the check stub—"OK, you're not selling drugs." You're gonna have to learn sooner or later about labor, about work. This here really is like training for what's gonna be out there. You learn what bosses want, what they want you to do—how you supposed to act, how you supposed to talk and walk. Outside the building you can do what you want to, you can talk the way you want to, but once you in the work area, you gotta act civilized—you can't be running around *messing* with everybody. You gotta do your job. That's *it*, point blank. If you wanna make the money, you gotta *do the job*.

After I take this GED, I'm gonna go ahead and apply for a college, or go into a city college, so I can expand my education. A GED just ain't gonna do it. My uncles and cousins, they're gonna help me with the money so I can reach my goal—to be the first male in my family that ever went to college. I got family members who dropped out of high school. So I'm thinking, "I ain't gonna be like them: I'm gonna *graduate*, I'm gonna get a scholarship, I'm gonna go to *college.*" I'm gonna make my family proud of me—say, "Yeah, *my* son went to woo-woo college."

I would like to own my own company, something little, something to help people. Open up a new company so people can have jobs. Live OK, make sure my family's OK. Make sure that all my priorities are straight. That's what I really want.

Javier Salazar

Onset, Massachusetts

H*is parents have a large, ram-shackle house, a block from the harbor. At the moment the living room is full of props and furniture from the set of a play they've just produced locally. Javier is wearing a baseball cap backwards, baggy shorts, and a T-shirt. Although somewhat laconic, he is very gracious about giving up time on this summer's end day—school starts the next morning. He is fifteen.*

I'm going to be in tenth grade. I like school. If I had to stay home all the time, there's nothing to do, nothing to do. I read for school, when I have to. I listen to music a lot, usually to rap—it's just like putting a poem to music, to a beat. That's all it really is, just rhyming with a beat. A lot of it is about life stories, how they live in the city. I like to hear those stories.

My dad's Puerto Rican and my mom's Irish. My father speaks Spanish, but he never got around to teaching me—at home he speaks mostly English. He speaks Spanish when he's up in New York, when he's talking to my grandmother. I wish I knew how; it's always good to learn a second language. I see myself as more a Puerto Rican than as an Irish person. I don't know why—it's just, everybody else sees me as Puerto Rican, that's why. When I fill out forms, I put "Hispanic." I feel like I'm just Puerto Rican and nothing else.

My father does carpentry, all different stuff. My mom is a school-teacher in the next town over. But they both like doing theater, they do plays. I'm not really interested in theater, and I don't really pay attention to what my parents do. They want me to go see every play at least twice, and I don't feel like going, but I do it anyways just to make them happy.

We come and go and eat whenever we can. We never had really a set dinnertime. Usually they give me money, I go down the street. I don't miss sitting together around a table, it's too bothersome—like, you gotta be home at this time to eat. My friends, most of them, they don't have a time either. It's just go in, look and see if there's anything to eat, cook it up, and eat whenever I get home. I can cook spaghetti, hot dogs, anything that we have. I can cook steak. Cooking's kind of easy: you just put it in and wait until it's done . . . [laughs] It's just something to eat, something to keep me going, keep me walking.

I was born in New York and lived there for about one year, and then we moved. We lived on the Lower East Side of Manhattan, and my grandmother, she lives in Brooklyn. I visit her, and then I got an aunt that lives in Manhattan, in the Village. I'm really close to both my grandfathers and both my grandmothers. My mother's father was a news reporter for the *Boston Globe*, and he'd tell me all different stories about how it was. My grandparents in New York, we go out and have fun a lot. My grandmother's got a really good gambling craze— she goes up to Atlantic City. My grandfather, he doesn't like gambling, he doesn't want her to gamble, but she does it anyway . . . [laughs] She takes me to places in New York. Illegal places, really, with one-armed bandits—slot machines. They're in stores, in the back. She knows all the corner stores, they got a back room. I would have rather grown up in the city, there's more action. The city, it never sleeps—it's *always* doing something.

Onset is kind of countrylike. It's pretty nice around here, but it's kind of boring, there's not much you can do. Usually we go up to the towns over, we visit people. We go to the mall, walk around, go into stores, look around, see what there is, hang out.

The media goes kind of over the top about teenagers. They're trying to give a stereotype that all teenagers do bad stuff all the time, and it's not like that. Some are real bad and some aren't; some people don't do nuthin at all. Teenagers, we don't get in all that much trouble. I mean, we do get in trouble—every teenager's gotten in trouble once or twice

—but there's all this "They're killing people" and this and that, and that's not how it always happens. In big cities, in the bad parts of big cities, yeah that happens, but not all over. Not in Onset. [laughs]

But *wherever* you go there's drugs. There's drug dealers in Onset now—there's crack dealers. As long as people want drugs, there *always* will be drugs. Wherever you go, from Mayberry to the South Bronx, you can't escape it, you can't stop it. Guns? I bet you everybody in our school could get a gun if they really needed one. The town over, down the street, New Bedford, you can get a gun there for a hundred and fifty dollars. I could, a kid could. You can get a gun anywhere, anytime—*anybody* could. There's not gangs in Onset, but there's people I know that have come from gangs. A guy that lives right down the street—he was in the L.A. Crips. He wanted to get out of L.A. before they killed him, probably . . . A lot of people in Onset came from other places, so I hear a lot—and, plus, going up to New York, I see a lot.

I have no brothers or sisters. You get kind of spoiled: people give you a lot of stuff. But also, when you come home there's no one there, you have nobody to talk to. All my friends, they only have one parent; I'm the only one that has two parents. One of my friends, the father is in jail; the other two, they just don't live with them. Sometimes I think they envy me that I have both parents. We make fun of each other, just for fun—it doesn't go to the heart—and they always talk about my father. I don't say nuthin about their fathers because I don't know 'em. I always think they joke about mine because they don't have one.

I got a friend that's Jamaican, another that's Cape Verdean, and African-American, and white. Who you hang out with is usually about the music you listen to, actually. The people that listen to heavy metal, they go off among themselves, and people that listen to rap, they talk amongst themselves. It's not like, "Oh, you're white, we don't like you"—it's more like we don't like the music you listen to . . . 'Cause usually we're talking about music, different stuff, clothes. The clothes we wear are different from what someone that listens to heavy metal would wear. They'd wear rips in their pants and skin-tight pants, and usually we wear baggy stuff. The way you talk is another thing. We do "dap," instead of "high five." Like, people that listen to rock use the word "dude" a lot, and we don't like that, we usually say "dawg"—like, "What up, dawg?"

We talk to girls, we go see girls and everything, but we don't usually hang out like we're buddies and stuff—unless they're somebody's sister or cousin, and then they'll hang out, kind of like one of the guys. We all usually get together, a whole bunch of us, and just go to a party or something. It's not like going out on a date. There's only four-hundred people in the school, so we all know everybody in our grade.

My mom sat down and talked to me about sex, and my dad talked to me about drugs. See, the thing is, my father moved to New York when he was five, from Puerto Rico. So he lived his whole life in New York until we moved here, and he's seen a *bunch* of stuff. His cousin was a heroin addict, and he died from AIDS. He was telling me all this stuff, and he told me *never* to try it. He was trying to scare me. Just to think of it—getting high by sticking a needle into your arm! A lot of people smoke marijuana. Last year they had a thing at school about recovering alcoholics and drug abusers: they had four people get on stage and do this acting thing. They made it funny, so the kids took interest. It works to use humor.

I go to a vocational school—you take a trade. I'm taking plumbing. I love plumbing—I *love* working with pipes and everything. My great-grandfather, on my mother's side, was a plumber. My mother wanted me to take plumbing. [laughs] She said it's always nice to have a plumber in the family, and my dad said it's really good to have a trade. I think you become a licensed plumber when you get out of the school. You get your diploma, and you can go on to college after that. I'd like to go to college, if I could get a scholarship. I'm hoping for one in soccer, because I play *really* well. This past year I did well in sports: I have two varsity letters and I played freshman basketball, and I was co-captain of the team. I was supposed to keep everybody from getting in trouble, even in school, during school. If I saw somebody getting in trouble, I made them do laps! [laughs] I'm not too sure, really, what I'd want to study in college. I just got to get through high school first, and then think about college and the rest of my life.

Actually, I can't envision myself being old—I just can't think of being like forty or thirty or whatever. You can't tell how it's gonna be, anything could happen: you could die before you get to that age;

things could happen, you could be different, do different things . . . I'd like to have kids, but I just don't know what's going to happen. I'd probably want to live in a city. Not in the worst part of the city— I wouldn't want to go where all of them gangs are, where it's dangerous. I wouldn't want to live way out in the country where it's long distance to call your neighbor. [laughs]

At school, in plumbing I work real hard, try to get all the stuff down. I work hard in my school work—you have to. If you don't work hard in your school work, you're never going to get an education, and you have to have an education. If there *is* work, you're not going to get it unless you've got an education: it's obvious. That's the reason why I went to the vocational school—so I could have a trade. By the time I graduate, jobs might not even be out there still. I don't want to have nuthin to fall back on. I hope things get better, but if it really would get that bad that you can't find any work, I'd probably move to another country. Psychologically, you *have* to work, you just *have* to do something to keep you sane, to keep your mind working straight, or else you kind of go crazy. You gotta work; *everybody* has to work.

Coming From,
Going Toward

Gavin Brownstein

Chicago, Illinois

Gavin, *in Chicago on a break from college, was supposed to come to my house the previous week, but he called and canceled, saying he had to leave town suddenly. In previous conversations he'd sounded good-natured, spunky, a bit cocky, but in this call he sounded terribly upset. He is athletic in appearance, with short brown hair mostly hidden by a backward baseball cap. He chomps on gum, is wired by nature, and on this day, by grief. He is eighteen.*

I grew up in, I guess you could call it, an "upscale" suburb north of Chicago. It's about thirty thousand people, very pretty, lots of large houses, and trees—middle- and upper-class. I live with my mom and my stepdad. I'm an only child by title. [laughs] My stepdad's four kids all moved out of the house—they're older.

My biological father divorced my mom when I was two. He wasn't exactly a model father: he didn't pay child support much, and he had some skirmishes with the law—I think for writing bad checks—like writing checks out to himself from other people's checks. That's, I guess, some of the things he's done. I have no idea of other things; this is just what I've been told. He's now married to his third wife, and he works not too far from my house. I don't talk to him at all. When I was a little boy, he'd say he wanted to see me, and we'd talk, see each other a couple of times, but then he just wouldn't call again. About a year ago, I gave him another chance—'cause he sounded like he actually cared. I told him, "If the same thing happens that's happened before, that's it—I don't want to see you." And it happened again . . . What was stupid on my part was that I actually *believed* that he cared.

Before he was married to my mom, he was married to another woman, and they had a son named Peter—my half-brother. Peter died on Monday. He was twenty-six. That's my father's first son, and he hadn't seen him in twenty years. He wasn't at the funeral—he wouldn't have been welcome. I was very, very close with Pete. He grew up in Arizona. I don't know how we got to be so close. [He laughs and brightens.] I went to visit him a lot when I was younger, and in the last five years I went out there regularly. He was the head of graphics at a TV station, and I thought he had the greatest job ever.

[He looks very sad, and his voice thickens.] Uh, he had cancer, let's just say. So, it was pretty tough. He was sick for a couple of years. I basically went to college in Arizona just so I could be near him . . . You know, it really hadn't hit me until yesterday, basically. The funeral was yesterday morning, and everyone from the station was there. It was really nice, but it was pretty tough.

He didn't want people to know that he was sick, 'cause he didn't want people to get that upset. I was one of the few people on my side of the family that knew. I knew he was sick with cancer—he told me a year ago when I went out and saw him. He didn't say it was AIDS . . . and he never did tell me he was gay. His friend Dennis always spent time at the house; and eventually two plus two was added. Yesterday was the day that I basically learned everything about my brother. In September I guessed, 'cause I saw purplish lesions all over his face and his body—and I saw Dennis wearing a pair of shorts, and he had the same purplish lesion down his leg. That's when I was like, *Whoa!* It took me a little bit to get used to the fact that he had AIDS, but, I mean . . . I wasn't gonna to treat him any differently . . .

Yesterday was the day that Dennis and I got real close. He told me everything about what happened, and that Pete was gay all his life— he started dating when he was sixteen. He saw Dennis for almost five and a half years. Dennis tested positive, anonymously, three years ago. Pete developed Kaposi's Sarcoma about a year and a half ago. That's the cancer; that's all I was told about. The cancer was inside his body, though. When it goes inside you're in some trouble.

I saw him a lot this year, this first semester, because he was only two hours away, which isn't that far—especially the way I drive! [laughs] I'd drive up all the time. Then when I saw him Labor Day, with his friend Dennis, that was just a very weird situation. I'd met Dennis before, but I had just never thought—you know? So I kinda had to— I left town . . . [little laugh] I just couldn't stay. It was a lot to handle at that moment of time . . . I'm not homophobic at all—I never have been. I didn't look at him any differently. Me knowing something about him isn't going to make me change the way I look at him and the way I feel about him. But it was a weird feeling, the *knowing*. Thinking that he just had cancer, and then realizing it's AIDS. No matter if you're homophobic or not, it's a tough thing to realize, because cancer can be defeated, you know—AIDS can't.

The thing is, though, I couldn't say anything to him or to Dennis, because God forbid I was *wrong*. Think about it: I take my brother aside and ask him if he has AIDS, and he doesn't. I was just in a very weird position. I tell my mom everything—so I told her, and she figured it was AIDS. So when Dennis and I were talking yesterday and he told me everything, it didn't surprise me. And also, on the in memoriam sheets, on the bottom it said, "If you want to make a contribution, make it to the American AIDS Foundation." Silently, it basically said everything. . .

My mom's always been there for me to talk to, and that's good. It's a way to channel my feelings and emotions instead of keeping them in, which is not necessarily a good thing. When she got remarried, at first I was intimidated by my stepdad—he's a big guy. He would roughhouse with me—in fun, though. I know now that it was in fun. [laughs] But someone who's only a few feet tall thinks that a guy that's like six one, six two, is kinda large, and he scared the *crap* out of me. Through my years in grammar school, it was easier for me to blend in with the family, and we slowly but surely became one family. And then, because the other kids were older, they were moving out one by one; and when I was in seventh grade, I was the only child in the house.

You have a lot of advantages living up in the suburbs. It's true that we live in a sheltered life, that's for sure . . . People in the city learn a lot about life in one way, whereas people in the suburbs learn a lot about life in a different way. Growing up in the suburbs, there's not nearly as many, I guess a good way to put it is, *distractions,* as there are in the city.

I'm more than prepared for college from my high school, but socially I *hated* it. Gossip is huge—word spreads like wildfire at anything that is done. It shouldn't be that the whole world has to get in on your personal life—that's just bullshit. And that's not just the high school but the town itself. It's very snobby, very glitzy, the ladies in that town are some of the most ruthless human beings *on earth.* Like one time, in probably the nicest section of town—if you're absolutely loaded, you live there—this girl's dad was shot and killed. Rumor had it that her mom had the Mafia kill him. And the rumors that went around the high school, around the town . . . you heard *so many* different stories, ranging from he killed himself, to it was a love triangle, to he owed money. I looked at the other side and saw how awful they must have felt, that family. Oh God, it had to be *terrible* for them.

I had a relationship for a year and a half with this girl in high school. You want to hear a funny story? [grinning] We were having sex on a constant basis, basically. We went away for the the weekend. My mom and my sister were in my room, just looking around . . . They hadn't been in there in a long time—I'm pretty private, I don't like people going into my room. So, I kept the condoms I used behind a picture of me which was on the wall. It's hard to describe, but you'd have to move some stuff to get to it. [amused] My sister takes the picture down. "Wow, look at this picture." My mom is standing there, staring at this box of condoms. It was like one of those with seventy-two—the discount boxes—and there were like eight left! [laughs]

I came home, and she was all, [feigns edginess] "I hope you had a good time this weekend . . . Your sister and I were in your room . . . " I didn't see it coming—it caught me off guard. I was like, "Yeah, OK, you were in my room"—I hid 'em well, I figured. [shrugs] She goes, "Uh, we saw what was behind your picture." [chuckles] Just like that. [abashed] And I'm like, "Yeah . . . " [laughs, cheeks redden] Though she was *not* thrilled that I was having sex, she was happy at least that I was being responsible. And I always have been, because there's too many diseases out there. I don't think too many moms are as open about that as my mom is.

I used to be an athlete. [laughs] I used to play baseball—I mean, baseball's my claim to fame. I was the number-two pitcher behind a guy who's on the Mets now. We were the greatest team ever: we *never* lost. I was serious, but I was not at all a jock star. Basically, I was very lazy, and I didn't use my athletic abilities to their fullest, and I did things I shouldn't have—like drink and smoke pot. I could have—had I really, really applied myself—done something special. I tried out for the university team, made the final cuts, but not the *final* cut.

So now my friend's on the Mets, and I'm at a university . . . [laughs] *Whatever.* [grins] I'm happy, though—I'm very happy. I'm the kind of person that was like the practical joker of the team: I always tried to put things on the lighter side. I didn't believe that there should have been any pressure on us. Though high school athletics should be taken seriously, we're still only in *high school.* That's basically how it went for me in high school. I'm my own person: I don't follow anyone else—I do what I feel like doing, when I feel like doing it. I don't hold back on how I feel, I *always* say what I feel . . . [laughs] In the proper time. . .

I don't enjoy coming home from school, because they still treat me as if I'm in high school: my mom always asks me what time I'm going to be home. If I say, "Four or five in the morning," she'll go, "*What? What are you doing?!*" But that's, you know, what I do. It's hard, 'cause I'm on my own at school, and then I come home to, like, prison . . . [laughs] At school I feel like an adult; here I feel like a five-year-old.

In the sixties, there was the Vietnam War, Americans were dying every day, and it was really a terrible thing. There's nothing like that now. Like the environment: if we don't take care of it, it's eventually going to get back and kill us. But a lot of people say, "If it's not gonna hurt us in our lifetime, then who cares?" Politics is the same kind of thing. You won't get a very civilized conversation about the Republicans taking over Congress with most kids, just because they don't care enough about it. Things have changed since the time of the Vietnam War: people list their priorities a little different. TV maybe is a bigger issue, as in what time are the Power Rangers on. Sports is huge—that's all a lot of people think about.

Journalism is my major. I want to try to get into broadcast journalism, if I can, and go from there—probably sports . . . When you're a kid, it's just a big blurry vision of what you're gonna be when you grow up; and the older you get, the clearer it comes in. The way I was, if I saw a road, I wanted to see where it took me—I explore a lot. And even though I might not get to where I want to go, I always learn something on the way. Each different niche or road that I explore gets me more in tune with what kind of person I'm gonna be, what kind of person I *want* to be.

An example would be, why did I go out with that girl for a year and a half? She's nothing but trouble for me. Why did I go out with *any* girls in high school? Did I learn something? In terms of friends—if a friend is gonna do something really stupid, or bad to me, you know not to hang out with those kind of people. You exclude things, you know what *not* to look for in life. The way I live my life now is kinda gonna tell how I'm gonna be in the future.

I want to get married, but I don't think about kids. If I have 'em, I have 'em, if I don't, I don't. I don't look that far ahead, I gotta concentrate on *now.* You gotta live in the present. To live in the future— you just can't.

I'm not like my normal self right now. I'm most definitely not my normal self. [He bends at the waist, arms resting on knees, and hangs his head. He stares at the floor for a moment, then takes a deep breath and sits up.] It's the first time I've actually been able to have a normal conversation for a while. [grimly] It's, it's . . . it's really hard on me. It's the toughest thing I've ever had to deal with. I mean, I still have to deal with it *today.* Yesterday, you know, the funeral was nice, and the ceremony . . . the cemetery was at a beautiful, beautiful place. Yesterday was probably the hardest day I've ever had. I went to my brother's funeral, and I was told the entire truth about his entire life. And then I flew three hours home. [laughs weakly] You know what? A lot of it—it just leaves me speechless. There's so much, I just can't say anything. . .

Rebekah Evenson

Manhattan, New York

W*e meet in a West Village cof-feehouse. She is very thin, with Peter Pan–length hair, and a nearly tangible glow of vitality. She is nineteen.*

I grew up in Northern California, about two hundred miles north of San Francisco, in the Redwood country—wild country. I spent most of my time outside. The experience of walking through a Redwood forest is a religious one—it's a spiritual feeling unlike anything else. There's a sense of time passing, and yet of certain things remaining somewhat . . . not *static,* but *permanent.* Certain things that are part of this earth. You have drought years and flood years; you have wars and peace pacts and governments overthrown; and then there's a tree that stays standing through it all. You feel part of something. The smells and the sights and the sounds, all going through an ancient forest. It is an ancient forest. And now they're all being torn down.

We were about fifteen miles out of town, a mile up a dirt road, in an old farm homestead. It was just my family: my mom, my dad, my sister, my brother, and myself. My brother's now thirty, more or less; my sister is two years older than me. By the time I came along, the cabin was mostly built—we lived in a one-room cabin for a while. We didn't have electricity, and we didn't have any of the amenities: no telephone, no television . . .

When I was about six we expanded the house and built another bedroom, a living room, and a kitchen. My grandmother said she wouldn't come and stay with us anymore if we didn't have facilities, so finally we got a bathroom. When I was around eight, we got a telephone. We *made* all of our electricity for running the house, and we still do. We grew vegetables and had an orchard for fruit, and we had animals: sheep and cows and goats and ducks and chickens and eggs, and you name it. My sister and I had Indian horses, and we used to ride to school. It was a little like *Little House on the Prairie*.

The community I grew up in was made up of people who wanted to create for themselves a society and a culture that was giving and caring, and really emphasized the values that they thought were important, rather than those of the greater society. My father graduated from Berkeley in the sixties and was very politically involved, and my mother's an artist. The two of them decided to be part of the back-to-the-land movement, and to homestead. They were together for about twenty years, and most of it was spent on the farm. Both of them ran it—we all worked on it. We made a little bit extra—we'd sell milk or barter—and there was a co-op in town where we could buy things, like rice and flour, that we couldn't grow.

I went to a Montessori school that the parents developed. The parents, and the kids too, we built it with our hands. It was this one-room schoolhouse, in the shape of an octagon, made out of wood—a lot of salvaged lumber. It was a *great* school—all different ages—and that's really how I got to where I am today, which is being a nineteen-year-old college grad. There were no grades or grade levels—so, when I was ready to read a book, I just read it; and when I was ready to do tenth grade math, it didn't matter that I was in fifth grade. There was no competition in terms of doing better than other people. Cheating wasn't something that you would even think about doing, because [laughs] you wouldn't get anywhere with it—there'd be no reward whatsoever. Your achievement wasn't measured in terms of anything but how you are doing, and how you can do versus how you are doing. It made school fun, it took the edge off learning. I didn't have any idea that school was supposed to be boring and you were supposed to hate it—until I went to public school in sixth grade.

When I was twelve, my parents split up—at Christmas. I was pretty shocked—they never fought. It was very traumatic, although it wasn't as horrible as what some of my friends went through. My parents still respected each other a lot, and were friends, and they are now very good friends . . . But [She sighs, and continues sadly.] At the time, there was a lot of bitterness. The worst part was, I guess, that my parents each felt the need to convince me that they were in the right, so while not consciously trying to turn me against the other parent, they were edging in that direction. And that made me so unhappy and bitter.

I'm not exactly sure what all the direct effects were. Adolescence is such a tumultuous time in anyone's life, and I was going through so many things. I turned outward and became very social, and spent a lot of time with my friends. My mom moved into an art studio in town; my brother was out of the house; my sister and I moved in with my mom; and my dad stayed on the farm. We lived fifteen miles apart, so I could visit him for the evening or a couple hours. I didn't spend as much time as I should have, probably, but I was doing my own thing: I became involved in school activities—sports, and all sorts of clubs.

When I went into seventh grade, junior high, I was incredibly awkward. I didn't look right, my hair wasn't right, I didn't have the right clothes . . . My parents didn't have any money, so I couldn't *buy* the right clothes. I had no concept of, like, matching my sweaters to my socks, and these very basic things that everybody was doing. People were nasty to each other, which was something I wasn't used to *at all*. It was a real shock to me that kids were so competitive and cruel. There was a sense that you could only further yourself by being mean to other people. I didn't know how to do it, and it would just make me feel bad.

In eighth grade, all of a sudden I had a figure: I had hips, and breasts, which was like a complete revelation to me. At a certain point I became glad about it. I thought, "Gee, I'm hot shit!" Boys all of a sudden started taking notice, and it was confusing and sort of bewildering and nice. It was fun realizing that I could actually look good, because I always thought that I was wretched-looking: I was *so* skinny, I couldn't fill out anything. It was always something that separated me from the rest of the girls, because everybody else would complain about being fat. I used to wish, *oh*, how I wished that I was fat! [laughs] Not that any of them were fat, but they thought that they had an extra bit of padding here and there. And I had bony knees and my thighs were the size of my calves. Being able to sit around and say,

"Oh, I'm *so* fat; look at the weight in my thighs," was something that brought girls together, and that I had no part in.

I had friends, but they weren't, like, the cool kids—and in junior high, there was definitely a hierarchy of who is really popular. In my school there were two distinct groups: there were the rednecks and the hippies. The rednecks were mostly children of loggers and law enforcement, and the hippy kids were the kids from the hills, and their parents were pot-growers or farmers or artists. I was *definitely* a hippy kid, and in junior high everybody, in desperately trying to conform, wanted to be like the redneck kids. I wasn't an outcast per se, but I definitely wasn't part of the in-crowd. My group of friends was a little more homely and less well dressed; we were kind of the smart kids, I guess. That was also when I realized I was smart. The teachers always said, "Good job," or, "You could have done better on this, Rebekah, why don't you do this again?" It didn't sink in at first: I thought *everybody* got all As; you just did everything the best you could, and that, of course, would earn an A. [laughs] It was very simple! I was very, and I still am, opposed to the grading system.

Realizing I was smart, I was proud of myself, and I sort of wanted to brag. But on the other hand, it was *really* not cool—not only to brag but to be smart. You wanted to be *stoopid,* and you played it down: you giggle a lot, flirt, and ask questions as if you don't know the answers. So I ended up doing that—I playacted a bit—in order to be able to talk to people who really, I guess on reflection, probably weren't as stupid as they were acting. It was more OK for boys to appear smart, although the quote-unquote popular boys didn't appear smart—that wasn't their thing either.

Intelligence is a weird thing, and it only gets to be more socially acceptable as you get into college. In high school it was the same thing: you're not supposed to be terribly bright. I guess what it really is, is that you intimidate people. [laughs] People thought that I would be looking down on them; and people would also ask me to do their work for them. It was horrible—I thought that's *completely* unconscionable. But, by the same token, I didn't want to say no and give myself more of an outcast status. "Why not? You know how to do it and we don't."

Sometimes I broke down and did it, and felt really bad about myself, but made temporary friends through that kind of thing. And then sometimes I would say, "Screw you." I would never do somebody's work *for* them—I felt much more comfortable talking them through it, and explaining how to do it. But sometimes kids would copy my work, and it made me feel horrible, so at a certain point I stopped doing that. By the time I was in high school I was much more comfortable with myself, and I had a good group of friends—I didn't feel that inferiority thing. I have no idea why kids cheat, except to perhaps point the finger at the achievement-oriented society. If you don't do well in high school, you won't get into the right college; if you don't get into the right college, you're not going to get the right job . . .

I found my high school so unchallenging academically that after my second year I was ready to get out of there. I decided I wanted to do an exchange program. I was fifteen at the time, and it was 1989, just before all the major changes that happened in Eastern Europe. There were some rumblings that the iron curtain was about to fall, the communist bloc was about to crumble. I was very interested in politics and international affairs—because of my parents, I suppose. I was fascinated by Eastern Europe, and I knew that it was the end of an era, and that this would be my last chance to see Eastern European countries as they were under communism. Which ended up being what happened in the fall of the year that I went to Hungary: they dropped the communist mantle and became a democracy. I witnessed the first elections ever, and it was an incredible experience.

I lived with a family in Budapest, and went to an English high school. I ended up teaching at the school; they asked me to teach a first-year English class, and so I had my own little class and curriculum. Being there gave me a whole new reality, and a whole new perspective on life and on living, and being a teenager, because their lifestyle was so very different from ours. Like I remember talking about sex and drugs and all that with my parents, and with my teachers, and at school. Talking about sex—what is it, and why people do it —and about drugs was never taboo. And I didn't have sex, which was unusual among my friends: most people were sleeping around. Most of my friends were two and three years older than me, and fourteen or fifteen when they started having sex. I knew I wasn't ready, and it was an emotional, not a physical thing. All through high school I thought sex was something that was special, not something to just do. There were definitely times when I wanted to, and I said, "Wait, this is not it —he's not the one." I had to wait for the right person, and I did.

In Hungary the kids were, at least in my school, much more wholesome. The boy situation was *very* different there. Most of them had not ever dated—many of the girls had never kissed a boy. So I went from my friends who are sleeping around to these girls who aren't even kissing! [laughs] We'd go to bars, and have a beer, but for the most part we had parties. We'd have a few bottles of wine, and play games, and talk. There wasn't that driving thing to get totally wasted. First of all, drinking always was legal, so *that*, for them, wasn't a big deal. Most of why people do it is because it's taboo. Marijuana would grow wild by the side of the road in Hungary, and they didn't know what it was. So nobody was doing any drugs, and alcohol was not a big deal—there wasn't that kind of destructiveness.

There are such deep, traditional values in Hungary. People love their history; people knew their history from about fifteen hundred years ago. They knew all of their kings, and they knew all of the transitions in history, and all of the different cultural and social changes. They're *very* proud of it. Knowing gave them a certain depth, and roots and ties that brought everyone in the culture together. There was a tremendous amount of respect for elders. There was a huge hierarchy of respect—there were about eight different ways to say "hello," for example. There's a very specific thing that you would say to your grandmother, as opposed to what you'd say to your mother, as opposed to your aunt, or your professor, or a friend, or an acquaintance. A certain commonality, shared traditions, brings all of these people together, makes them respect their elders; and makes them more stable in a certain way. Whereas Americans kids have no idea of their history. American kids, there's no respect for elders, or for each other. In Hungary, anytime somebody gets up to get themselves a second helping, they ask everyone at the table, "Can I get you anything?" And in America, kids are elbowing each other aside.

I was in Budapest for a year. When I come home I went through major culture shock. The shiny newness of everything was one of the things that my eyes couldn't get used to seeing. Everything is old in Hungary, and much more sedate, quiet, decrepit—old cars, and smoggy, dark skies. [laughs] And when I came back to America, everybody's driving brand new cars, and everybody's got new clothes —fashion, right up to the minute. And the food . . . anything you could possibly eat, any time. Walking into a supermarket, the shelves are all stocked with so many different brands, of so many different things. I thought it was kind of grotesque, but I also thought that it was wonderful. [laughs]

One of the things that hurt me the most upon coming back was the stark differences between the poor and the rich. Because you didn't really have the same poverty in Hungary. I mean, everybody was poor and struggling, but you didn't have homeless people. There's a different kind of desperation, or depression, about life. In America it's *so* glaring. It's sad to see people starving. You look around and see all this wealth, and think why not redistribute the wealth? [laughs] I heard a statistic today that in the last ten years, the top 1 percent shifted from having 32 percent of all household assets to *40 percent*. The top 1 percent in this country has 40 percent of household assets, and they're talking about capital gains tax cuts?! [laughs] I mean, that is just *absurd!* It's *complete* greed. And somehow the conservative element in the Republican party, and in the Democratic Party, have been able to convince poor, working-class Americans that it's in their best interest to subsidize this top 1 percent, and to help them keep getting richer.

It's extremely important for young people to get a sense for what else is out there in the world. I don't think most American teenagers have that sense, and that's very limiting. Traveling is a chance for self-discovery, as well as a chance to experience different cultures, and different ways that people treat each other, and eat, and live. When you are able to step back from your high school or your group of friends, it enables you: it enabled me to really be able to find myself. I couldn't have done it had I been in the same setting the whole time. I mean, America is very homogeneous in a strange way.

Growing up without television has been one of the most important factors of my life in allowing me to develop intellectually. I never sat in front of a TV when I came home from school: I read. I *devoured* books. TV kills imagination, because you don't have any brain activity: your eyes glaze over, and it's all input and no output. Even still I don't live with a television in my home. But it creates a cultural barrier between me and the rest of the world: I don't understand most of the inside jokes that Americans share. I probably have a slight superiority kick, like, "What? This is a waste of time, and I'm not wasting my time on this." And a little feeling of being left out, I guess. But television is stupid; it panders to the lowest common denominator. The highest-quality thing on TV today is the advertising, because the most money and skill goes to designing these quick, incredibly fast sells, that are very scarily effective. They're so tailored to their specific audience, to have all the imagery perfect to suck you in and spit you out, another consumer.

After Hungary, I was gonna go back to high school, and then I thought, "There's no *way*. It would be a complete setback: boring, horrible—I would regress to my old, childish, high school ways." I applied to Simon's Rock, which is a four-year college that accepts students who have not graduated from high school. After a year there I decided to transfer. I wanted to go to a small college with the resources of a university. Columbia was very attractive to me, and Barnard is part of the university, so I transferred there. Another reason I chose it is because it's a women's college. I was very aware of the difference in the way that teachers and people and students, everyone, treat women and men, and that angered me. I think it's very subconscious, but people tend to listen to a masculine voice; there's something about the tonality we are conditioned to listen to, pay more heed to, give more respect to. And to shut up when men are speaking. Men don't shut up when *women* are speaking. And so even people who consider themselves feminists, I think, engage in activities which have the result of silencing women. And in a women's college, that is just not a factor: you're accorded a certain level of respect, and that's that.

I worked all the way through college, and had tremendous scholarships. At Barnard they push you to get internships. Most of the good internships, the ones that lead to the good jobs, weren't paying, you had to volunteer. Most kids there had more money than I did, and they *could* volunteer. The whole system—the way it's set up—is a perpetuation of the class system, and also racism. It's total discrimination. You get these internships because you have money enough to afford to do them, and because you have the connections, because you know people: your uncle happens to know somebody who's working there, blah-blah-blah. It just made me in tears.

But finally I found an internship at an organization called Human Serve. Their goal is universal voter registration. I entered in 1992, and what we were working on was passage of what became the National Voter Registration Act of 1993—most people know it as the Motor-voter Bill. [proudly] I've actually worked on writing laws in several states. [with a trace of disbelief] My own words are in legislative language! Most recently I've been working with the U.S. Department of Justice. Attorneys from there call me up and say, "Rebekah, Louisiana just submitted a form, and it has this question on it. What should we do? How should we react?" [laughs] It's very exciting. I'm making a difference: I'm doing work that really means something to me and I think *will* mean something to the country. It has incredible potential. This law could register 95 percent of the people in this country, and studies show that 90 percent of eligible voters vote.

I graduated from college this year with admission to Yale Law School! [giggles, beaming] I'm proud of myself—it was a long shot. It's the only law school that I wanted to go to—they don't have grades, class ranking, or competition against each other, and they have total loan forgiveness for public interest work, which is what I'm gonna do. I'm postponing going a year to keep working at Human Serve.

At a certain point in high school, I had three things I wanted to do: to go into genetics, because I was fascinated by microbiology; to go into graphic arts, because I love art, and I could spend hours doing nothing but drawing and painting; and I wanted to be a lawyer, because I thought I'd be a damn good lawyer. [laughs] And also, I have always felt the need to do something with my life that would be a part of social change—that would make the world a better place to live. Going to Hungary, my desire to do political work was only heightened by seeing the changes that were happening, and how individuals could be part of that change. It was also the year that South Africa sort of shed it's apartheid, and there were things happening all over. I slowly forgot the genetics and the graphics. By the time I got to college I *knew* that I wanted to do political stuff. I started out thinking I'd do international human rights, but I think I'm going to go into civil rights law: I see the necessity for a lot more civil rights work in this country. My main interest is poverty issues, because it draws together women's rights, and the rights of minorities in this country, and welfare issues. The Contract with America is trying to cement very conservative, and I would say *un-Christian* values, into federal, national policy—it's the decimation of social programs which hold this country together. And it's most clearly epitomized by their attack on welfare. Poverty is a central issue, and if poverty is not solved, nothing else will be.

I definitely want a family some day. I love children, and I'd like to have some of my own—although sometimes I have these massive doubts about bringing more life into this miserable world, and so on and so forth. But I think that it's something that I want to do. It's hard to think of finding the right man. My parents' divorce made me more cynical about my own prospects, but it also cemented in me the idea that when I got married, I was going to be together with my husband forever. But I'm tremendously demanding, and I want myself, you know, in a male form—with a couple of modifications here and there. I'm probably not going to find him. [laughs]

Akili Merritt

San Francisco, California

Akili still has the face of a sweet child, sitting somewhat *incongruously atop his six-foot, bean-pole frame. He is fourteen.*

Ever since I was young, I always felt I had to be older than I was. Especially 'cause when you're tall they automatically give you a year or two more. [laughs] I've always tried to, not exactly, be the man of the house—but I always felt that I had to step up and be older. They assume that you're a teenager, you're gonna be wild and crazy—the whole way they market things to you is based on the assumption that you're gonna act this way. They want you to play the role. And I admit, sometimes I do. Like when my mom says things that just tick me, I'm like "What are you *talking about?*" Sometimes I think she's asking too stupid questions: I'll come home and I'll have a frown on my face, and she'll say, [sweetly] "In a bad mood?" and I'll be like, [disgruntled] "*Man!*" Like, "GET OFF MY BACK!" [laughs] I'll get sarcastic like, "No—I'm *happy.*" [laughs] I can't name why, it just rides in me, this annoyance.

People have a lot of expectations about you when you're tall—they automatically assume you can play basketball. I think that they would not make as big an assumption if I was white. [laughs] I don't identify much with mixed people, because most of my life I've just been treated like a light-skinned black man. But I do feel like I'm in two worlds sometimes—especially when I go home to a white mother. But when I'm out in the world, society names me as a black man, a black teenager.

I have a little brother, he's twelve; and two half-sisters from my father, they're in their twenties—they live in Chicago. My mom kicked my father out when I was two; I don't even think they're technically divorced. He became abusive, and he would play Russian roulette and stuff with a gun. I don't remember this, but this is how they split up: they were in the car, he slapped her, and she went to the police station, had him restrained, and we drove off. Then all that night she sat up with a shotgun. That's what she told me . . . And that was it. I don't really feel like a big part of my life is missing because in order to miss somebody that you love, you have to have memories of them, and spend time with them—they have to be part of your daily life. I have one memory: it was in a gym, and I saw him playing basketball. That's the only memory I have.

Me and my brother, we don't talk about him . . . Except for if he gets mad at me. Like if I try to keep him in check, he'll say, "You ain't my daddy," and stuff like that. [laughs] We're close, as close as brothers can be at our age. You know, we step on each other's toes. When you're so immature, and you don't see that somebody's copying you, maybe from envy, you say, "They're just trying to get on my nerves"— so he'll copy me, try and dress like me, talk like me, try to do what I do. I'll be like, "Get outta my face, man!" [laughs] Then we start to argue. It's just ignorance, and being young.

I've always kind of been the star as far as doing things—and basketball, and I like to perform, sing, act, whatever. He's like in my shadow, and I just hope he doesn't give up, and say, "Oh, I'll never be like that, never be good at sports," or whatever. And then I'm taller—he's constantly looking up to me—so he thinks he's short; and I just hope that doesn't keep him down. But I'm pretty confident that he'll do the right things. He kinda has a little sassy mouth on him. [laughs] He'll hurt your feelings if he wants to—he can clown with the best of them. [cocky] He can't get to *me*. [laughs] I'm a *pro*. He can try, but I *always* have the upper hand. You know, like for adults maybe two years isn't nothing, but to us that's like twenty years. So I'm ahead— he *knows* not to mess with me.

I feel I gotta take care of him. Lately he doesn't like the math teacher at his school, so I said, "You're gonna have to deal with these people all your life. If they're ignorant, then that's just how they are—they can't help it. Don't let it shorten you, what you're trying to do in getting your education." Advice like that. Try to keep him on the right track.

I go to a private school—small, under four hundred kids. It's my first year, freshman year. It's predominantly white—there's a clump of black kids. They say they got all these minorities, but if a white person's grandmother is black, then they're considered a black person, 'cause of their ancestor. So for studies, when they present it to whoever they have to answer to, they become a diverse school. If you just *look* at the place, it's a white school. It ticks me off. They need to have more everybody getting a good education. And the way society *says* it is, if you can afford to get it, then go get it; but if you look at reality, most people of color can't afford it.

I went to a black middle school, but I transferred to a private white middle-school in eighth grade year so that I could get into a good high school . . . [He sighs; when he continues, his voice is weighty.] It's a lotta pressure. And I'm on full scholarship, so you can't mess up, you can't slip for one second, 'cause it could be gone in an instant. You're scared. There's *so many* ways I could ruin my life right now. Like this white dude could get on my nerves, and I could just, from instincts, knock him out, man, just start whuppin his ass. And then I'm expelled. What I'm gonna do? I could get violent, or I could start acting a fool in class. I could play into their stereotypes at school, and that would not only ruin my future but ruin *other* black peoples' future who're gonna have to deal with it—because I'm just strengthening the stereotypes. That's the way that a lotta private schools can get rid of people of color: they say, "Yeah, you can *still* come here, but now you gotta *pay* for it." I could try to get into that world and try to be as white as I could be, and then come home, and every black person I know disown me—and then I'll have to go to therapy years down the road because I don't feel I'm with my roots . . . Since I identify as a black person, I could stay away from my roots as a white person—and *that* could mess with me! So, you . . . [His voice trails off in a strangled sigh.]

I'm constantly trying to do the best I can. Young black teenagers nowadays, when we're at private schools, we don't have none of that Black Panther stuff, we don't have no NAACP, or nothing like that. We stay together only to survive, only to keep our blackness. But we don't never make a real change to make the place better—we don't complain. We just bear it and grin it, we just go on. Even in our conversations, we don't talk about how bad the system is, or how bad the school is, or how ignorant these people are. We go around like nothing's happening. We sit there, we joke, we say, "Oh, did you see this on TV last night?" And that's why we're not making no progress.

We feel isolated. In assembly we sit in the back, in one corner in the back. And that's basically where all the people of color are, and the rest of the auditorium is white—so we feel segregated there. Where we eat lunch, we eat all the way in the back, and all the white kids are in the front. That's just how it was when I came there, and I automatically went to that area. I think it's ignorance on both parts, and fear of what's at that other table. If I went and sat with the white kids I would feel uncomfortable; I wouldn't know what to say, I wouldn't know what they wanted me to say. And especially with teenagers, you want to say the right thing.

Where I came from, my old school, I could just breeze through and get As—but it's kind of a con, because you don't have good work habits. Then when I get to this situation where I gotta *really* work for it—the first trimester I was drowning. People cheat in school . . . I stay away from *that*. I look at it as a drug, or like stealing: if you get away with it, you're like, [breezy] "Oh, I can do this all the time." It may start off with just looking over somebody's shoulder and then, the next thing you know, you're gonna be buying tests off of people, things like that. The tests are supposed to test what you *know*, first of all, so you gonna short *yourself*—it's not worth it. Plus, I feel that I have an obligation to prove that I can get that point without cheating. Because most people, they'll say, "Oh, that's a black person, of course he's gonna be cheating—he gotta get ahead, he's got to find his advantage." So I think it's my responsibility to keep my self in line.

This may be a stereotype, but liberals think that black students in white environments need to be treated special, they need to be coddled, and all that. There's this subtle racism that a lot of black people get frustrated about. With conservatives, they just plain say, "This thing is genetics: you're *stupid*," so you can go and throw that in their face. But you can't deal with subtle racism. Like if somebody makes a remark, they don't even mean it, how can you deal with that? It's not tangible: you can't hit it, you can't boycott it, you gotta just sit there and stay frustrated, stay in this *rut*.

When I first got there, a lot of white people, when they would try to come up and talk to me, they'd say, "*Yo, what's up homey?*" [laughs] Now to them, they was just trying to be friendly, but to me that was just madness! I was ready to knock people out. I was like, "*What?!*" Subtle racism like that: you can't get mad at them, that's just how they were raised. If you do something like yell at them, or punch 'em, then they're not gonna learn anything, they're gonna write you off: "That's just another angry Negro." So, you gotta educate them. I explained to them why I talked like this: I said, "Basically, because when my ancestors were slaves, they were taught broken English to keep them ignorant. They carry it on today." And then they would say things like, "Well, why couldn't you just unlearn it?" And I said, "If you live in a Spanish-speaking home, you're gonna speak Spanish. Same thing with me, what it's like."

My mom works for the city—sometimes in the daytime, she can ride in the city van. She picked me up from school one time, and this girl said, "That's your parole officer?" I said, "I don't have no *parole officer!*" [laughs] I was, "*What?!*" I have to stuff down a lot of anger —*all* the time. [He shakes his head and laughs.] Yeah. It's like, you gotta keep it down, and you're always scared, because sometimes it'll just come up. [with emotion] And you can literally feel it coming up, and it comes up in your head and you're just surrounded by this . . . [He spits out a violent grunt.] So you're sitting there, and it's like right here, [grabs throat] but then you gotta push it down, go to the bathroom, whatever. Just go to the bathroom and calm down, cool out. Push it back down there.

You just gotta say it's worth it. You're gonna deal with a lot, all your life. I'm always thinking of how I have to handle myself. I might get frustrated one day, like, "Forget all these people, man! They're *getting on my nerves*—they don't understand *nuthin.*" I'll go to the corner, ask somebody for some weed, come back, get high, then turn into a dope fiend—just 'cause of that frustration, that anger that's built up. And those are the things I'm trying to be cognizant of, so I don't fall into those traps.

A lot of people told me, they said, [a devil's whisper] "OK, you're smart, but don't worry, they're gonna getcha some day. You're going away to jail someday. You're gonna sell drugs someday." That's black people, and as a matter of fact, some white people would discourage me. [pained laugh] If I said I wanted to be a doctor, instead of saying, "Great, I'm all for you, more power to you," they say, "You know how many years it takes to get there?" and all that. Like, [pompous] "You know, if you're gonna be a doctor, you'll just be studying every second of your life." Like they assume that you automatically *hate* studying. Yeah, I get stuff like that.

Like police, man. *Police*, they have just messed with me *all* of my life. If you walk near the scene of a crime, and the description is a "young, black man," that's you. As soon as you hear something going on, you might as well just go raise your hands, because they're coming. There's no doubt about it. [snaps fingers] Like clockwork: *"Hey you!"* I've been stopped three or four times in my life. Twice when I was in *elementary school!* That kinda messed with my mind. The worst time, I think I was eleven. I was walking home, and all of a sudden there was this, *"Hey you!"* It could be anybody, so I kept walking—and then it got closer and closer and closer. Pretty soon there was this police all up on me. "Have you heard about a car radio being stolen?" I was like, "No." He said, "Are you getting sassy?" So then I was all up on the wall like this. [He spreads his arms up and out.] Maybe I pissed him off, I don't know, but he started calling me names, *nigger* this, *nigger* that. I was kinda naive, and I was like, "You can't call me nigger." [nervous laugh] At one point he had a gun to the back of my head. It was *at my head!* At that point I was like, *"Nossuh. Nossuh nossuh nossuh."*

I got stopped a couple months ago. If you say *sir*, they think you're trying to get smart with them. If you say *sir!* If they say, "Do you have any drugs on you?" You say, "No, *sir,*" they'll be like, "*What?*" I just stare at the ground, and say, "No." You say it like in slave days, when black people couldn't look up at white folks. That's how you gotta play it. You just gotta look down, like that. [He assumes an abject posture, then continues with the voice of an old man.] It's just to put fear, let you know, "You might be smart, but I'm still gonna have this gun, and I'm still gonna have this badge and I do what I want." If you conduct yourself as an educated person, they think you're just trying to get wise with them—like, "Yeah, OK, fine. You're gonna be somebody—I'm *still* gonna whup your ass on the way home from work, man."

That's how they try to get you when you're young, and implement it in your mind. In school, you're not supposed to be *anything*. That's mostly what that poor education is about. It makes you feel like you got no chance. The only chance is gonna be to sell drugs, steal cars, gangbang, whatever. I always had a good home, so wherever I was, I knew I could come back to something good—but what happens to all the people that *don't* have good homes? They don't come home to good parents, and so they go out and get their love somewhere else; they go to school, and folks tell 'em they can't be nuthin there *too*. You get stopped by the police, he tell you you ain't shit. You start to believe it, and then you're gonna be on that corner, selling dope or smoking it, whatever, drinking . . . Just going to jail.

A strong aspect of my personality is *I wanna know*. I'll get in good with people older than me so they can tell me what's the game, how do you play it. First you see all of the sex and drugs in your community, and see what it's doing, so you know you don't wanna do *that*. You see all these pregnant teens, and somebody comes up to you and says, "If you want to have to drop outta high school, get a job, be nothing, work manual labor, just get a girl pregnant . . . *Use* a condom, or just don't have sex at all." A lot of people who've been through it themselves—have babies at the age of fifteen and stuff—they'll tell you. They have to say *nuthin*—just go to they house, see what they doin', see how they livin': you're like, *not for me, not for me*.

When I was in seventh grade, I hung out with this guy named Claudell, and he was just a young gangsta in *every* sense of the word. It seemed like he was my guardian angel, because no matter how bad he was, he would *always* show me how to do the right thing and how to handle myself. Because there is a way that you can handle yourself, and people respect you—but it doesn't necessarily have to be off of fear. He gave me the way to carry myself: to be educated, but not like *totally* sold out. He taught me how to get that respect without having to shoot nobody.

He showed me all the horrors of the life of a gangsta. He showed me how paranoid he was all the time, how the only way you can not drive yourself crazy off of that paranoia is to drink and smoke weed. He showed me dope fiends, he showed me fights, he showed me guns, he showed me all the nonsense, all the madness that you're gonna have to go through. And then when I got into a situation—somebody bumped into me, like, "What's up, man? You got a problem?" He said, "Look, I'm sure"—see, he wouldn't disrespect you—"I'm *sure* you can duke it out with him, but I'm also sure that he has a gun under his coat, and he will shoot you with no hesitation if you try *anything.*" So he would just say, "Keep walking." Except for sometimes, man, when he was drunk, he'd be, *"I'm gonna whup his ass!"* [laughs]

He showed me drugs and how it was done: how to cook it up, cut it up, sell it, who to sell to, who's a narc, who's all this . . . But soon as he went out dealing his dope, or whatever, I went home. He'd always say —this was my cue—"Ain't you got some homework to do?" And I would know it was my time to go. I appreciated him for all of that. He was in County jail a couple of months ago, but I saw him when he came to my eighth grade graduation. [pleased] That was cool. He was all laughing at me, "Why you up there with all them *white* folks?" [laughs] That's how it's gotta be, man.

Affirmative action—people think that there are millions of black people stealing jobs from white people, and it's really not true. I mean, yes, they might get to the interview and get the job, but the chance of a black person getting to that interview is like, [He holds his hands out, palms up.] He's not gonna really get there, because of all the traps that've been set up, like alcohol and drugs, poor education. That's how it usually works out. First, say you're born into a project: you're gonna go to a bad school; you're not gonna get good medical attention—you might suffer from lead poisoning. Then you got drugs on the corner. Every time you get frustrated, don't worry, there's some alcohol right across the street, and they're just dying to sell it to you. Maybe you get past high school—most high school students don't go to college in the people of color's community: they gotta go to work to *feed* the *family.* So I don't see why everybody's tripping off of a certain amount of people that actually make it through and get to that interview, and now they want to take that away from them.

This Muslim guy once told me that America was born on blood, tears, and other people's sweat, and that's how it's gonna go down.

And that really made me think. We still got this great military, and we have this prestige and ego trip that we're the top in the world. I don't think we'll become a third-world country or something, although in some cases we *are;* but I *do* worry that the problems are gonna get so bad that it's gonna call for revolution someday. And then you gotta think, we're killing the ozone, right? Ozone's gone, deforestation—are we even gonna have *oxygen* to *breath* in order to be mad at each other? [laughs]

I thought I wanted to be a doctor for a long time. I wanted to be a whole lot of things in my life: a journalist, a lawyer—I wanted to be Spiderman at one point . . . [laughs] I think that good education means a lot of opportunities to do what you want to do. I want to go everywhere—I want to see the world. If I become a doctor, I want to see what I'm trying to help; if I'm a lawyer, I want to see what I'm defending; I want to see what I'm writing about. I just want to see it—to *see* it.

I want to get married and have kids. All people who don't have a father, or had an abusive father, they all wanna be the perfect parent. That's how I am. I always talk about, "Well, my kid's gonna have all of this, and they're not gonna have *no* problem." And I know in the future that might mess me up, because I might be overprotective and all of that—but, yeah, I always dream about having that perfect family.

I'm gonna marry a black woman. I think the reason why black women get mad at men with white women is because the system is trying to make sure that we don't reproduce ourselves, they're trying to kill us off. Do I feel that genocide is being practiced? That's *exactly* how I feel. I try not to let it run my life, because you'll drive yourself crazy and be like, "*People are trying to kill me, people are trying to kill me!*" [small laugh] So black women are like, "You got liquor stores, gun stores, whatever, and now you're gonna go date *they* women!" That's basically their whole frame of mind.

I always had it a little rougher—in a group of black kids, the lighter-skinned one is gonna be the punk of the group—and I have to prove myself every time I get into a new situation with new black kids. I really don't want my kids to go through that. I don't know about genetics, but I don't want my kids to come out on the line, where they don't know what they are. I appreciate love is love and all that, but it's really not good for kids to have that kind of confusion. And it'll just be a more comfortable life for them, and I want to provide a more comfortable life for my kids, so they're gonna come out *dark*. [laughs]

Sometimes my mom will say things—she has some subtle racism in her—and I'll be like, "Dang, man, *white* people." [laughs] I won't be able to deal with her because I'm just *mad*. Some white people have the tendency to over explain things to black people because they'll think they don't understand—she does that a *lot*. Sometimes I think that's just part of adults. But you can turn it into a racial thing too, and it's kinda frustrating going through life thinking, "Is this person explaining this to me because I'm black or because I'm *young?*"

Sometimes I think it would help if my mother was black, but I think it would take away from her identity and who she is. And what she's given me is based on her personality, and it would be different, and I don't want to be different. I don't think I would change her— except for the stubborn part. [laughs] I'm stubborn, and I think I got it from her. It really doesn't work with teenagers when your parents are stubborn, 'cause you're trying to come into your own, and do what you wanna do, and then they come in and they have this idea, and they stick to it. [He laughs, then continues, with frustration charging each word.] Say you think that driving is something *you'll* be able to do when you turn sixteen, and then they go *on and on* about privileges, and it's *stuck* in their head that you have to be *perfect* in order to drive. And "I want straight As, I want you in by this time," and all of that— and so that gets *frustrating*.

But she's pretty respectful. I had to put her in check a little while ago. One time I said, "Mom, don't pick me up from school, I can catch the bus home." And *here* she come, in front of all my friends, man, *driving* up, *honking* her horn, and I was like, *"Oh, what* am I gonna *do?"* Honking the horn, [yells] *"Akili!"* I was like, "Mom, please. Look, we're gonna have to get something straight: if I say I can catch the bus home, I'm catching the bus home."

Single-parenting is good for your kids, because you'll become their hero. She was my hero for a long time—she still is. She would never let anybody think she was vulnerable—she's *tough*. But it causes tension, because you're constantly tired: you're keeping a home together, and you're going to work—so you get grumpy, and *that* causes a lot of arguments. It's not good for the kids to be growing up constantly trying to figure out, "Is she gonna be mad tonight?" But you really have to admire a person that would take that kind of responsibility. In my house we got this chart, who cooks dinner when. I cook, my brother cooks, and then my mom cooks. At first I didn't like it, but now it's like no big thing: at first I didn't like doing laundry, but now it's like second nature. And if you give that to your kids, they're gonna be able to take care of themselves. That's the thing: the kids are gonna cook too, in my house. [laughs] Shoot, all they gotta do is do homework, *man*—they're gonna cook *me* something.

But I think I wouldn't work as much when they were younger, because you gotta be there and all that. That's where all their education is gonna come from, the first years of their life. That's where you can really give them values. Because then they're gonna go off to school, and they're gonna go and learn all these other things. To be general, this is kind of the land of opportunity: if you work hard, you can *be* something. [with passion] But for black children, they're constantly told that they're nothing, and then they get blamed for it later when somebody says, "Why do you always blame white people, man? Why couldn't you just do this on your own? Pull yourself up by your bootstraps." Basically we need to change the whole way that we educate young black kids—education is the *key*. And the environment: it's just most of the environment that they're gonna be dealing with is in the schools—that's where they need the most support. It's a cycle, and if you fix one part, then it will eventually carry into the next part. So, I may have entered into a world where I was told I wasn't shit, but at that part of the cycle at home, I was being told that I *could* be something, therefore, I'm gonna be something. And then I'm gonna tell my kids, so then they won't have to deal with shit, man, 'cause they gonna *know*.

I just go about it like this: I have a funny name. A lot of people make fun of that name, but I figure some day they're gonna be naming their kids after me.